Treasure
AND THE COMING
Temple
of God

FINDING THE ARK & ASHES

LONNIE SHIPMAN

Other books by the author:

Secrets of Prophecy Revealed:
Keys to Jesus' Second Coming

Heaven's Orchestra:
The Stars Sing Praise to God

© 2023 Treasure and the Coming Temple of God
By Lonnie L. Shipman

All Rights Reserved. No part of this publication may be reproduced, stored in a retrieval system, or transmitted, in any form or by any means, electronic, mechanical, photocopying, recording, or otherwise, without the prior permission of the author. Final editing by Lise Cutshaw, Cover design and layout by Ginny Tallent.

For more information contact:
Beacon Street Press
500 Beacon Drive
Oklahoma City, OK 73127
1-800-652-1144 / www.swrc.com

Printed in the United States of America

ISBN: 978-1-933641-82-9

Endorsements

These pages are remarkable in the enormous extent of information Lonnie Shipman includes. While I am not competent to fully judge the accuracy of every detail, it is reverently and thoroughly written to honor and magnify the Lord Jesus Christ and to prepare us for His return. It is a riveting description of the rebuilding of the Temple in Jerusalem and the return of the Lord in the Rapture. This book is typical of the remarkable mind and grasp of intricate details the author has shown in all his books. These pages of the coming Temple and the return of Jesus Christ for His church excite me to look at the clouds on this day and pray, "Amen! Come, Lord Jesus!"

Dr. Jimmy Draper
President Emeritus—Lifeway

This exhaustive treatise, *Treasure and the Coming Temple of God*, by Dr. Lonnie Shipman is a treasure within itself. It is first a scholarly work with comprehensive Biblical insight into a tangible edifice that will be the physical abode of the infinite God Himself. The compelling illustrations encourage the reader to anticipate a day in the near future when we as believers can witness the embodiment of God's plan to demonstrate His radiant glory in tangible dimensions.

But the book is more than this. The author dramatically leads us to the point where we want to see the God of Redemption in Person. What more could we ask in our day of converging prophetic fulfillment than to be led to yearn, "Even so come Lord Jesus!"

Thank you, Dr. Shipman, for leading us on this incredible journey.

Carl E. Baugh, M. A., M. Div., Ph.D., Th. D.
Founder and President
Creation Evidence Museum of Texas
Glen Rose, Texas

Founder and Original Host
Creation in the 21st Century
Trinity Broadcasting Network

Since his youth, Lonnie Shipman has – among his many endeavors – had a passion for understanding the Book of Revelation and the teaching of the end-time events. He has sought the Bible teachers and leaders in the field. In addition to that, he has visited with those who have studied the history, archaeology, and culture of the Middle East, especially of Israel in particular. His is more than a second-hand experience. It's not an exaggeration to say that the larger body of eschatology writing is original. His prodigious mind well equips him to research, think, and then write about the Biblical end-times.

You will find in this book a trove of information that is the result of his work on the subject. He has assembled the material in a way that assists scholars and lay students in broadening their understanding of Revelation. You will find in this book the tools, carefully organized and presented, to answer many questions commonly asked of Bible students and inquisitive disciples.

All this while he also excels in the piano, combining Christian hymns and anthems with the great classical works of the past three centuries.

I heartily encourage you to get this unusual book. You will find it a great help in your own studies, and, if you're a teacher, an indispensable tool for the student.

Terry Spencer
M.A. in Medieval History, Wayne State University
M. Divinity in Systematic Theology, Bible Baptist Seminary
D. Humanities, Louisiana Baptist University

Dr. Terry Spencer was President of Faith Bible College, Norfolk, Virginia, Vice-President and Academic Dean of Arlington Baptist University, Arlington, Texas, has pastored five Baptist churches in Michigan, Texas, and Virginia, has been married for 48 years and has two children and four grandchildren.

Acknowledgment

I would like to acknowledge the great work and indispensable help others have made, without which this work would not have been possible.

I would like to thank my many Bible teachers who have inspired a deeper study of the Bible such as my father, Dr. Donald E. Shipman, along with Dr. Luther C. Peak, Dr. Roy A. Kemp, Dr. Earl K. Oldham, Dr. Terry Spencer and Dr. James Combs.

Special thanks must go to Aubrey L. Richardson, a Bible and Music authority, engineer with Lockheed Aircraft, and project initiator for an archaeological dig in Israel. He organized my 1992 evangelistic tour of Israel and has personally led me on several tours through the caves of the Dead Sea Scrolls and underground Jerusalem. He has been an invaluable resource for materials and support. This book is a direct result of that tour, meeting top rabbis, archaeologists and dignitaries, and the research and study that resulted.

I would like to thank the many people who have helped in typing and editing such as Ronnie Shipman and Dr. Elvena Shipman. Special thanks is due to Dr. Terry Spencer for his considerable help in helping edit the final draft. Each of these people have made a contribution of tireless work and effort to bring this project to fruition and their labors are deeply appreciated.

Thanks are due to Dr. Donald E. Shipman, Dr. Elvena Shipman, and Ronnie Shipman for production and final details of the book. Unless otherwise noted photographs and charts are by the author. All others are in the public domain.

May this book bring glory to the living God through the fine efforts of others

Dedication

I dedicate this book to my mother, Dr. Orlie Elvena Shipman, who nurtured me in this world, taught me the Bible and how to live for God, who has consistently prayed for me, and who has been an invaluable source of guidance and encouragement.

> [17] "Thine eyes shall see the king in his beauty: they shall behold the land that is very far off."
>
> [20a] "Look unto Zion, the city of solemnities: thine eyes shall see Jerusalem a quiet habitation, a tabernacle that shall not be taken down;"
>
> [21a] "But there the glorious LORD will be unto us a place of broad rivers and streams;"
>
> [22] "For the LORD is our judge, the LORD is our lawgiver, the LORD is our king; he will save us."
>
> (Isaiah 33:17, 20a, 21a, 22.)

Preface

On rare occasions, a publication emerges that seizes and keeps the attention of the reader. Such is this work authored by Lonnie Shipman, theologian of more than ordinary scholarship and concert pianist of the highest rank. As an academician myself, I know a good pen when I see it.

Many people of our time are caught up by a spirit of eschatological fervor, whether those of genuine Christian faith or those infected by a Godless atheism. We embrace much more about climate control, exploding global population, and the shortage of food and nourishment in many parts of the world. All this is in addition to unbridled violence in our streets and schools, and most heartbreaking of all, murder and mayhem in our homes. Observers of all kinds are stymied as to what to do. Sociologists, educators, and even theologians, at least some kinds, fail to find answers to our social problems.

Treasure and the Coming Temple of God goes a long way in showing that only God and the Christian faith offer a genuine solution. I have carefully read this engaging work and I do not know of any other works that are more eschatologically comprehensive, and in my view, more accurate in engaging last-time events. I recommend this work as one of the very best available.

Eugene H. Merrill
Professor of Old Testament Studies (Emeritus),
Dallas Theological Seminary
Ph. D. in Old Testament Studies, Bob Jones University
M.A. in Theology, New York University
Ph. D. in Ancient Near Eastern Languages and History of the Ancient Near East, Columbia University

Foreword

In this volume written by Evangelist Lonnie L. Shipman entitled, **Treasure and the Coming Temple of God**, he has presented the glorious new Jerusalem and the center of its worship as it is prophesied in the Bible. The coming of the Lord Jesus Christ for the second time from heaven and all the details that surround the denouement of world history and the setting up of the kingdom of our Lord are marvelously and gloriously presented in these pages.

The illustrations are beyond compare. I have never seen their like in any published volume I have ever looked upon. They brilliantly illustrate and present what this new kingdom and the new temple of God will look like. They are worth the volume in themselves.

God be praised for the scholarly study Lonnie Shipman has poured into this depiction and description and understanding of the coming temple of God. You will be imminently rewarded in reading and studying the book.

Dr. W. A. Criswell
Dallas, Texas
Senior Pastor, First Baptist Church
Chancellor, The Criswell College

Table Of Contents

ENDORSEMENTS i
ACKNOWLEDGMENT v
PREFACE ix
FOREWORD xi
TABLE OF CONTENTS xiii
LIST OF ILLUSTRATIONS xxi
LIST OF COLOR IMAGES xxii
INTRODUCTION xxv

CHAPTER ONE
Are We Living in the Last Days?

The Last Days Events 1
The Preparations for the Temple 4
Events that Lead to Rebuilding the Temple 6

CHAPTER TWO
The Mysterious Ashes of the Red Heifer

The Command for the Red Heifer Sacrifices 9
The History of the Sacrifice 12
The Special Requirements for the Red Heifer 13
The Preparation of the Priest for the Red Heifer Ceremony 15
The Ceremony of the Ashes of the Red Heifer 22
The Sprinkling of the Ashes of the Red Heifer 26
The Biblical Picture of the Red Heifer Sacrifice 27

CHAPTER THREE
The Modern Importance of the Red Heifer Sacrifice

The Ashes and Temple Worship 31
A Historic Interview with Rabbi Shlomo Goren 33
Are the Original Ashes Needed? 41
What Happened to the Ashes? 48
Are the Ashes Hidden in Qumran? 49
What About the Temple Mount and the Mount of Olives? 53
Could a Gentile Provide the Red Heifer for the Temple? 59
The Breeding of New Red Heifers 61
The Coming Kingdom Age 67

CHAPTER FOUR
Where is the Lost Ark of The Covenant?

The History of the Ark 71
The Importance of the Ark of the Covenant 81
To Where did the Ark Disappear? 82

CHAPTER FIVE
What Happened to the Ark?

Did Nebuchadnezzar Take the Ark to Babylon? 89
Did Jewish Kings Take the Ark? 93
Was the Ark Lost or Stolen? 96
Is the Ark in Heaven? 96

CHAPTER SIX
Unusual Theories of the Ark's Location

- What About the Vision of Masada? 99
- Does the Pope Have the Ark? 101
- Did the Ancient Romans Take the Ark? 103
- Was the Ark Hidden in the Nea Church of Israel? 106
- Was the Ark Found During the Crusades? 108
- Is the Ark in England or Ireland? 110
- What About Ein Gedi? 112
- Will the Real Indiana Jones Please Stand Up? 113
- Did Indiana Jones Really Find the Ark? 116
- Is the Ark Hidden at Gordon's Calvary? 119

CHAPTER SEVEN
The Primary Possible Locations of the Ark of the Covenant

- Was There More Than One Ark? 125
- How Many Arks Exist? 126
- The Ancient Ethiopian Legend 128
- Is the Ark in Qumran by the Dead Sea? 137
- Did Jeremiah Hide the Ark on Mount Nebo? 142
- Is the Ark in Jerusalem? 152
- Was the Ark Hidden Under the Dome of the Rock? 156
- Was the Ark of the Covenant at the Dome of the Rock Location? ... 165
- Where Else on the Temple Mount Might the Treasure Be Hidden? ... 167
- Digging for the Ark 169
- Why Do the Muslim Arabs not Retrieve the Ark? 178
- Eyewitness to the Discovery of the Ark 179

Reflections on the Ark's Discovery and the Coming Temple 181

CHAPTER EIGHT
Peace in the Middle East 185

- The Mid-East Peace Agreement 185
- The Dead Come to Life 186
- The Regathering of Israel 187
- The Coming Messiah 189
- God's Covenant of Peace 189
- God's Sanctuary in the Land 190
- Peace in the Temple 191

CHAPTER NINE
Will the Jewish Temple be Rebuilt? 193

- What Does the Bible Say? 193
- The Second Coming of the LORD 194
- The Liberal Objection 194
- The Manner of Jesus' Coming 195
- When Will the Temple Be Rebuilt? 200
- The Seventieth Week of Daniel 201
- The Temple is Desecrated 204
- The Jews Flee to Petra 206
- The Battle of Armageddon 207
- Jesus Descends to Earth 211
- Christ Will Establish His Throne 212

CHAPTER TEN
Temple Preparations Today

- Jewish Priesthood Schools 215
- Playing the Temple Instruments 217

Laying the Temple Foundation Stone 218
Finding the Holy of Holies..220
Why Rebuild the Temple? 220
A Peaceful Goal 222
Guardians of the Sanctuary...222
Many Rebuilding Developments...223
Discovering the Oil of Anointing...224
The Search for the Lost Ark and Ashes 225

CHAPTER ELEVEN
The History of the Temple

The Tabernacle in the Wilderness..227
The Temple of Solomon..229
The Temple Measurements 230
The Holy of Holies 231
Jewish Temple Terms 232
The Temple is Attacked...233
Rebuilding the Temple Under Cyrus 234
The Turbulent Reign of Antiochus Epiphanes.....................................234
The Maccabean Revolt..235
The Temple Mount Proper 236
The Roman Invasion 236
Herod Remodels the Temple 236
The Second Temple Destroyed 238
Preserving the Western Wall...238
The Bar Kokhba Revolt 239
The Temple of Bar Kokhba..240
The Size of the Temple Mount Platform 241
The Roman Pagan Temple 242
The Coming of Constantine..243

Building the Dome of the Rock 244
Crosses Adorn the Dome of the Rock 244
The Al Aqsa Mosque 245
The Coming of the Crusaders 246
Shrines Returned to the Muslims 248

CHAPTER TWELVE
The Tribulation Temple

The Tribulation Period 249
The Time of Rebuilding 250
Obstacles to Rebuilding the Temple 250
The Christian Objection 251
The Arab Objection 252
How Will the Obstacles be Overcome? 252
The Antichrist's Covenant of Peace 253
Gog and Magog I 254
Will the Al Aqsa Be Removed? 255
Where Will the Rebuilt Temple Stand? 256
The Northern Location 256
The Southern Location 258
The Traditional Location 259
The Foundation Stone as the Site of the Holy of Holies 260
The Foundation Stone as the Site of the Altar 261
What will the Temple Look Like? 263
The Bar Kokhba Temple 264
The Temple of Ezekiel 265
A Description of Herod's Temple 266
A Walk Through the Tribulation Temple 267
Differences Between the Tribulation and Solomon Temples 268
The Tribulation Temple Destroyed 269

CHAPTER THIRTEEN
The Millennial Kingdom

The World in Chaos	271
The Judgment of All Nations	272
God Establishes His Kingdom on Earth	274
The Blessings of the Millennium	279
Topographical Changes in the Middle East	279
Changes in Jerusalem	280
The Dead Sea Comes to Life	282
The Nile River is Stopped	283
New Boundaries for Israel	284
Jerusalem is Given a New Name	284
God's Political System	285
Ruling and Reigning with Christ	287
Will David Be King Again?	288
Beneficial Climate Change	290
Increased Fertility and Productiveness	291
The Disappearance of Physical Disease and Deformity	292
Longevity of Life	292
The Barrier of Language	294
Peace in the Animal Kingdom	295
God's Special Love for the Jewish People	296
God Building His Temple	297
Stone is Provided for Building	297
Sacrifices Renewed in the Temple	298
The Later Gog and Magog War	299

CHAPTER FOURTEEN
The Millennial Temple

What Will the Millennial Temple Look Like?...301
Ezekiel's Description of the Temple...302
The Inner Temple 305
The Altar of the Temple...306
The Temple Thrones of Judgment..307
Other Possible Temple Designs..309
The Purpose of the Ark and the Temple...313
The Glory of God on the House 315

EPILOGUE
The Hidden Meaning of the Jewish Sacrifice Revealed.................................319
How Do You Accept Eternal Life?..321

BIBLIOGRAPHY 325

ABOUT THE AUTHOR..333

List of Illustrations

1. The Highlights of Prophecy Chart
2. A Messiah street-sign, New York State
3. The Temple Mount with Herod's Temple and the eastern bridge
4. Tomb of the Kings, Jerusalem, Israel
5. A map of the Catacombs of the Tomb of Queen Helena
6. An overview of the Vatican and St. Peter's Basilica
7. The Arch of Titus, Rome, Italy
8. The menorah inside Titus' Arch
9. The Byzantine Nea church of Jerusalem
10. The Oasis of Ein Gedi near the Dead Sea, Israel
11. Vendyl Jones and the two caves he surveyed
12. The skull face, Gordon's Calvary, Jerusalem
13. The Memorial Church of Moses, Mt. Nebo, Jordan
14. Inside the cave called the "Well of Souls."
15. Ritmeyer location of the Ark at the Dome of the Rock, Jerusalem
16. The Seventy Weeks of Daniel Chart
17. The Jewish Temple superimposed over the Temple Mount
18. The Temple of Solomon, built in 950 B.C.
19. The floor plan of Herod's Temple
20. Cave eleven of the Dead Sea Scroll caves
21. A floor plan of the Temple scroll Temple
22. The northern plan of the Temple of Herod
23. The southern plan of the Temple of Herod
24. The Temple plan with the Rock as the Holy of Holies
25. The Temple plan with the Rock as the Altar

26. The Temple Scroll Temple
27. Model of Herod's Temple
28. Model of Tribulation Temple
29. A topographical map of the changes for the Millennial Temple
30. The Gates of the Millennial Temple
31. A half-mile vista down the outer court of the Millennial Temple
32. The Corner Court compared to the St. Paul's Cathedral of London, England
33. The Inner Temple
34. The Millennial Temple Covered with the Shekinah-glory Cloud
35. A Jewish Model for the Millennial Temple
36. Another Jewish Temple Model
37. The Millennial Temple concept from *Israel My Glory*

List of Color Images

1. An example of a red heifer
2. The Eastern Gate, Jerusalem, Israel
3. Lonnie Shipman at Cave III, Qumran, Israel
4. Qumran, and the Dead Sea Scroll caves
5. Lonnie Shipman inside Cave IV A, Qumran, Israel
6. The Mount of Olives with the Church of All Nations and the Russian Church
7. A representation of the Ark of the Covenant
8. The Ark from the tomb of King Tutankhamen of Egypt
9. The Tabernacle of Israel
10. The Second Jewish Temple with interior vessels
11. A depiction of ancient Babylon
12. Masada, the desert fortress of Herod

13. The "Holy Blood" of Brugge, Belgium
14. The Ark of the Covenant procession, Aksum, Ethiopia
15. The Wailing Wall with Wilson's Arch, Jerusalem, Israel
16. The Rabbinical Tunnel in Jerusalem
17. The Dome of the Rock on the Temple Mount in Jerusalem
18. The Treasury of Petra, Jordan
19. The valley of Megiddo, Israel
20. The articles of the Temple Institute
21. A harp from the Harrari harp factory of Israel
22. The Temple of Herod
23. The Al Aqsa Mosque, Jerusalem, Israel
24. The Temple of Ezekiel

Introduction

The study of the soon coming of Jesus Christ to this world in judgment is fascinating. The purpose of this book is to show the many interconnected events with the prophecies of the end of the world, especially the rebuilding of the Jewish Temple.

In our current time, the topic of rebuilding the Jewish Temple is of great importance. In the decades of the '80s and '90s with the fall of communism in parts of Eastern Europe, although it remains in power in Russia, China, and other areas, and immense changes in world economy and military policy, the subject of Mideast peace became a prominent goal of future world change. This peace process in Israel is intimately involved with reconciling differences of Jewish and Islamic faith. To the Orthodox Jewish mind, a future peace in Israel must involve a rebuilding of the Jewish Temple and a complete reinstitution of the Jewish Law which would include a full sacrificial system of worship. Toward this end, the Jews are tirelessly working today. Together with the rebuilding of the Jewish Temple, the continued search for the Ark of the Covenant (to ensure God's presence in the Temple) and the ashes of the red heifer (a sacrificial ash used to cleanse the Temple and priests) is explored to see its importance to the events.

The Bible tells us that in the end-time the Temple of the Jews would be rebuilt. Thus, the timing of the rebuilding gives the reader clues to the fulfillment of many other end-time prophecies such as the Second Coming of the Lord Jesus and the establishment of His Kingdom on Earth.

As a young man growing up in Dallas, Texas, it was often my privilege to hear many sermons on biblical prophecy and a love for these topics was instilled in me from an early age. As I grew older, a pursuit of a more intense study of prophecy was a thrilling part of my growth in Bible study.

In 1992, it was my great privilege to preach and concertize across the land of Israel in an evangelistic tour. While traveling in the land, I had the unexpected opportunity to meet many leaders in politics, religious faith, and archaeological study. Also, I was given a tour of eight of the eleven caves of the Dead Sea Scrolls and underground Jerusalem.

After viewing first-hand the current events leading to the rebuilding of the Temple in Jerusalem, I began to speak on these subjects in many churches. People began to suggest that I write about these topics to alert others to details about the soon return of our Lord Jesus. I present this study humbly to you. This book is certainly not the last word on these subjects, and I do not claim to be a final authority. The book is merely a result of my personal Bible study and travels.

I offer it to you with the hope that you will receive as much enjoyment as I did, learning these things of prophecy. I pray that this study will awaken many Christians to serve God more fervently, and that other people may hear the gospel and be saved before it is eternally too late for their souls. May God bless you as you read.

CHAPTER ONE

Are We Living in the Last Days?

Prophecy is one of the most electrifying and popular subjects today. It seems that people everywhere are searching for answers to such questions as, "When is Jesus coming back?" "Will there truly be a Battle of Armageddon?" and "When is the End of the World?" The subject has been popularized in many current books and even secular movies such as *The Omen* and *The Day After*. People seem to look for the soon return of Jesus everywhere, and events such as the beginning of the new millennium are just one of many examples of end-time signs. And the continual occurrence of wars, famines, various pestilence (including illnesses like the Coronavirus-19), and continual new false teaching all point to the end time scenario. Yet, when will Jesus return? What will happen to the world and how can we prepare for His coming?

Are there answers to these questions? Does God declare the outcome of world events? The Bible gives us answers in a detailed account of end-time events.

The Last Days Events

The Bible defines several coming events that divide the end-time into sections. These sections are the Rapture, the Tribulation Period, the Battle of Armageddon, the Millennial Reign of Christ, the Great White Throne Judgment, and the

HIGHLIGHTS OF PROPHECY

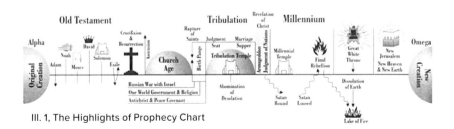

Ill. 1, The Highlights of Prophecy Chart

New Heaven and New Earth. There are also many other related events to these, some of which happen simultaneously.

Students of the Bible refer to our world's current age as the New Testament Church Age. Jesus of Nazareth, the living Son of God, came humbly to Earth as a virgin-born babe. He lived a sinless life, growing into manhood and fulfilling the law. As prophesied in the Old Testament, the Lord Jesus preached the gospel and performed untold miracles, and was later betrayed and tried for crimes He did not commit. Men took the Savior to Calvary where He died on the cross for the sins of the world, providing salvation for all who would believe. He was buried for three days and nights and triumphantly arose from the dead the third day, later ascending to His heavenly throne. The disciples of Jesus then went throughout the world spreading the good news of salvation through Christ, building churches as they went.

The Bible speaks of a time at the end of this Church Age when Jesus will come back to Earth to claim His church and all believers. The Rapture is the event where Jesus descends back to Earth for His saints with a shout, with the voice of the Archangel and the trump of God. At this time, all the bodies of the Christians who have previously died will rise from their graves. Christians who are still alive on Earth will be raised to meet the Lord in the air. Their bodies will be changed into a glorified body like unto the resurrected body of the Lord and then they will enter the glories of Heaven, being in the presence of Jesus forever (1 Thess. 4; John 14; 1 Cor. 15)!

At that time, the Antichrist will come to power on Earth as a great world leader. He will first appear to be the most wonderful of all rulers, possessing a magnetic personality and the most brilliant mind ever known. Soon though, his true identity will be revealed as the "man of sin." He will literally be the embodiment of Satan. Then will commence

CHAPTER ONE

a time of judgment never before seen on Earth. Cataclysmic events will be commonplace as God will judge the world. This period of time is the dreaded Tribulation Period and will be the greatest time of war, death, famine, and disaster in all of human history. This time of prophecy is also called "Daniel's Seventieth Week" or "The Time of Jacob's Trouble (Jacob's Sorrow)" because of the dealing of God with the nation of Israel proper (Rev. 6-18; Dan. 9; Matt. 24).

The Great Tribulation will culminate into the Battle of Armageddon. In this Battle, the armies of the world will be gathered strategically at the Valley of Megiddo, also called Armageddon, to fight against God Himself! Jesus will descend from heaven, accompanied by ten thousands of His saints, and gloriously defeat the armies of the world. After overcoming His enemies, He will descend on the Mount of Olives, which will divide in half at His coming. This will cause a series of geographic transformations in Israel and especially at Jerusalem (Rev. 19; Zech. 14).

Jesus will then ascend to Mount Moriah (the Temple Mount), entering through the Eastern Gate. Mount Moriah and Mount Zion will be merged into one huge mountain as the result of a great earthquake, and it is there that God will establish the seat of His throne. This will mark the beginning of the Millennial Reign of God on the Earth where He will rule the nations with a rod of iron. All nations will worship Christ Jesus in the Temple of Jerusalem at this time (Rev. 20; Zech. 6).

At the end of the Millennium, all the unsaved dead will be judged at the Great White Throne. These unsaved people will be sent to the Everlasting Lake of Fire to be punished for their sin of not believing on Christ for salvation (Rev. 20).

God will then melt the elements of this world with fervent heat and the heavens will be engulfed in a flame that will flash across the sky. This will make them appear to roll up like a scroll. After this, God will form a New Heaven and a New Earth. In this New Heaven and Earth, all those who have believed on Jesus as Savior will live eternally in a perfect state, with perfect bodies, in a perfect world (Isa. 65:17-25; Rev. 21:1-8).

The Preparations for the Temple

Thrilling days are surely ahead for the Christians and many stirring events are yet to occur. In these "Last Days," the prospect of rebuilding the Jewish Temple in Jerusalem is very exciting. The Rebuilt Temple is a subject for which the Jews look, the Arabs fear, and Bible students are thereby intrigued. The Orthodox Jews in Jerusalem are awaiting a soon-coming Temple of worship. Priests are being readied, Temple garments are being replicated, and signs are placed on the streets proclaiming, "Messiah is here!"

Amid this air of expectancy and exuberance, the leaders of the Jewish Rabbinical system are quietly preparing and waiting for a soon-coming event, the advent of the Messiah! This Messiah the Jews seek is not necessarily Jesus of Nazareth. The Orthodox Jews do not generally believe in Jesus as their national Messiah and personal Savior. They are seeking another religious and political leader.

Ill. 2, A Messiah street-sign, New York State.
Photo by Gaby Grossman stljewishlight.org public domain

CHAPTER ONE

An example of this action is a movement in recent times among one group of Orthodox Jews named the Lubavitchers who followed a Jewish Rabbi living in New York named Rabbi Menachem Mendel Schneerson. This man was in his 70s and in very poor health. Notwithstanding, he seemed to be such a wise and holy man that some Jews believed him to be the coming Messiah and were awaiting his arrival in Jerusalem. A poster in the Jewish Quarter of Jerusalem proclaimed, "Long live our master, our teacher, and our rebbe king Messiah forever and ever!" While some Jews put their faith in this New York rabbi, others did not follow him. Then he passed away in 1994. These Jews now look for another political and religious world leader that is soon to be revealed.

There have been many cases in history where Jews have claimed to be the Messiah who would bring peace and an everlasting kingdom to the Jews. Of all the "false Christs" who will appear on the scene of history, the most evil is yet to arise. Bible-believing Christians often think of the Antichrist as this coming world leader.

The Bible says that Israel will make a covenant with the Antichrist during the Tribulation Period. This Antichrist will seem to be the greatest world leader of all time. He will assemble all the nations into a one-world political and religious system. And he will establish peace in the Middle East between the Jews and Arabs through a special peace covenant he makes with Israel. Yet, in the midst of the Tribulation Period, the Antichrist will break his covenant with Israel when he enters the Temple and commits sacrilege to God. This event is often referred to as the "Abomination of Desolation." As a result of this event, Israel will realize that he is not the true Messiah and will turn away from him (Dan. 9; Matt. 24).

Thus, two distinct systems of thought by the Jews and the Christians will ultimately culminate. The believers in Jesus of Nazareth as Savior are awaiting the coming of Christ in the Rapture to take them to heaven in a supernatural instantaneous event. They believe a false Messiah will then arise who will be defeated by Jesus at His coming as King to reign for a millennium in Jerusalem as King of Kings and Lord of Lords. While the most conservative Orthodox Jewish groups look for another Messiah (or Christ) to usher in the reign of their King and Kingdom.

The Bible tells us that Israel will be living in the land again and have returned in unbelief. The Bible also tells us that they would be operating a temple in the future which means they must have Jerusalem in Jewish control. The State of Israel declared its independence on May 14, 1948, and they regained control of Jerusalem in 1967. Now we are awaiting the replacement of the Jewish Temple.

Jesus had prophesied the destruction of the Jewish Temple in Matthew 24:2 where "not one stone is left upon another," and yet He also told us that in the last days, the Antichrist will commit the abomination of desolation "in the holy place" (Matt. 24:15), which implies that Antichrist will desecrate a future Temple. This occurs three and a half years into the Tribulation period, yet the Rapture occurs first. Thus, if we are close to the time of the future Temple, we are even closer to the Rapture. Although no specific date is given in the Bible about Jesus' return in the Rapture, because the Jews are trying to rebuild the Temple in this modern age, we are closer than ever to the Rapture!

Events That Lead to Rebuilding the Temple

Two modern-day trends that lead us to this event are the preparation for the rebuilding of the Jewish Temple and the Jewish anticipation of a soon-coming Messiah. Of the many interconnected events that accompany the coming Temple and Messiah, perhaps the most intriguing are the search

CHAPTER ONE

for the lost Ark of the Covenant and the Ashes of the Red Heifer. In the Jewish mind, these events will happen at about the same time. Orthodox Jews believe that the Messiah will come when the Temple is rebuilt. For worship in the Temple to resume, they must have Moses' original Ark of the Covenant to place in the Temple. They must also have the Ashes of the Red Heifer to cleanse the priests who will serve there. Yet, what are the Ark of the Covenant and the Ashes of the Red Heifer? Where are they hidden? Why are they so important? In recent days, several amazing clues have come to light. Surely, we are living in the "Last Days." Let us be awakened to the soon return of the Lord and proclaim, "Even so, come, Lord Jesus!"

CHAPTER TWO

The Ashes of The Red Heifer

In the Old Testament, the Jewish Levitical priesthood was charged with the responsibility of administering the offerings to God. The five main types of offerings were the burnt offering, meat offering, peace offering, sin offering and trespass offering. There were also several other lesser-known offerings such as the heave offering and wave offering.

The Command for the Red Heifer Sacrifices

Probably the least familiar offering was the mystical sacrifice of the Red Heifer. A description of this sacrifice is given in Numbers 19:1-22. The Bible introduces us to this sacrifice:

And the LORD spake unto Moses and unto Aaron saying,

This is the ordinance of the law which the LORD hath commanded, saying, Speak unto the children of Israel, that they bring thee a red heifer without spot, and upon which never came yoke:

And ye shall give her to Eleazar the priest, that he may bring her forth without the camp, and one shall slay her before his face: (Num. 19:1-3)

This sacrifice was unusual for several reasons:

1. It was the only female sacrifice, (Num. 19:2).
2. It was, of necessity, a red heifer, (Num. 19:2).
3. It was to be without spot or blemish, which had never previously been yoked, (Num. 19:2).
4. It must be burned without the camp. Later, it was burned outside the city walls, (Num. 19:3).
5. It must be burned in its entirety, leaving only the Ashes of the sacrifice. It was the only Biblical offering that was entirely consumed by fire, (Num. 19:5).
6. The blood of the sacrifice was sprinkled seven times before the Tabernacle of the congregation as in the offering on

the Day of Atonement, the most holy sacrifice in Israel, (Num. 19:4).
7. Articles added to the offering were cedar wood, hyssop and scarlet thread of wool, (Num. 19:6).
8. The high priest was made ritually unclean for offering the sacrifice, as well as his assistant, (Num. 19:7, 8).
9. The Ashes are used to purify one that touched the dead, (Num. 19:12).
10. This sacrifice was only made seven times in history. Some Jewish scholars believe that it was made as many as nine times.[1] (It is believed that one or two priests each offered two sacrifices, thus seven, eight or as many as nine times.)
11. The sacrifice was offered so that the Ashes could be used to cleanse sinners. Sinners were ritually cleansed in a ceremony that included mixing these Ashes with water. A sinner who needed cleansing was defined as anyone who was defiled by a dead body (Num. 19:16), or who touched a bone or grave of the dead (Num. 19:14).
12. This sacrifice was to be a perpetual sacrifice for the nation of Israel. Even in A.D. 70, after the great Temple in Jerusalem was destroyed, the priesthood had ceased and Israel's people were scattered, the ordinance was still in effect. Also, when the book of Hebrews was written, sometime in the first century, the sacrifice was mentioned in Hebrews 9:13-14, showing its continued importance.

This purification was specifically given to purify those people who might have been contaminated and became ritually unclean by touching the dead or the bones or grave of the dead. The commandment was first given after the Israelites had suffered the death of 14,700 rebellious Jews by plague, mentioned in the book of Numbers 16:49. Under hot desert conditions, the bodies would require immediate burial in

---
[1] Parah 3:5

CHAPTER TWO

graves. It was at this time that God gave the instructions to Moses and Aaron regarding the red heifer. The significance of the red heifer to cleanse from the defilement of death came at a most impressive time. The connection between sin and death could hardly be more apparent!

Thus, someone who touched the dead or grave of the dead must be cleansed, giving a picture of death as being the greatest result of impurity, just as it was in the Garden of Eden, (Gen. 3; Rom. 5:12). However, this cleansing was also applied to cleanse someone for the office of priest, for cleansing lepers and others healed of sickness, for cleansing everyday worshippers in the Temple, and for cleansing members of the Sanhedrin, (Num. 19:9).

The Sanhedrin was the assembly of ordained Jewish scholars that functioned both as Supreme Court and as legislature in Israel before A.D. 70. With the destruction of the Temple and the end of Jewish independence, the Sanhedrin ceased to function.

The process of cleansing was very simple. The priests would take a small amount of the Ashes (a pinch held between the fingers) and sprinkle it into a basin of water, which was used for the cleansing. The mixing of this special Ash made the water ritually clean. This water was then called "The Water of Purification" and sprinkled on one who needed to be made clean. The Ash was stored in a *kalal* for use at a later time.

A *kalal* was a pot or pitcher made of stone used in Biblical times for all purity purposes. These stone vessels were used by the priests in their daily eating and drinking and for storage of needed items. Therefore, it was also the only kind of vessel used to hold the Ashes of the Red Heifer, sometimes referred to as the vessels of purification. This word is mentioned in the Aramaic dialect as *klal* in the Copper Scroll of the Dead Sea scrolls, and is sometimes interpreted to mean the pot of the Ashes of the Red Heifer, although its use in that way in the Copper Scroll is debatable, and is probably not true. However, in this instance, the word means "vessel, or jar" and could refer to any urn containing a substance. The meaning in the Copper Scroll is not clearly implied, and several interpretations exist.

This Ash was also used to cleanse vessels and places (Num. 19:14-15, 18). Not only did the people need to be clean to serve God, but they must also use clean vessels and worship on holy ground. This Ash must be found to cleanse the area of the Temple and the Temple vessels for use in a later rebuilt Temple. Even if the buildings were built, they could not be used for worship until they are first cleansed.

The Temple Mount is a place where many battles have taken place. During ancient times, many thousands met their death on this holy Mount. Moreover, profane worship places have been built on the Temple Mount and sections of the Mount were even used as places of refuse in earlier history. The Ashes will be used to cleanse the future priests and Sanhedrin of Israel and the everyday worshipers, to cleanse the Temple vessels, the ground of the Temple Mount and the rebuilt Temple building itself. In the Jewish mind, it is essential that these Ashes be found or at least reproduced.

The History of the Sacrifice

When God first commanded this sacrifice, the people of Israel were still wandering in the wilderness and God's presence was manifested at the Tabernacle in the pillar of cloud by day and the pillar of fire by night. Moses himself prepared the first sacrifice. Ezra prepared the second, and seven sacrifices have been prepared since that time. The last was prepared shortly before the Roman invasion of A.D. 70.

The Mishnah teaches that up until the destruction of the Second Temple, ashes had been prepared from a total of only nine heifers. Moses by himself gave the first–as the verse states, "...have them bring you a red heifer." The prophet Ezra offered the second after the days of the First Temple, and during the Second Temple only seven more heifers were used for ashes. This was to provide enough ash for the nation's needs for purification throughout all those years.

The names of all the High Priests who prepared those seven heifers during Second Temple times are recorded by the Mishnah: Simon the Just and Yochanan each made two; El'yhoeini ben Hakof, Chanamel HaMitzri of Egypt and Yishmael ben Pi'avi processed one heifer each. Thus, from the time that Moses received the commandment of the Red Heifer from God until the destruction of the Second Temple, purifying ashes had been produced by the hands of these famous Jewish leaders from a total of nine red heifers.

The Special Requirements for the Red Heifer

The ordinance of the red heifer has detailed requirements that must be met. Some of these are directly related in the Biblical verses of Numbers 19. Many others were transmitted orally to Moses and then passed down by the rabbis throughout the generations, until the present day. These extra-Biblical requirements are expounded upon in the Jewish writings of the Oral Tradition.

The religious Jews believe that the Oral Traditions are just as sacred as the written Word of God and that God gave it to Moses while he was on Mount Sinai as part of his revelation to man. Christian believers might view the Oral Tradition as very important reference material, but would still view it only as tradition, not actually the very Word of God.

First, the heifer must be three years old and perfect in redness. This means that the presence of as few as two hairs of any color other than red will render it invalid for use as a sacrifice![2]

---
2   Parah 2:5.

The difference of certain Jewish authorities on this point is varied and almost comical. For instance, some rabbis believe that there must not be even one hair that is not red. Another said if it had two black or white hairs growing from a single hole or hollow it is invalid. Rabbi Akiba said it could have as many as four or five if these hairs were disbursed and they pulled them out. (Can you imagine that scenario?) Rabbi Eliezer says it may have even fifty. Interestingly, Rabbi Joshua b. Bathyra said that if it had only two hairs that were not red, and one was one its head and the other on its tail, then it would disqualify.[3]

Because the heifer must have fewer than two hairs (or no hairs) that were not red, it was always rare and expensive to acquire. Even the hooves and eyelashes must be red. It must be totally free from any physical blemish or defect, whether internal or external.

While the offering of the red heifer is not slaughtered in the Temple as other sacrifices, it is required that the heifer should have no blemishes which make any sacrifice invalid—such as those recounted in chapter 22 of the book of Leviticus. The red heifer also has an additional, unique requirement: it must never be used to perform any physical labor. That is the interpretation of Numbers 19:2, "...upon which never came a yoke" and it is believed that any labor of the animal in any physical sense at all would make it invalid, even for the least, most minor thing. This would include riding her, *or even leaning on her.*

The only exception would be some action which is intrinsically necessary for the heifer's own well-being, such as tying her for her own safety. But if a yoke were placed upon her even once, even if she was not used to plow, this would be enough to make the heifer unfit for use.

---

3   Parah 1.2.5.

CHAPTER TWO

A red heifer that meets these requirements and others could be used to provide the ashes for the purification process and fulfill the commandment. This heifer must be brought to the "Mount of Anointment," a precise location on the Mount of Olives, opposite to the original eastern gate of the Temple Mount where they have erected the Miphkad Altar. At this place, the heifer must be slaughtered and burned. Afterward, its ashes are mixed together with natural spring water for purification. These "waters of sanctification," would be used to sprinkle on those who were impure.

The Preparation of the Priest for the Red Heifer Ceremony

The process of preparing the priest for the sacrifice is quite interesting. Seven days before the burning of the sacrifice, the priest that was to burn the heifer left his house and family and went to a special chamber. Opposite the northeastern corner of the Temple buildings was a chamber called the House of Stone. For seven days, the priest would prepare himself through prayer for the sacrifice. During this time, other priests would sprinkle him with purification water from

Color Image 1, An example of a Red Heifer. Red Heifer

the Ashes of earlier sacrifices and read aloud to him from the Torah and Talmud. He would be presented to the elders of the priesthood on the eve of the holy day in order for him to be taught in the most precise manner the incense service. Then he is escorted by the elders to the Chamber of Avtinas, where the priestly Avtinas family formulate the incense according to their secret tradition. While there, he would be taught the incense service from the senior priests and swear that he will follow the Pharisee interpretation.

Before the High Priest would serve in the Temple on the Day of Atonement, he would leave his home and family a full week before the advent of Yom Kippur, and withdraw to his chamber in the Holy Temple. This was following the first example, for Aaron, the first High Priest, who had also separated himself (Lev. 8:33).

In some ways, the priest entrusted with burning the heifer has a similar status to the High Priest, who must separate from his wife and family as part of his preparations for Yom Kippur. This was in order to ensure that he would be in a state of purity when the awesome day of sacrifice arrives. In the same manner, the Mishnah teaches that the priest for the red heifer ceremony also separates himself to the Chamber of Stone. The chamber and all vessels the priest would use are fashioned exclusively of stone because this was the only material mandated by Biblical law to be impervious to impurity.

There were several other extra measures that were taken to safe-guard the priest from inadvertently becoming defiled during the course of the week, thus rendering him unfit for attending to the heifer.

One precaution was to sprinkle the priest during the course of the separation, with a mixture of the "waters of separation" which had been prepared from ashes made earlier. According to the Mishnah, the priest was sprinkled every day from a mixture of all the ashes that had been produced until then and previously mixed with earlier heifer ashes back to the heifer of Moses. Each time a heifer was burned, one-third of the ashes were saved and kept by the priests for future generations.

Why was this sprinkling done? During the time the priest had been in the chamber of stone, he had not been allowed to come into contact with anything that could defile him. But before the priest went to the chamber, it is possible that he had unknowingly been defiled or exposed to other impurity. According to Numbers 19:12, someone that is exposed to death must endure the sprinkling of the ashes on the third and seventh days after his exposure. Thus, the priest is sprinkled every day of this week, in case this happens to be the third or seventh day after an exposure.

According to the *halachic* concept of a grave which may be buried deep within the earth, whose presence is unknown because it cannot be detected from the surface of the ground, Biblical law concerning the impurity of death is quite exclusive. If a grave is hidden from sight, buried far below the ground with no suggestion of its existence on the surface–the power of the impurity is such that it radiates upward and out through the ground. So, even if someone is careful never to come near the proximity of the dead and has always been careful not to be exposed to impurity, he may still be impure due to at some point passing over an unknown grave under the earth.

When preparing the "waters of purification," even the water used was very specific. In Biblical times, this water was taken from the Siloam (the Shiloach) spring in the City of David. This spring is Jerusalem's original water source, located at the foot of the Temple Mountain, at the end of the water tunnel of King Hezekiah that collected water from the Gihon Spring on the eastern slope of the *Ophel*. It has always had great spiritual significance and was used as the Festival of Water

Libation during the Feast of Sukkot (Tabernacles). During the celebration of this Festival at Temple times, the priests and all the participants would descend to this spring, and there fill a golden vessel with its clear waters, to be poured out on the Temple's altar at the first rays of dawn.

Recently, this very service was reenacted in commemoration of the early Temple times and to encourage the soon return of the Temple. Priests gathered in the area of the Wailing Wall wearing their priestly garments, with the golden pitcher for the water, and with trumpets, harps and other musical instruments. Accompanied by a large crowd, they made a peaceful celebratory walk to Siloam and back, stopping a few times for singing and exhortation. The priests gathered the water and returned to the Temple area which they later offered together with wine on a specially prepared altar.

The Jews refer to the Western Wailing Wall as the Kotel ("wall," from *kathal*, "to join together, make into blocks"). The Wailing Wall, popularly called *Ha-Kotel*, "The Wall," is a section of wall that was the only remnant of the Temple (a retaining wall) accessible to Jewish people after the destruction of the Second Temple. Although it is a section of the mountain retaining wall, not of the building itself which stood on top of the mountain, it is sacred to the Jews and first became accessible to Jews for worship in modern times on June 7, 1967.

One interesting question is, who is pure enough to collect this fresh water? The person must be indisputably pure, or else he would render the water unfit upon contact! How can water which he collects be used to mix the solution for sprinkling on the isolated priest, who will in turn be burning a new red heifer to make new ashes …if he might also be tainted?

The Mishnah recounts that during the days of the Second Temple in Jerusalem that this problem was solved in an

CHAPTER TWO

unexpected way. Children were raised in specially prepared homes built with many arches separating them from the possible impure ground. They were never exposed to ritual impurity, where they were raised to grow up and perform the purification ceremony of the red heifer.

Dr. Randall Price, the famous Christian Biblical scholar, interviewed the Jewish Temple authority, Rabbi Chaim Richman, on June 23, 1991 about this problem and the rabbi tells of geographic isolation:

> *The Torah describes how in the time of the Temple there were certain courtyards, which because of their unique geological make-up, shielded from ritual impurities. Stone prevents impurities, and that is why there are walls in the Jewish cemeteries, and why the ashes were kept in stone vessels. In these courtyards the wives of the Cohanim priesthood went to give birth, and they left the child there until he reached a certain age. To reproduce this today, there have to be all the services for those children in the courtyard–nursery, grocery, everything. It's a whole concept of a society within a society…but it seems to me to be the only vehicle for preventing children from being exposed to impurities. This is obviously a mammoth undertaking… but this work may in fact be being done right now.* [4]

Reports concerning the fact of this work are not reliable, but what has been rumored is that special Israeli houses have been built on double arches, resting on solid bedrock to raise the building off the ground so that it does not come into contact with the land. This is because the land is possibly defiled, and contact would cause the inhabitants raised in the house to incur ritual impurity. In Biblical times, a hollow space of one *tefach* (the Biblical measurement of a hand breath, approximately 10 centimeters) was left underneath, between the floor of the courtyard and the rock.

---
[4] Thomas Ice, Randall Price, *Ready to Rebuild*, (Eugene, OR: Harvest House Publishers, 1992), 137.

It is believed that the children born to these Cohanim are being kept there in a state of quarantine and are being trained to perform the ceremony of purification. If such places exist, these children are waiting for the day when the red heifer becomes again available, and for the fulfillment of their destiny as future priests, preparing the way for the rebuilding of the Temple.

From the time of the Old Testament, children raised in this manner would gather the waters for the solution of "waters of sanctification," when the time came to purify another priest assigned for the work of burning a new heifer and preparing the ashes. When the children came of age, they left the special platform homes in an unusual way. Oxen were brought forth, and boards were placed across the oxen. The children rode these oxen out of the courtyards, sitting on the boards and carrying stone vessels to hold the water they would collect. The space below the boards, like the hollow space underneath the courtyard, protected the children from the possibility of any exposure from impurity coming up from within the Earth's depths that may cross their paths, while in route to the Siloam spring.

Color Image 2. The Eastern Gate, Jerusalem, Israel. Golden Gate (Jerusalem). (2023, February 12). In Wikipedia.

When they arrived at the spring, they would dismount and fill the vessels with water. Here, they could stand on the ground with no suspicion of impurity rising from below, since people are not accustomed to burying their dead under running water. (Actually, one Rabbinical opinion maintains that they were so extremely cautious they did not even dismount but remained upon the oxen and lowered the vessels down into the spring by a cord).

After gathering the water, the children remounted the oxen atop their boards and rode to the Eastern Gate of the Temple.

This gate is a double gate where each side represents the Gates of Mercy and Repentance, which was built by Sulieman the Magnificent in the sixteenth century on top of an earlier gate from Solomon's time. The gate beneath the present sealed double gate is also called the Golden Gate. The term "golden" was mistakenly applied to this gate because of the reference in Acts 3:2 to another inner Temple gate, the impressive Nicanor Gate, used the word *hóraia* ("beautiful"), which was misunderstood as *aurea* ("golden"). According to the Mishnah, this was the only gate on the east side of the Temple Mount.

The actual Beautiful Gate inside the Temple complex was called so because the lintel and sill were made of silver, the doors were made of bronze and it stood about seventy-five feet tall! There was also some confusion between commentators because the Beautiful Gate also faced east. It is thought by some researchers that this Eastern Gate might also be the Double Gate mentioned in the Copper Scroll, in which are possibly hidden the red heifer urn and a scroll describing the red heifer ceremony. This inner Temple gate, the Nicanor Gate, is what the priest would look through to view the Temple at the heifer sacrifice.

At the Eastern Gate and Temple Mount, there would be no fear of contamination—for the Temple with all its chambers was built with a hollow space below. Also, the entire Temple Mount complex was built with overlapping arches, as was the bridge leading from the Eastern Gate to the Mount of Anointment (the Mount of Olives). Holding their water-filled vessels, the children walked to the gate at the entrance to the Women's Courtyard. There, a stone vessel known as the *kalal* was kept at all times, which held the ashes of the red heifer. A child would then take these ashes and mix in the proper amount of water, preparing the "waters of sanctification." Finally, these children would then sprinkle the attending priest.

The Ceremony of the Ashes of the Red Heifer

After the children had gathered the "waters of sanctification" and cleansed the attending priest, the priest would make his way over a special bridge leading from the Eastern Gate on the Temple Mount to the "Mount of Anointment." This location was the spot on the Mount of Olives, directly facing the gate and aligned with the entrance to the Sanctuary where the purification process was conducted.

The bridge was built of overlapping arches supporting a smooth roadway, so that there were hollow spaces under the walkway that the people would cross. Impurity was stopped and sanctity ensured by having an open space of support between the earth, as detailed in Biblical law. Annually, this same bridge was used for the scapegoat as he was taken out of the Temple and into the desert on the Day of Atonement after the blood had been applied.

In this picture, the Temple is centered in the Temple Mount, in line with a "centered Eastern Gate," the Shushan Gate. There is a large causeway or eastern bridge that was built from the Temple Mount to the Mount of Olives on the far side where they would perform the ceremony of the red heifer. On the western side of the Temple Mount, facing us, there is a smaller bridge across the Tyropoeon Valley. The last large

CHAPTER TWO

arch in this western bridge as it connects to the Temple Mount Wall is Wilson's Arch, next to the current Western "Wailing" Wall. The current ground level at the Wailing Wall is much higher today, thus only the last arch is visible on the western side, which is used as a rabbinical study and is a great underground hall.

When the time was ready, a Red Heifer without blemish was brought forth. The red heifer, the attending priest who would be burning it, and all those who would be aiding or assisting in the ceremony would make their way outside the eastern city gate. This group would cross a causeway (or bridge) built from the Temple Mount called Mt. Moriah to the Miphkad Altar, ("the appointed place") on the Mount of Olives. The priest, and all that aided him, then led the Red Heifer with them to the altar. The causeway itself was built so that the priest could travel from one mountain to another without desecrating himself by passing over a grave in the nearby cemetery.[5]

On the Olivet Mount, in a specified place, the sacrifice was made. The place of the sacrifice had to be rather high on the side of the mountain in a direct line east from the door of the Temple. The High Priest had to be able to look at the door of the Temple through one of the gates on the eastern side of the Temple Mount (the Shushan Gate or more likely the Nicanor Gate). Consequently, the sacrifice was made directly across from one of these two gates near the bridge exit on the Olivet Mount. Somewhere across from the entrance on the Mount of Olives is where the Red Heifer sacrifice was made and the Ashes might also be hidden nearby.

The Jewish elders and all the city leaders awaited the arrival of the procession at the Place of Burning. Once the attending priest reached them, the Mishnah records that an unusual practice took place. After being guarded from impurity in a

---

5   Parah 3:6.

separated chamber with special vessels and being purified the entire previous week, the senior priests would deliberately contaminate the attending priest!

Some would view that the Sadducees were stricter in adherence to the Bible because they would require the attending priest to wait until sunset after his immersion to begin the ceremony. Because of a dispute with the Sadducees, the attending priest was deliberately contaminated before he began the process of burning the heifer, thus rendering him impure. This was to demonstrate that by his immersion in a *mikveh*, he might immediately begin the ceremony of burning the heifer, without having to wait for sunset of the same day.

The elders of Israel placed their hands upon the priest's head. Some rabbis hold that it was by this laying of the hands that they made him impure. Other authorities maintain that they touched him with some other source of impurity. To enable immediate purification from this contamination so that he could burn the heifer directly without waiting, according to the prevailing opinion of the rabbis, there was a special

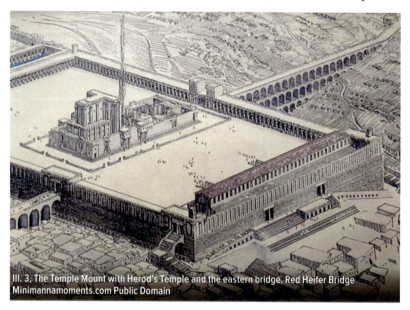

Ill. 3, The Temple Mount with Herod's Temple and the eastern bridge, Red Heifer Bridge Minimannamoments.com Public Domain

CHAPTER TWO

mikveh bath (similar to a church baptistry) built at this spot for the *kohen* priest to immerse himself before beginning his task. With their hands upon his head, the elders would cry: "My master, High Priest! Immerse yourself at once!"

Next, the priest descended into the Chamber of Immersion and purified himself by immersing himself in the water, and then came up and dried himself. Through this process of contamination and purification, witnessed by a large assembly in the presence of the elders of Israel, "the influence of the Sadducees and their illicit, unfounded rulings were silenced." At the same time, with the exception of this necessarily deliberate device that had its emphasis on the one specific *halachic* point of not waiting until sunset, the hallmark of the entire procedure was purity in the highest degree. The most elaborate precautions had been undertaken for that purpose.

At this location, a special altar is prepared, made from cedar, pine, cypress, and fig trees stacked like a small tower of wood and lit from the west side. The heifer is then bound to the altar with cords made from reed-grass, which do not become impure. It is placed on top of the wood arrangement with its head on the south side, and its face westward–toward the Temple–and the priest stands on the eastern side, also facing west.

Based on the instructions in Numbers 19:3, we recall, *"and ye shall give her unto Eleazar the priest, that he may bring her forth without the camp, and one shall slay her before his face."* Eleazar was the assistant to his father Aaron, the High Priest at the time this commandment was given. This tells us that the actual slaughtering of the heifer is performed outside the Temple ("without the camp"), and that it can be carried out by a lay kohen priest. It is not required exclusively to be done by the High Priest, though in reality the high priests always guarded the honor zealously within their own ranks.

When ready, the priest stands atop the altar, slaughters the heifer and uses his right hand to sprinkle the blood seven times in the direction of the Temple, as the verse states: *"toward the front of the Tent of Meeting."*

Next, he descends from the altar, lights the fire, and then the heifer is placed upon the fire.

The priest wraps the hyssop together with the cedar inside the crimson wool and throws it into the belly of the heifer–for as it is written, *"…and he shall throw it into the fire of the heifer."*

After the fire is finished and all has been completely burned, everything is ground down and crushed–including the wood, and all parts of the animal. The entire black mass is beaten with rods and sifted, because these are the ashes that will be saved and used for purity.

The Ashes would be divided into three sections. One part was reserved for safe keeping in the Temple, inside the wall at the front of the Women's Court. Another part was kept at the burning station on the Mount of Anointment. The third part was divided for use between all the priestly shifts serving in the Temple. The attending priests would then use their individual portions to purify the people in their respective part of the nation, while the allotment that was on the Mount of Olives was not used but was to be saved for the future priest who would later come to burn a new heifer.

The Sprinkling of the Ashes of the Red Heifer

According to the Bible, one who has had contact with the dead is impure for seven days. During the course of that week, on the third day and on the seventh day, the individual would be sprinkled with the waters of sanctification, that is, spring water mixed with a pinch of ash.

They are to use a vessel that is filled with "running waters," which is water flowing from a natural source, like a spring, not a stagnant pond or "still waters." Some of the ashes are thrown into this vessel, and the mixture of ashes and water are sprinkled on the body of the man on the third and seventh day after sunrise. It was also sprinkled on clothing or vessels that became impure by having been within the same tent (or any enclosure) that contained a dead body.

How did the priest do the sprinkling? One who was previously purified administered the waters. This was not done by hand; rather, the one who purifies the others would tie a bundle of three stalks of hyssop. Each twig must have one bud, and the tops of the buds were dipped into the solution in the vessel. He then uses the hyssop to sprinkle the water onto the persons or the vessel.

It is not necessary for a large amount of the sanctified waters to come in contact with the impure. As long as a slight amount of the water touches him, it is sufficient to purify. Even if a tiny drop touched only his fingertips or lips, it would be enough.

However, all the people who are involved with the heifer and its preparation, from beginning to end, become impure from contact with it, as well as their garments. They were required to immerse themselves and wash their clothing in order to be reinstated. And it is this concept–that the very same agent that brings purity to those who are lacking it renders the pure impure–that is the mystery of the commandment, beyond the grasp of understanding. This is a mysterious and deep paradox–that the same tool can have opposite effects.

The Biblical Picture of the Red Heifer Sacrifice

This sacrifice was always seen as the most difficult sacrifice to interpret and understand. It is thought of as a *chok*, a Biblical command for which no explanation was given and that remains a mystery above human understanding.[6]

The great Rabbinical scholars of Israel consider this precept to be the deepest mystery of the Torah. For example, the

---
6   The Jewish Chronicle, (Nov. 5, 2008), "Chok," Accessed on February 4, 2023, https://thejc.com

sacrifice includes a great contradiction. The ashes of the red heifer have the inexplicable power to cleanse all who have been rendered unclean, but contact with the same ashes for those who are pure has the opposite effect–it makes the ritually pure unclean!

King Solomon was given special wisdom from God, as he prayed that God would give him the wisdom to lead the people of Israel. God not only blessed him with wisdom, but also with riches, power, and a great kingdom. He is often referred to as the wisest man that ever lived (apart from Jesus Christ, of course). According to Jewish tradition, King Solomon was the wisest of all human beings who ever lived, and he understood every aspect of God's creation. So great was his knowledge and wisdom that this tradition also relates that he understood even the languages of all the animals.[7] (If true, he was the apparently the first Dr. Doolittle!) Yet, he was not able to fathom the secret of the red heifer. As he said, after contemplating upon it, *"...I said, 'I will be wise, but it was far from me'"* (Eccles. 7:23).

However, for Christians who understand the work of the cross and its picture of Jesus' accomplished salvation, the mystery is now revealed. The sacrifice of the Red Heifer pictures the atoning sacrifice of Jesus in the most exact manner.

1. It was a female offering. Jesus was virgin-born, made of the seed of a woman (Gal. 4:4) He was the only virgin born person in all of history!
2. It had to be a pure sacrifice. Jesus was the sinless Son of God, in whom they would find no guile. (John 8:46a, 1 Pet. 2:21-22)
3. The sacrifice was burned without the camp. Jesus was crucified at Golgotha, outside the city walls of Jerusalem and near the Damascus Gate.

---

[7] Abraham O. Shemesh "And God gave Solomon wisdom: Proficiency in Ornithomancy, Ariel University, Israel, Accessed on February 4, 2023, https://scielo.org.za, Pesitka de-Rav, Ecclesiastes Rabbah

4. The sacrifice was burned in its entirety. Jesus died completely. He did not just swoon or faint, but experienced final death to become the propitiation for our sin and to appease the wrath of God. (The ancient Jews believed that you were not completely dead until you had been dead for three days and three nights.)[8] Jesus fulfilled this "complete death" by giving Himself completely to pay for our sin. He gave His all that all who repent and believe on Him might live!

5. The blood was sprinkled seven times, picturing, by the number seven, completeness and perfection. This showed how God shed His blood for our salvation, to provide a one-time, complete and perfect offering for sin.

6. The articles that accompanied the sacrifice were pictures of Jesus' sacrifice. The cedar wood pictures the cross on which the Savior was nailed, the hyssop pictures the cleansing given by the sacrifice and the scarlet thread pictures the blood of Jesus shed for our redemption to accomplish our salvation.

7. The high priest was made unclean by offering the sacrifice and in like manner Jesus took our sin upon Himself to redeem us, becoming a curse by hanging on the tree.

   "For He hath made Him to be sin for us who knew no sin that we might be made the righteousness of God in Him." (2 Cor. 5:21)

   This sacrifice accomplished our purification of sin. This removal of sin that Jesus accomplished for us was more than a ritual cleansing. We were given complete and full cleansing, once and for all, from sin and all its consequences of death, hell, and the grave (Heb. 9:11-14).

8. The sacrifice is obviously a cleansing from death because it cleanses someone from touching the dead. Even more so, it is also an example of how God can make the dead come back to life in the resurrection.

---

[8] Tanhuma, Miqetz 4, Pequdei 3, Babylonian Talmud Sanhedrin 90b-91a

This sacrifice not only pictures our cleansing from sin and death, but our ultimate victory over sin, death, hell, and the grave through the redemption of the body. We have been promised the hope of a new glorified body like unto our Lord's body and we earnestly wait until the coming of the Lord when we will also receive the redemption of the body. (Rom. 8:23)

9. The sacrifice pictures how we should now live a continually pure and holy life, one of total dedication to God. It not only pictures a one-time cleansing of a person from sin, but also how he must continue in holiness as a servant of the Lord.

   The Bible tells us, in Hebrews 9:12-14: *"neither by the blood of goats and calves, but by his own blood he entered in once into the holy place, having obtained eternal redemption for us. For if the blood of bulls and of goats, and the ashes of an heifer sprinkling the unclean, sanctifieth to the purifying of the flesh: how much more shall the blood of Christ, who through the eternal Spirit offered himself without spot to God, purge your conscience from dead works to serve the living God?"*

   The picture in Hebrews 9:12-14 shows how the sacrifice in Old Testament offerings and Jesus' fulfillment of its typology is to cleanse our conscience from dead works to serve the living God now. We are to realize His ultimate and supreme sacrifice for our salvation and be motivated to serve the Savior with our all and to live our life for Him by taking up our cross daily to follow Jesus.

10. Jesus' sacrifice is an eternal sacrifice in its effect. Jesus gave Himself once on the cross for the sins of the world. This one-time sacrifice paid for all the sins of the world, both past, present, and future. So, by this sacrifice of Christ, the salvation of men's souls is both perpetual and eternal.

CHAPTER THREE

The Modern Importance of the Red Heifer Sacrifice

While this is an interesting study of Old Testament typology and fulfillment in the atoning death of Jesus Christ on the cross, why is it an important issue today in modern Bible prophecy?

The Ashes and Temple Worship

There is a strong movement in Israel today, especially in Jerusalem, to rebuild the Temple and to re-establish the sacrificial system of worship in Judaism.

The Temple Institute of Jerusalem is currently busy making replicas of the Old Testament Temple vessels, priestly garments, and worship instruments. Two different rabbinical schools in Jerusalem are again teaching the precise Old Testament priestly methods of sacrifice, including how to prepare each sacrifice and its accompanying rituals. In addition, there is a movement in Jerusalem to rebuild the Temple on the Temple Mount. On October 8, 1990, Temple activists called the Temple Mount Faithful attempted to lay a cornerstone for the third Jewish Temple to be built on the Temple Mount. Although they were not successful, this incident certainly illustrates how earnest certain Jews are about rebuilding the Jewish Temple.

For Biblical prophecy students, this incident is quite interesting. The Bible is very specific that during a later event of the Tribulation period, the Antichrist will enter the Temple and commit the "abomination of desolation" to signal his insult and attack on the Jews and to center all worship on himself. This abomination of desolation is generally viewed as the Antichrist entering the Temple and sacrificing a sow (a female pig, considered by the Jews as an unclean animal) on the altar and then setting up his image in the

Temple. The Antichrist will then command that everyone on Earth commence worshipping him. (Dan. 9; Matt. 24) This sacrilege will reveal the Antichrist's true character as being "anti-God" and it will mark the beginning of his blasphemous self-worship and his intense attack and persecution of the Jews and Christians. For this event to occur, there must be a Temple in Jerusalem.

Although, today there is no Temple as of yet, there is a strong move to rebuild one. This Temple the Jews are attempting to rebuild is the very building which the Orthodox Jews believe will be the Temple of the coming Messiah of Israel. And this is where the importance of the Ashes of the Red Heifer becomes so apparent. The re-institution of Temple worship and the sacrificial system would be impossible without the ashes of this special heifer.

While commenting on the unique importance of the red heifer ashes, Rabbi Chaim Richman said:

> *In our own times, the commandment of the red heifer takes on more and more significance. For without it, the Divine service of the Holy Temple cannot be resumed. There is a spiritual renaissance today in Israel; after almost 2,000 years, Israel is clearly moving towards the time when the Holy Temple on Mount Moriah–the prophesied Third Temple–will be rebuilt.*
>
> *But the sages of Israel enigmatically stated that when Messiah arrives, he will stand atop the roof of the Temple and cry out: "Humble ones! The time of your redemption has arrived!" Thus: The Temple will be built before the Messiah arrives.*
>
> *What does a heifer have to do with any of this? Perhaps it would be difficult for some to believe that a cow could be so important. But in truth, the fate of the entire world depends upon the red heifer. For God has ordained that its ashes alone are the single missing ingredient for the reinstatement of Biblical purity–and thereafter, the rebuilding of the Holy Temple.* [9]

---
9   Chaim Richman, *The Mystery of the Red Heifer: Divine Promise of Purity*, (The Temple Institute, 1997), 6, 8.

CHAPTER THREE

While the prospects for the Jewish Temple's rebuilding are clearly on the horizon there is an interesting hindrance to its reconstruction. In an interview by Aubrey L. Richardson (project initiator for an Archeological dig in Israel) with Rabbi Shlomo Goren, the Chief Rabbi of Israel, the Rabbi was quoted as saying, "Without the Ash, it will be very difficult from a religious point of view to renew the worship of the Temple. So, we have to find the *kalal*." [10]

The *kalal* is the vessel, carved from stone, used to hold the Ash, containing a remnant of the Ash of the Red Heifer from the time of Moses. Each of the set of Ashes from the sacrifices of the Red Heifer was mixed with earlier sacrificial Ashes, continuing the Ashes of the sacrifice of Moses. It is important to note that the main purpose of finding the Ashes is not so much to replace the Temple, but rather to renew the worship of the Jews. The Ash is to be used to purify the people, especially the priests to enter the Holy of Holies on the Temple Mount. Even today, most Orthodox Jews will not enter the Temple Mount for fear of accidentally treading the area of the former Holy of Holies and that this action might cause a spiritual loss of their soul. The Ash is also to be used to purify the Temple Mount itself and the rebuilt Temple.

An Historic Interview with Rabbi Shlomo Goren

In the late 1980s, General Dynamics (now Lockheed Martin) of Fort Worth, Texas, sent Aubrey L. Richardson to Israel to be the chief engineer of a defense project, building the F-16 fighter jet for Israel. He had earlier attended the Bible Baptist Seminary in Fort Worth with my father, had been a life-long family friend and was even present the night my parents first met. And he was the major reason that I was able to come to Israel to preach on my first missionary tour. He heard that I was traveling to Belgium and the Netherlands to preach and perform piano concerts and he insisted that I also come to Israel

---
10   Personal Interview of Slomo Goren by Aubrey Richardson, Jerusalem, Israel, 1988.

to continue my evangelistic ministry. Aubrey provided all the connections, virtually organizing my missionary tour. While there, I met many of his wonderful contacts, such as dignitaries, government officials, engineers, rabbis, and archaeologists–and this study was the result!

Because Aubrey was already trained in Biblical study as well as scientific study, he became interested in many of the archaeological discoveries and their prophetic significance. And this led him to an interest in the red heifer (among other things). On May 31, 1988, Aubrey had an interview with the chief Rabbi of Israel, Rabbi Shlomo Goren, the former military general and hero of the Six-Day War who personally measured the Temple Mount during the '67 War but has since passed away. Among the things that they discussed were the search for the ashes of the red heifer and its importance in rebuilding the Temple. This historic interview is especially important for our study and has never before been published. This amazing interview is quoted as follows:

Aubrey   Rabbi Goren, for my future reference, do you believe that the red heifer sacrifice and the discovery of the old ashes will force the Jews to replace or rebuild the Jewish Temple?

Rabbi Goren   The *Parah Adumah* [the Red Heifer] and the ash that you are looking for–these have nothing to do with the evidence to **replace** the Temple. No. This is only a method to purify our people–an order of purification to enter the Holy of the Holies of the Temple Mount, where the Temple was built and then the ashes prepared the people to enter the temple.

Without the ash it would be very difficult from a religious point of view to renew the worship of the Temple, so we have to find the *kalal*. This is the ash of the Red Heifer–the *Parah Adumah*. This is just an instrument by which we can come closer to our purpose of building the Third Temple.

CHAPTER THREE

Aubrey   Does the ashes or are the ashes that will be found, do they necessarily have to be the remnant of the ashes of the seventh *Parah* [heifer]?

Rabbi Goren   They must be the remnant of the ashes of Moses' heifer.

Aubrey   Perpetual...

Rabbi Goren   Moses prepared the first one and his heifer's ashes shall remain 'til the end.

Aubrey   ...Because there's a succession?

Rabbi Goren   During the First Temple, they did not make any attempt to prepare a new *Parah Adumah*. Just at the time of the Second Temple, they started preparing seven of the others; so, the main one still remains, the *Parah Adumah* [red heifer ashes] of Moses.

Aubrey   The main one is carried through? From Moses' time?

Rabbi Goren   Part of it was hidden somewhere but where we don't know.

Aubrey   Is this in the Rabbinical Talmud or where do you find that it will be found?

Rabbi Goren   It is not mentioned where.

Aubrey   No, not where they will be found, but it does mention that the ashes that were in the Second Temple will be found? That's in the Talmud somewhere?

Rabbi Goren   Yes, yes, of course.

Aubrey   Can you tell me, roughly, where it is in the Talmud?

Rabbi Goren   Yes, yes, in a special section telling of the *Parah Adumah*. I will show you.

Aubrey   O.K., Thank you.

Rabbi Goren   One minute–between the chapter–together with the Mishnah–(this interpretation of the Mishnah)–it is mentioning that the ash was divided into three parts. One part of the ash they put it in the jars prepared of stone, they were made of stone (not regular jars). They were attached to the walls, in the Temple Mount.

Rabbi Goren (con't)	This was the first part. The priest could use it when they needed the ash and the second part they put it somewhere on the Mount of Olives, not to be used. No! The third part was to be divided among the twenty-four divisions of the priests. They took and divided it throughout the country.
	The old priests in Israel were divided into twenty-four groups, every group got a specific week to come to Jerusalem and perform the worship in the Temple. They changed themselves on Saturdays; every Sabbath there came a new group to the Temple, and they took over the Temple–all performance and all worship. So, every one of the twenty-four groups of guards (they called each a guard), every guard performed the worship in the temple twice a year, approximately a bit more than twice. (Thus, you have the guards serving for forty-eight weeks a year, every guard twice…a little more than twice a year.)
	The priests were spread out over the country and were in charge, keeping the ash, the third of the ash divided into 24 parts for the priests, and whenever somebody wanted or needed to be purified, they went to their local priest and they performed the purification. Finally, one part of the ash on the Mount of Olives was not used.
Aubrey	Whatever happened to the one on the Mount of Olives? Was it put back in with the next heifer ashes?
Rabbi Goren	They buried it there somewhere. This is not mentioned. This is the most clear source… *The Parah* chapters. I will show you something else.
Aubrey	Am I keeping you from preparation of the wedding?
Rabbi Goren	Oh, no. Here, in the interpretation of the Bible, from the First century of the Bible, it says here: The part of the ash that was hidden on the Mount of Olives, it was used for purifying the High Priest, when they prepared themselves to make a new sacrifice. It was only for them to use, in order to make a new *Parah Adumah*. This one part, they used only this portion of the ash. Hidden, it served as purification of the High Priest.

CHAPTER THREE

Aubrey — This stayed hidden on the Mount of Olives?

Rabbi Goren — Yes, nobody could use it without the priest. He was isolated for a week in order to prepare himself for the new sacrifice, the making of the new Parah Adumah. This was before the first century. So, it was divided into three parts, the one in the Temple was used by the people. One opinion says that the other portion stayed hidden in the Temple Mount... this was to stay for the future generations, not to be used.

Aubrey — In your opinion, is that the portion that was taken and will be found one day? The portion that was in the Temple?

Rabbi Goren — Yes, no doubt. [Rabbi Goren refers again to the writings.] Here, the *kalal*, he said, they put the ash in a jar–a *kalal* made out of stone.

Aubrey — Could the ashes that were in the stone *kalal* be preserved without being enclosed in another vessel for protection–should it be protected?

Rabbi Goren — It was protected from being defiled. Nobody was allowed to touch it. No one was to touch it, so that it was only allowed to be touched by a priest–if a man would touch it, he would defile it.

Aubrey — But, Rabbi Goren, say, if this were the *kalal* [Aubrey is holding up a little container], the ashes were inside and they are hidden somewhere, would they have to be in another additional vessel to be protected?

Rabbi Goren — It's not mentioned, no.

Aubrey — O.K.

Rabbi Goren — It [the *Kalal*] was made of stone as a jar. Stone vessels were made out of clay–or they were not made of clay... There are a variety of opinions. Stone jars–of pottery, were made without fire. They didn't put it in fire or bake the pottery in a kiln. If the jars would be baked in fire and then someone would touch it, it would be defiled. If held in stone jars, without being baked in fire, it would remain pure.

Rabbi Goren (con't) There was part of the ash that was hidden on the Temple Mount, and the part that was hidden on the Mount of Olives–there is a chance to find one or the other. I will show you something else.

This is also in the tractate *Parah*, in the *Mishnah*. Seven Red Heifers were made in our history of the First and Second Temples. Who made them? Moses the first one, and together (with Moses) was eight. The first was Moses.

Aubrey Together with Moses was eight?

Rabbi Goren Yes. The second one was made by Ezra. Sheme [or Simon] the righteous was the High Priest, beginning at the Second Temple–he made the third one. And Yochanan the Priest, he made two. And El'yhoeini ben Hakof was a High Priest, and Chanamel HaMitzri, the Egyptian, and Ishmael the son of Pi'avi, they each made one. So, you have Moses' *Parah Adumah*...and you have eight altogether.

Aubrey You have eight?

Rabbi Goren Yes.

Aubrey Are we looking then for number eight to be found?

Rabbi Goren You are looking for...

Aubrey Number one... but carried over, really.

Rabbi Goren You will find one, and so you will find eight... or seven. There is a variety of opinions. One says seven, one says eight. If you will find the ashes, I assume all are hidden in one place. Somewhere on the Temple Mount and the Mount of Olives there will be portions of the ash. I'm not sure, but someone maybe later put it somewhere else–It's just an assumption.

Aubrey The idea that the *Parah Adumah* will be found is passed on from Rabbi to Rabbi to Rabbi...?

Rabbi Goren It is a tradition...**It must be found.** This is part of our faith. It must be found! We will start building the New Temple.

CHAPTER THREE

Aubrey The Temple will not be begun before the finding of the *Parah Adumah*? Or will it be found sometime, during the rebuilding of the Temple?

Rabbi Goren I believe so, I am not 100% sure, so it will be found before the building of the Temple, but I am not 100% sure.

Aubrey Are you going to read some more?

Rabbi Goren Yes. This is the Mishnah in chapter 3. (Mishnah 5 also mentions the *Parah Adumah*.) Maimonides tells us in chapter 3... He is the most authoritative... and in chapter 4. He says the part that was hidden on the Temple Mount was hidden specially to remain forever and from every one of the sacrifices, from **every** sacrifice, they took a part of it and put it in the place on the Temple mount. He says that nine heifers were offered, (thus, says Maimonides). The first sacrifice was made by Moses, the second one by Ezra, and seven afterwards–and then the tenth, **the tenth** will be made **by Messiah**!

Aubrey Made by Messiah?

Rabbi Goren By Messiah. This is His *Parah Adumah*, it will be the tenth one–the tenth!

Aubrey Do you agree with that?

Rabbi Goren I agree, it is authoritative–the tenth one will be prepared by Messiah...**The Jewish Messiah**!

Aubrey The Jewish Messiah, Yes, sir.

Rabbi Goren It will be prepared by Messiah, very soon–very soon He will appear. He says so–very soon He will appear.

Aubrey Soon after the ashes are found or soon now?

Rabbi Goren Soon–from after his time, the time of Maimonides, and it has already been close to nine hundred years after Maimonides wrote it.

Aubrey Messiah will bring the Skee-nah or shekinah glory and He will make the tenth heifer offering, the Ashes!

Rabbi Goren According to Maimonides, Messiah will build the Temple–the Third One. It is his opinion–another opinion–I can give you. This is the opinion of Maimonides.

Aubrey	I won't take much more of your time then. This is very interesting to me.
Rabbi Goren	I was going to the beach. Yesterday I fell while out walking. I fell down and hurt my side (my ribs) but I keep on walking. What can I do? I can't give in to things. [He then reads from another source]. Nine heifers were made throughout the Second Temple. The Tenth will be made by Messiah. Children were kept in a place of training to keep or preserve their purification. They went to bring the water from the Siloam spring. They were put on cows–on platforms on the cows–and the children got up on the platforms and down, they were not allowed to just go anywhere. It can be that they could become defiled if they got down–this was a special group of children.
Aubrey	Now, is there a group of children being prepared in Jerusalem?
Rabbi Goren	Yes–but now we don't have it.
Aubrey	Are they today being prepared?
Rabbi Goren	No.
Aubrey	But, if the ashes were found today...?
Rabbi Goren	If the ashes were found we would be able to purify them–today we cannot purify anyone.
Aubrey	You have to have the ashes in order to purify them.
Rabbi Goren	Yes, it is a vicious circle. We can't prepare without having the ashes–you will have to find the old ones. This is a very...difficult problem.
Aubrey	I would like to show you some pictures. [He displays a picture at Qumran of the Wadi Qumran and the city and caves below]. Do you see the *Kippah*? [He points to the rounded top of the mountain in the picture].
Rabbi Goren	Yes.
Aubrey	Here is the blueprint sketch of the Mercy Gate or Eastern Gate.

Rabbi Goren	I could have broken through the Mercy Gate. In one hour–during the War of Six-Days–but I didn't do it. I neglected to do it.
Aubrey	Here is a plan view and elevation view with dimensions in metric units. Do you have the measurements also?
Rabbi Goren	I have measurements but I can't give them away. I made measurements by myself.
Aubrey	Could I study the paper that you wrote on the subject?
Rabbi Goren	It is in Hebrew. I may publish it soon in *The Jerusalem Post*.

(The interview by Rabbi Goren and Mr. Richardson was to be continued at another time. Unfortunately, this interview was taken when Rabbi Goren was in his eighties, and he has since passed away. However, that makes this interview all the more valuable and important. The bold emphasis was added to reflect the Rabbi's own vocal emphasis in the taped interview, and the comments in brackets were added only for clarification.)

I conclude several things from this interview. In my opinion, Rabbi Goren definitely believed that the Ashes of the Red Heifer from the time of Moses would be found and that the Temple would be rebuilt sometime in the future. He seemed to believe that there were hidden ashes on the Temple Mount and on the Mount of Olives and there may have been as many as nine different *kalals* of ashes, one for each red heifer sacrifice. He believed that the ashes would be found near to the time that Messiah comes, and he believed that His coming was very soon. He also assumed that these ashes might have been moved but that they *would* be found.

Are the Original Ashes Needed?

The Bible recounts that God told Moses, "Speak unto the children of Israel, that they bring *thee* [or *you*] a red heifer..." From this passage we understand that the original heifer sacrifice was to be the beginning and most important of a perpetual offering for Israel. It is also clear that Moses was the first to offer the red heifer and that this first heifer was to be especially significant.

There is a Jewish tradition that all the heifers are sanctified through Moses' original heifer and a portion of those ashes were put away for the future sanctification of Israel. As Rabbi Richman said, "These words teach us that God told Moses, 'Even if all heifers throughout history are lost, yours will remain forever.'"

During the earlier preparations for the sacrifice in the days of the Temple, the priest who was to burn a new heifer was sprinkled during his week of separation with ashes that had been made previously, back through the generations. This was done as one of the extra measures of purity associated with the ceremony of the red heifer, even though he was known to be clean, and there had been no opportunity for him to become otherwise while he was in the Temple.

Some Rabbis believe that the newer ashes were always mixed with a combination of the previous ashes. One way of understanding this is to view this mixture of old and new ashes as being an additional precautionary measure... actually, as a kind of insurance policy for purity.

The ordinance of the purification has an almost unparalleled status for Israel; after all, the purity of the entire nation is dependent on it. But every man has his limitations, being only human. What would happen if the entire process had been carried through according to the letter of the law, but some detail which could make the procedure invalid had gone unnoticed and undetected? One scenario might be that a perfect red heifer has been chosen and found to be blemish-free, and all the other steps had been followed, exactly as prescribed. But unknown to those officiating, in reality the heifer had a blemish which disqualified it. If such a thing could happen, how can Israel's purity be protected?

CHAPTER THREE

One way would be simply to depend upon the ashes prepared by the leaders of an earlier generation, since those great men were considered wiser about spiritual matters than modern men. The Jewish sages taught a general principle, that as the generations pass in time, they would become weaker spiritually. This is a general principle taught in the Bible about many things. The previous generations were on a far more exalted and powerful level than those who follow. This belief may appear strange at first to our current generation, in light of all our technological advancements, discoveries and achievements.

In the last hundred years, the world has seen more advancements and scientific discoveries than the last thousand. However, if we are more advanced scientifically than our predecessors, that does not mean that we are more advanced spiritually.

According to conservative, Biblical Christian belief, we believe that we are born as depraved sinners, already condemned by the righteousness of God, in need of a Savior and on our way to hell. It is only by the Grace of God by believing in Jesus Christ as our Savior and in his blood to pay for our sins, that we can be saved from eternal judgment for our sin (Eph. 2:8, 9; Rom. 6:23; 10:9-10, 13). We believe that the Old Testament prophets witnessed to the world, Jesus himself preached to the lost people of the Earth, and during the time of the apostles, the entire world was turned upside-down with the gospel of Christ. Although many people became believers, there were still others who did not know the gospel or had not believed. Today, there are more unsaved people than ever before in the history of the world and the need to reach the world with the gospel of Jesus Christ is greater than ever before!

Thus, the world seems to get more sinful every day. Paul, the apostle warned us of these coming evil days, "...in the last days, perilous times shall come..." Surely, they have come in our generation!

The Jewish rabbis believe that the earlier Second Temple religious leaders' power was so great that they were giants among men. They did not have the machines and technology we have today because they did not need them. Their spiritual insight and righteousness were viewed as so clear that the rabbis would deem that the ashes prepared by them to have a greater level of separation. Thus, rabbis today believe the older ashes act as an "insurance policy" because men who were closer to the revelation of Sinai than we are prepared the ashes. Jewish leaders think the earlier men knew God and His commandments better, followed the Lord more heartily and so their actions help maintain the purity of the Ashes.

As Rabbi Richman tells us,

> The chances that something has gone wrong now are not that likely. However, if such as mishap has transpired, if we combine these ashes with a previous solution, we can rely on the majority portion of the mixture, which is certainly error-free beyond any doubt.
>
> Additionally, mixing the newer ashes we have produced now with those from olden times is a way of connecting through time with the original heifer that was slaughtered and prepared by Moses himself.[11]

Can the Jewish rabbis proceed in offering a new sacrifice without the original ashes? Even if a new red heifer could somehow be obtained, slaughtered, and burned, how could ritual purity be reinstated without the earlier *kalal*, the container of original ashes dating back from the time of Moses? Many people seem to realize that without these original ashes, it would be impossible to rebuild the Temple. This is because the original ashes would have to be mixed in with the new ones, as was done in the past, whenever a red heifer was prepared.

---

11 Chaim Richman, *The Mystery of the Red Heifer: Divine Promise of Purity*, (The Temple Institute, 1997), 60.

CHAPTER THREE

Because of this assumption, many people have been earnestly looking for the old ashes in various locations inside of Israel. These possible locations will be dealt with in the next section of this work. However, whether these ashes are found or not, are they needed for renewed worship in a rebuilt Jewish Temple? Opinion differs from various sources and even among the rabbis.

One organization searching near the Dead Sea Scroll caves of Qumran believe that the Copper Scroll gives clues to the actual location. Their claim is dealt with in detail in a later section of this work. However, their Internet site gives an intriguing quote about this question:

> *There are differing attitudes towards the need of the red heifer's ashes. A small percentage of Jewish people (and a few Gentiles) believes a new red heifer can be offered and its ashes used for the purification. To accomplish this, two herds of red cattle have been started in Israel in order to raise an unblemished red heifer born in the land of Israel. There are two problems with this.*
>
> *First, a new future heifer would have to be offered on the Miphkad Altar (currently in the hands of the Muslims) located on the Mount of Olives. Second, in order to have a new offering of the red heifer, ashes of the heifer that can be traced back to Numbers 19 would have to be used to cleanse the Miphkad Altar to have the required "clean place."*
>
> *This leads to the obvious conclusion that, even if a newly born, unblemished red heifer was to be offered today, ashes that can be traced back to the first offering of the heifer (Num. 19) would still have to be found for the continuity of the "perpetual and forever," as prescribed in this passage.[12]*

This is an exciting conclusion about the need for the original ashes. Yet, Rabbi Chaim Richman, of the Temple Institute and a respected authority on these matters, has a clear disagreement with the above quote. He tells us,

---
12 Chaim Richman, *The Mystery of the Red Heifer: Divine Promise of Purity*, Ibid. 62.

> Whatever their true intentions may be, the statement quoted above is a gross distortion of the issue and has no basis in the reality of Biblical law or Jewish practice. All of the information in this statement is false. More importantly, how does one who is not an authority on Jewish law come to an "obvious conclusion" that a red heifer cannot be made without the earlier ashes–unless he is driven by some other motivation?
>
> Assuming that some substance was found, and assuming that it could even be proved scientifically to be organic and possibly from an animal–how could it be proven that these are the original ashes, from the time of Moses? How could it be proven that they were not impure?
>
> If a portion of those ashes were indeed set aside for the future sanctification of Israel, then perhaps they shall be found. Or, perhaps they will be revealed through Divine intervention; perhaps when the Messiah arrives, he will identify their location. It would certainly be desirable for all of Israel if the original ashes could be located and proven to be authentic beyond any doubt.
>
> But in the meantime, let the truth be known: there is nothing to stop the people of Israel from raising a new heifer, from birth, and preparing it in the manner we have described, and raising children in purity to carry out the procedure–even without the original ashes. On the contrary: we may be in doubt as to the true nature of any discovery that is unearthed whose authenticity cannot be completely verified. But a perfect heifer, born and raised under a controlled environment, would be fit to be used for the Temple. And that is precisely what is being done today. [13]

Thus, it seems that the rabbinical sources conflict with each other on this point. As one famous Jewish writer stated, "If you have two Jews you will have three opinions" meaning that there are often differences of opinions among Jews, as among any other people. So, in this case it seems that if you want to follow the letter of the law you must find the original heifer ashes from the time of Moses. Yet, if you want to expedite

---

13 Chaim Richman, *The Mystery of the Red Heifer: Divine Promise of Purity*, 62-63.

CHAPTER THREE

the rebuilding of the Temple with as few complications as possible you might opt for a broader interpretation.

It is my opinion that you cannot use a broad interpretation for these issues because the Temple and the Red Heifer sacrifice will have to be acceptable to all Jews and that would only be possible if you follow the letter of the law to the smallest detail. Remember, the former Chief Rabbi Shlomo Goren believed the original ashes were essential and said,

> Without the Ash, from a religious point of view, it would be very difficult to renew the worship in the Temple. So, we must find the Kalal [of original red heifer ashes]" ... "It is a tradition...**It must be found.** *This is part of our faith. It must be found! We will start building the New Temple.* [14]

Yet, Rabbi Richman seems to be representative of those determined to begin the Temple worship whether they find the ashes or not. As he said, "Let the truth be known, there is nothing to stop the people of Israel from raising a new heifer from birth...and preparing it...even without the original ashes." "There is no prerequisite in Judaism that we have those original ashes."[15]

However, Rabbi Richman did also seem to believe the earlier ashes would be an "insurance policy" against any possible contamination of a new sacrifice and would be a way of connecting us with the spiritual depth and repentance of Moses himself, as mentioned earlier. And the Scriptures do teach that it is to be a perpetual sacrifice, a statute to be observed forever. "And it shall be a perpetual statute unto them," (Num. 19:21) and "for a statute for ever." (Num. 19:10) Thus, it would seem that the solution to this issue is best left up to the most authoritative rabbis; whatever they decide will undoubtedly be the most correct view.

---

14   Personal Interview of Slomo Goren by Aubrey Richardson, Jerusalem, Israel, 1988.
15   Thomas Ice, Randall Price, *Ready to Rebuild* Ibid., 136.

What Happened to the Ashes?

If we are to find the lost Ashes, we must first consider what happened to them. The sacrificial Ash was divided into three parts. The first part was put in jars made of stone, which were attached to the walls in the Temple Mount at the entrance of the Temple court, between the Rampart and the Court of the Women. This ash was to be used by the priests when cleansing was needed for the people. The second part was divided among the twenty-four divisions of the priests. These groups distributed the ash throughout the country of Israel. The third part was hidden somewhere on the Mount of Olives, not to be used. It is believed to be buried somewhere in Jerusalem, saved for the future and not to be used, thus guaranteeing a secure collection of ash for future sacrificial needs.

In Biblical times, the priests in Israel were divided into twenty-four groups. Every group was privileged to serve the Lord on a special week by coming to Jerusalem to perform the worship in the Temple. These priests rotated every Saturday. Consequently, every Sabbath a new group of guards came to the Temple to administer the sacrificial worship. Each of the twenty-four groups performed in the Temple approximately twice a year. (With twenty-four guards in fifty-two weeks it was actually a bit more than twice a year.) The twenty-four guards of priests were spread over the country, keeping charge of the Ash (the third divided into twenty-four parts). When someone needed to be cleansed, he went to the nearest priest in the land and the priest performed the purification. The priests also provided spiritual guidance to the people throughout the land.

Once the Ashes are found in the future, the Ashes from any of the nine former sacrifices are acceptable because all were mixed with the Ashes of the sacrifice of Moses. The Mishnah also makes it clear that no one could be ritually clean to begin a new Red Heifer Sacrifice without the earlier Ashes. This is due to the fact that even the priest administering the sacrifice has to be prepared for it by sprinkling the Ashes of an earlier Red Heifer sacrifice on him.[16]

When fearing an oncoming invasion, the priest would hide the Ash so that it would not be destroyed. Rabbis tell the story of returning from Babylonian exile, rebuilding the Temple and finding the Ashes that were hidden under the Temple Mountain during an earlier Babylonian siege. Thus, hiding the Ash was common practice among the priests. Furthermore, the Ash on the Mount of Olives always remained in hiding and possibly some Ash remained in hiding on the Temple Mount.

Similarly, the Ash at the Temple and the Ash held with each of the twenty-four divisions of the priests could have been put in hiding during one of the Roman sieges. This would make as many as twenty-six possible pots of Ash hidden in different locations. The mystery remains, where is the Ash buried?

Are the Ashes Hidden in Qumran?

It is believed that possibly one of these twenty-four parts of the one-third of the Ashes was kept at Qumran in Israel, the site of the finding of the Dead Sea Scrolls. This is not completely unlikely because evidence shows many of the Zadokite priests (high priests of the family line of Zadok, the High Priest of King Solomon) lived there. According to one hypothesis told to Aubrey L. Richardson, which is based largely on very slight evidence in the Copper Scroll, one *kalal* containing Ashes of the Red Heifer was possibly hidden or buried in the floor of Cave IV at Qumran.

The Copper Scroll was one of the famous Dead Sea scrolls found in the area of Qumran.[17] Although almost three hundred caves in the area were searched, scrolls of the Dead Sea were

---

16   *Parah* 3:1
17   Allegro, John Marco, *The Treasure of the Copper Scroll*, (New York: Oxford University Press, 1959).

found in only eleven caves. In Cave III, the Copper Scroll was found along with 274 other portions of manuscripts. The author is standing in the very place where the famous Copper Scroll was found.

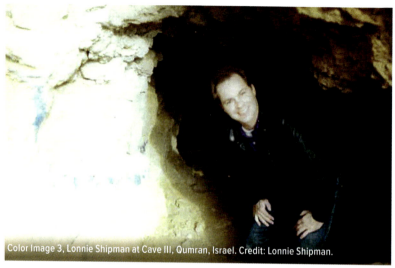

Color Image 3, Lonnie Shipman at Cave III, Qumran, Israel. Credit: Lonnie Shipman.

It is a special scroll that was written on copper and lists fantastic hidden treasure, scrolls and other articles. The exact hiding places of the treasure are difficult to pinpoint because often the scroll is written in certain cryptic phrases. One of these cryptic phrases is believed by some researchers to reveal a possible hiding place for the Ashes of the Red Heifer.

Item 26 of the Copper Scroll says,

> *In the inner chamber of the platform of the Double Gate, facing east, in the northern entrance, buried at three cubits, hidden there is a pitcher: in it, one scroll, under it, 42 talents.*

The word pitcher in English is *kalal* in Hebrew and is viewed by some to be the *kalal* of the Ashes of the Red Heifer. These same researchers also believe the scroll in Item 26 was hidden near the *kalal*, but not in it, and the 42 talents were hidden under the scroll. (They do not explain how they come to this very different conclusion of the *kalal's* contents, because the

CHAPTER THREE

Copper Scroll does not mention the ashes of the red heifer.) Many people have looked for this chamber in an attempt to find the lost Ashes. Vendyl Jones, a former Christian minister who later denied his Christian faith, claimed he had found this cave in another location. His claim will be dealt with in a following chapter.

Color Image 4, An overview of Qumran and nearby caves. Adobe Stock.

Aubrey Richardson has discovered evidence that Cave IV is the possible lost hiding place of Item 26. Notice the inner and outer chambers of Cave IV A in the left cave. The city's ruins lie in the upper middle section.

The caves are in the lower left extension of the mountain and in other nearby mountains. Each of these chambers has a doorway that faces east. The doorway for the outer chamber has now collapsed, but the sill of the man-made doorway is still obviously visible on the inside of the cave. It matches the description of the "chamber of the platform of the Double Gate." Also, notice that the cave previously had three chambers and that the one in the middle would match the description for the inner chamber with a northern entrance mentioned in the Copper Scroll.

Cave IV contained the most manuscripts found in the Dead

Sea Area. It is sometimes called the library of scrolls because in this cave they discovered between five hundred to eight hundred manuscripts. Several of these were complete scrolls. Also found were approximately one hundred thousand fragments of scrolls which varied in size from as small as a thumbnail to a legal sheet of paper.

As illustated in the next photograph, Lonnie Shipman is pointing to another lower very small interior room, possibly a storage chamber, of the man-made cave. This is the very chamber that some people believe once held the Ark of the Covenant, although this is extremely unlikely.

Color Image 5, Lonnie Shipman inside Cave IV A, Qumran, Israel. Credit: Lonnie Shipman.

In between Cave IV-A and Cave IV-B, there is obvious evidence of a former inner chamber now called Cave IV C which has since collapsed. This inner chamber between the two other caves would be aligned with the lower entrance floor levels of each Cave IV A and B and seemed to have also contained an upper, northern entrance, like the other two caves. The *kalal* was possibly hidden in the floor of this chamber. This *kalal* in the floor at Cave IV C is thought by some researchers to have held part of these Red Heifer Ashes because it is believed that the Copper Scroll listed these as part of the Temple treasure hidden at Qumran, although this seems to only be an assumption. Other treasure was mentioned to be hidden near Jerusalem and throughout Israel, but not the ashes.

The Cave IV-C chamber has now collapsed and eroded with the passage of almost two thousand years. Lost are the contents of the cave which possibly included other scrolls, since many Dead Sea scrolls were found in Cave IV A and B, (and this very remotely included the *kalal* of the ashes of the red heifer or other contents mentioned in the Copper Scroll.)

What About the Temple Mount and the Mount of Olives?

Where else might the Ashes be hidden? Possibilities exist throughout the land of Israel. These Ashes could have been hidden in any of the twenty-four stations of priests across the land, on the Temple Mount or on the Mount of Olives, where one *kalal* containing one-third of the Ashes was specifically hidden.

It is certain that the Ashes of a former sacrifice of the Red Heifer were hidden for future use. That was the specific reason to save the Ashes that remained on the Mount of Olives. This guaranteed a continual sacrifical rite. The Jewish Mishnah makes it clear that when the Jews returned from Babylonian captivity, that they found the earlier Ashes of Moses hidden away, and mixed them with the sacrifice made by Ezra. I believe they found these Ashes in earlier times on the Mount of Olives or the Temple Mount.

The Mishnah relates an interesting fact about finding the ashes when the nation of Israel returned from the Babylonian exile. This Jewish writing tells us about this earlier discovery:

> The Jewish leaders found the ashes of the Red Heifer that had been left in the Temple, safely hidden, when the nation went into exile. [18]

However, Jewish historical sources suggest that the ashes may have been carried with the Sanhedrin as it moved from place to place after the Temple's destruction in A.D. 70, and that

---
18 *Parah* 3:3

they may have been eventually deposited in Tiberias. Some scholars believe that the sacrifices continued for a time after the destruction of the Temple, and if so, the ashes would have been needed for an uninterrupted worship. And it is possible that Bar-Kokhba even rebuilt the Temple and re-instituted sacrificial worship during his reign in Jerusalem (A.D. 132-135). Evidence of the rebuilt Temple is suggested by the minted coins of the era which show a Temple and list the year of the High Priest Eliezer and new Kingdom inauguration. If Bar-Kokhba did build a new Temple, the ashes would have been required for renewed sacrificial worship.

It seems impossible to continue the Jewish sacrifice without finding the earlier Red Heifer Ashes. It is possible though, that the Ashes at one of the Twenty-four stations of the priests or on the Temple Mount still exist. It is also possible that the Ashes are still hidden on the Mount of Olives.

Color Image 6. The Mount of Olives with the Church of All Nations and the Russian Church. Credit: Lonnie Shipman.

The Mount of Olives has been used as a cemetery for centuries and it was so even in Jesus' time. It was also used as a garden (such as the famous Garden of Gethsemane) and as land for residences of homes. Although the cemetery area would be considered ritually unclean for the hiding of the Ashes, there were still areas on the Mount that were ritually clean, like the Gethsemane. Thus, one portion of the Ashes could be hidden on the Mount of Olives. Even though the Romans plundered Jerusalem in A.D. 70 destroying many buildings, the Ashes could have been hidden under ground in a secret chamber! For archaeological evidence of secret underground chambers, let us consider one example.

The Tomb of Queen Helena of Adiabene, of Northern Mesopotamia, mistakenly called the Tomb of the Kings, was built underground as a complex of catacombs in Jerusalem around A.D. 65 on nearby Mount Moriah, a little north of the Damascus Gate near to the Garden Tomb.[19]

Ill. 4, The Tomb of the Kings, Jerusalem, Israel. Public Domain.

Inside is a large complex of catacombs that include a secret stairway and chamber where the queen's sarcophagus was found. The tomb included a series of rooms and tunnels on at least two different levels. This tomb was unusual, not only because of its magnificent and impressive design, but because the sarcophagus of the queen was not placed in the main

---

19 Bahat, Dan, *Carta's Historical Atlas of Jerusalem*, (Jerusalem: Carta, 1986).

burial chamber designed for it.[20]

Evidently sensing possible plunder because of the First Jewish Revolt, the queen was hidden in a secret chamber known as room G.

This underground map identifies the specific rooms of importance and the secret chamber. In a small back room of the catacomb, concealed under a sarcophagus, a hidden stairway led to another underground room with a special stone door that could be opened mechanically only once a year. Her body was discovered there in recent years and is now on display at the Louvre in France.

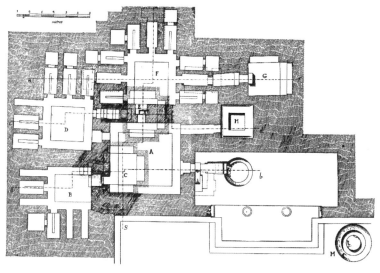

Ill. 5, A map of the Catacombs of the Tomb of Queen Helena. Tomb of the Kings bible.archaeology.org

To reach the tomb, you enter a grand stairway that leads to a large open courtyard. The sides of the stairway contain recesses for huge cisterns. In the center of one side of the expansive courtyard was the columned tomb, at one time topped by three ornate pyramids. The entrance to the tomb is very small, but opens to a large center chamber, the chamber

---
20   Murphy-O'Connor, Jerome, *The Holy Land*, 3rd Edition, (Oxford/New York: Oxford University Press, 1992), 144.

CHAPTER THREE

for the criers. To the right of this chamber is another large chamber which was originally intended to hold the queen. Passing through a series of underground chambers and hallways, to the rear is a small and little-noticed chamber. This was the chamber that held Queen Helena's body.

This chamber (room G) was entered by a secret stairway below the floor of the *kokh*, a Middle Eastern-style grave. This entrance was so small that the burial servants had to knock off the corners of the sarcophagus lid in order to get it into one of the lower chambers. The servants were also able to disguise the entrance so well that it escaped casual notice.

In describing this legendary tomb in the late second century A.D., the ancient chronicler Pausanias wrote:

> They have contrived to make the door of the tomb, which is stone like all the rest of it, so that it opens only on a certain day of the year; at that moment the machinery opens the door on its own, holds it open for a little while, and then closes it up again. [21]

Aubrey Richardson and I have explored this eerie tomb together. It is an intriguing site with a piercing darkness so black that standing behind someone holding a flashlight will block from view any illumination of the room, leaving you in utter darkness. The rooms themselves are quite surprising. Some rooms are rather large and some very small. They are arranged in a complicated layout of underground vaults. At the back of these vaults is the hidden stairway. The whole complex is much larger than one might expect, leaving one awed with the First Century engineering ability.

If First Century Jews had the ability to dig underground rooms with secret stairways and special mechanically operated stone doors to hide the body of a queen, it could be possible that they had a special underground chamber or series of vaults to hide the Ashes or other Temple treasure such as the Ark of the Covenant on the Temple Mount or Mount of Olives.

---
21   Pausanias, *Guide to Greece* 88: 16.4-5.

The hiding place on the Temple Mount would probably be in a secret chamber that was entered by a hidden stairway from the area of the Temple. It is already known that several stairways led underground from the Temple area, including some used only by priests for service in the Temple. There have also been rumored legends of other secret stairs. With all of the underground tunnels and secret stairways, this would have been a very good place to hide the Red Heifer Ashes.

Experts say that before A.D. 70, there were likely several different complexes of secret chambers in other areas of Jerusalem, as well as several large catacombs with extensive layouts dug in Olivet Mountain. There could also have been a special chamber or series of tunnels dug to hide these lost Ashes on the Mount of Olives. If so, the entrance was probably in the area where the sacrifice was made, near the Place of Burning. This is due to a fear that contamination would restrict the Jews from transporting the Ashes too far.

The most logical entrance to this hiding place would be on the Mount of Olives, directly across from either of the eastern gates. This would have been at the Golden Gate, or just slightly to its south and across, at the later gate, mistaken as the Shushan Gate.

We know the sacrifice of the Red Heifer was made at this location on the Mount of Olives, directly across from either the Golden Gate or the Shushan Gate. The priest had to look across the Kidron Valley through the gateway to the doors of the Temple when he committed the sacrifice. My opinion leans toward the area opposite the Shushan Gate as the place of the sacrifice and hidden Ashes because Solomon's Temple must have stood in line with the Dome of the Rock, although both positions are highly possible.

Thus, I believe that a *kalal* of the Ashes of the Red Heifer were hidden in secret chambers on the Temple Mount, near the

Women's Courtyard and also on the Mount of Olives, near the Place of Burning. I also agree that there were twenty-four other locations of small *kalals* around the nation of Israel, such as the one that was possibly hidden at Qumran in Cave IV-C, perhaps mentioned in the Copper Scroll. But this *kalal* is now lost, or destroyed, because the chamber possibly holding the container of ashes collapsed to the valley below long ago.

Could a Gentile Provide the Red Heifer for the Temple?

Red heifers have been raised in other parts of the world for centuries (although finding such a perfect red heifer is extremely rare). Could a Gentile be involved in contributing to the Jewish Temple service?

During the Second Temple era, many kings such as Darius of Persia and Ptolemy of Egypt donated large portions of their wealth for the honor of the God of Israel. King Monobaz II of Adiabene donated gold for the Temple vessels and his mother, Queen Helena, offered a huge golden lamp that was suspended over the entrance to the Sanctuary. Most famous among these ranks of Gentile donors is Nicanor, who donated the brass gates that were the main entrance of the Sanctuary and were known as the "Nicanor Gates."

The Mishnah recounts an engaging narrative about the red heifer that was used at that time. A non-Jew and righteous gentile named Dama ben Netinah provided it.[22]

Once, one of the stones of the High Priest's breastplate became dislodged and was lost. The rabbis of the Sanhedrin were naturally concerned to replace the stone immediately, since the garment could not be worn without all the stones in place, and the High Priest was unable to serve until it was fixed.

The sages heard that in the town of Ashkelon lived a man named Dama ben Netinah, who possessed a collection of

22   Mishnah *Peah* 1:1, 15c; *Kiddushin* 1:7, 61b

precious gems. A delegation of their number traveled to his home to ask him if he happened to own the stone they sought and if he might sell it to them for use in the Temple.

When they arrived in Dama's house, they told him of the mishap that had befallen the High Priest's breastplate. Dama ben Netinah told them that he did possess the stone they needed, and he would be happy to sell it to them. The sides settled on the price of one hundred gold coins, and the deal was concluded.

The rabbis were overjoyed that God had granted them success in their mission, and they would be able to repair the breastplate. Dama excused himself and went into the next room to get the key to his strongbox, where the jewel was locked for safekeeping.

But when he emerged from the room, he regretfully told the delegation that he would not be able to sell it to them after all! He apologized profusely for disappointing them but explained that when he went into the room to remove the key, he discovered that his father was sleeping, and the key was under his pillow. There was no way that he was going to disturb his father. Perhaps if he would try to remove the key from under his head, however gingerly, it would give his father a start! No, he could not risk disturbing his father's sleep.

The sages thought the man was bluffing, in an effort to drive the price up. They were not concerned with the price at all, but only with obtaining the stone. So, the men quickly doubled their original offer, and told Dama ben Netinah they would be willing to pay two hundred gold pieces. But to no avail; Dama refused their offer. The delegation offered three hundred, and then four hundred, and continued raising the price until they reached a price that was ten times the original amount they had offered. But Dama ben Netinah remained undaunted and steadfastly refused to sell the stone. "For all the money in the world," he told them, "I would not disturb my father's sleep."

The sages left the man's house discouraged and dejected and began the long journey back to Jerusalem. After having had been on the road only a short while, the Jews recognized the figure of a man who advanced towards them rapidly, finally overtaking them. It was Dama ben Netinah. He explained to the shocked men that shortly after they departed from his home, his father awoke of his own accord, and once he had awoken, Dama retrieved the key and opened the box. "Here is the stone," he declared, "I am now prepared to conclude the sale, just as we discussed."

The rabbis were naturally delighted and immediately presented him with the sum of one thousand gold pieces–the last offer they had made before they parted company with Dama.

But Dama ben Netinah refused the money. "I was perfectly content with your original offer of one hundred, and I had then made up my mind to sell you the stone. I had no intention of seeking to raise the price, but only to honor my father. Why should I profit in this world for honoring my father? I shall sell you the stone for one hundred gold pieces, as agreed."

The great sages were intensely moved to see the true honor and respect this man had for his father. Because he did not want to receive monetary reward for this, he was rewarded by heaven with the ability to fulfill another of God's precepts. Soon, a red heifer was born to his cattle, and he provided this heifer for the use of the Temple and Jewish worship.

The Breeding of New Red Heifers

Reports are occasionally received about attempts to raise a new breed of Red Heifers. The Temple Institute in Jerusalem and various new agencies have revealed attempts to raise the future Red Heifer for this sacrifice in different parts of Europe, America and Israel.

The birth of a new red heifer in the religious village of Kfar-Hassidim (near Haifa, Israel) was truly exciting. On a farm in northern Israel (raised in the mid 1990s), a red calf named "Melody" roamed blissfully in a green pasture, unaware of the controversy that surrounded her very existence. "Is this the "holy cow" of the Bible?" the priests wondered.

Several months later, a commission of twenty-five religious experts, including Rabbis Yisrael Ariel and Yoseph Elboim, visited her farm in northern Israel to determine if she qualified for the Biblical sacrifice. They concluded that she did indeed meet the Biblical specifications for this unique sacrifice and that she is the first such red heifer to be born in Israel in two thousand years! "We have been waiting two thousand years for a sign from God, and now he has provided us with a red heifer," said Rabbi Yehudah Etzion, the leader of Chai V'Kayam who was also present during the examination. "There were a couple of little white hairs which worried us, but the rabbis were satisfied that it is the red heifer referred to in the Bible," he related.[23]

The birth of the animal to a black-and-white mother and brown bull was being hailed as a "miracle" by activists who want to rebuild the Third Temple and prepare the way for the Jewish Messiah's entry into Jerusalem. While recently commenting on this new birth, an Israeli Biblical historian, Professor Ory N. Mazar said:

> The finding of such a rare, red-colored heifer is extraordinary. Such a cow is extremely uncommon; one may be born among 50 million or more cows... In the entire world, only one such calf has been confirmed to match the biblical requirements, and intriguingly, it was born in the Holy Land. [24]

According to archaeologist M. Leen, "should the Temple of God be reconstructed... such a Red Heifer would be necessary

---
23 London's *Sunday Telegraph* of March 16, 1997. London, UK
24 *Jerusalem Christian Review*, April, 1997.

CHAPTER THREE

for the Temple rituals to function." And Gershon Salomon, of the Temple Mount Faithful, said, "The red heifer is one of the most important signs that we are living in a special time."

If the animal did not disqualify, then she could be sacrificed just before Rosh Hashanah 5759 (September 1998) or any time during the Jewish year 5759.

Reports of this new red heifer from Israel were widely reported in the news media around the world. Sentiment about the heifer is mixed even in Israel. Some people believe that this new red heifer would lead to extreme reactions, rioting and chaos from certain more extreme Jewish factions. These critical observers would like to kill this red heifer to destroy the possibility of renewed Jewish worship on the Temple Mount.

Recommending extreme measures, such as shooting the calf, the liberal *Ha'aretz* newspaper wrote, "The potential harm from this heifer is far greater than the destructive properties of a terrorist bomb." Calling Melody's birth "a very delicate situation," Menachem Friedman, a sociologist at Bar-Ilan University stated, "We don't know how radical groups...will use it. People are looking for those signs, and talking seriously about it."[25]

Shmaria Schorr, the rabbi of the agricultural village of Kfar Menachem in Northern Israel, said hundreds of people have flocked here to catch a glimpse of Melody. Melody's mother is from a group of visually unremarkable black-and-white Holsteins penned down the hill at Kfar Hassidim. An anonymous bull in Sweden, who sired the calf, was used to artificially inseminate this mother. Shore takes pains to point out that Melody, who is darkish red, may not be the genuine article because of several imperfections that later appeared. As he examines her, he said, "Here, you see some white hairs," pointing to the tail. "And here–her eyelashes only start off red but turn to black."

25 "Red Heifer Causes Worried Reaction," *Ha'aretz*, March 16, 1997.

And recently, the red heifer has become officially disqualified for this red heifer sacrifice because a few hairs have appeared on the tail that are not red. So, at least the future of this red heifer calf is relatively safe from attack.

New heifers are also attempting to be bred in Mississippi and Texas. A red heifer from Texas named "Geula" started to make headlines. She was even being touted on the Temple Mount Faithful website. But the red heifers from Mississippi raised by Reverend Clyde Lott are the most significant.

In the spring of 1989, after reading the account of Jacob's spotted and speckled cattle in Genesis 30:31-32, Rev. Lott was intrigued with the question of where Israel gained the cattle for the red heifer offering. He wrote to the United States embassy's agricultural attaché in Athens, Greece, who were responsible for the entire Middle East about this matter. They sent the letter to the United States embassy in Tel Aviv, Israel, who in turn sent it to the Ministry for Religious Affairs for the State of Israel, who continued it on to the Temple Institute and Rabbi Chaim Richman. Thus began a connection with American cattlemen and Jewish rabbis.

Then the following year, a small group of expert cattlemen and pastors from Mississippi, Arkansas and Texas traveled to Israel to meet with the rabbis of the Temple Institute to discuss the red heifer. The group discussed the requirements for the red heifers and an overall exploration of ideas and expectations for a joint project. Several more meetings ensued, an in-depth study of the land, cattle and climate of Israel was begun, and several locations were explored in Israel for a cattle ranch location for breeding the new red heifers.

Although the group had initially planned on participating with several kibbutzim in the area of the Golan Heights, the central part of the country was later examined as a location for a pilot cattle program. The group's goals are presented by

CHAPTER THREE

Chaim Richman:

> The program involves the establishment of a livestock purebred production farm in the United States. The farm will utilize scientific methods of embryology and semen collection and distribution. It will also conduct its own grass and feed tests on its cattle in order to achieve genetic superiority with Red Angus cattle.
>
> These are the very variety of cattle which can produce the red heifer needed for reinstatement of purity and the resumption of Temple service. With success, the operation will actually transform Israel from a country dependent upon importing inferior beef from other countries, to a leading exporter in her own right. In our own generation, Israel, with its natural resources and geographic location, could become the leading livestock producer in the Middle East. [26]

Then, in the fall of 1994, Rabbi Richman made a trip to America to examine the red heifers at the home of Clyde Lott in Canton, Mississippi, and to present his view of these things and the rebuilding of the Jewish Temple to American audiences. After Rabbi Richman viewed the heifers, Rev. Lott relates the event:

> At mid-afternoon on November 11, 1994 the Rabbi walked into our barn in Canton to inspect 4 heifers. Almost immediately, he was drawn to one heifer in the middle stall on the north side of the barn. These heifers had been washed and groomed for the Rabbi. They were immaculately clean, for we wanted the Rabbi to be able to examine the heifers down to the skin, hoof line, the eyebrows and even into the ears. He began to study this particular heifer from the tip of her nose to the tip of her tail. He would back up and then come close to the heifer. This went on for at least 10 minutes.
>
> Finally, the Rabbi backed up to where my brother was standing outside the stall and looked at him and said, "This is the heifer that will change the world."
>
> There is no way to measure the importance of this moment when

---

26   Chaim Richman, *The Mystery of the Red Heifer: Divine Promise of Purity*, 71.

the heifer was verified and certified by the Rabbi. This, as well as the other things, confirmed to us that we were called of God to fulfill this work.[27]

Rev. Lott is not discouraged by the birth of Melody or other red heifers that might be possible candidates. They have shipped several of their own heifers to special Jewish farms in Israel. This group plans to continue breeding red heifers and exporting them to Israel to continue to be used in breeding programs there, so that a perfect specimen might be born in Israel.

Recently, several red heifers were sent to Israel from a ranch in Bono, Texas. Byron Stinson, a Christian supporter of several Christian and Jewish causes and head of Boneh Israel ("Building Israel"), became interested in helping to provide the possible heifer needed for a future sacrifice. On September 15, 2022, Stinson shipped five heifers to Israel which was lauded with much public news exposure on television and in newspapers.

When approached by the rabbis of the Temple Mount Institute about helping supply the red heifer, Stinson said,

"I wasn't expecting that…and it was shocking to think about it. But I know a lot of ranchers and I know a little about cattle, and being in Texas, I always say yes to these Jewish rabbis because they're my friends and I love them, and why not?" "The criteria is to make sure every hair is clearly red all the way through. There's no playing around with it. On top of that, the animal could never be used for work. And then the biggest one that almost disqualifies everyone is it can't have a blemish."

These heifers are each under a year old and will be shipped to two Israeli ranches to wait until they are the appropriate required age and then checked to see if they still qualify for the sacrifice.

---

[27] Chaim Richman, *The Mystery of the Red Heifer: Divine Promise of Purity*, 72.

CHAPTER THREE

Stinson hopes that one of the five heifers will continue to be acceptable and become the first heifer in two thousand years qualified for the sacrifice. "I think with five of them, we have a really good chance of that," Stinson said.[28]

When the heifers arrived at the airport in Israel, they were greeted by Temple Institute officials Rabbis Chanan Kupietzky, Tzachi Mamo, Yisrael Ariel and Azaria Ariel along with Byron Stinson and Jerusalem and Heritage Ministry director-general Netanel Isaac. "I didn't set out to do this, but right now, I am probably the best red heifer hunter in Texas," Stinson told *Israel365 news*. "The prophecies came true, and the Jews are back in Israel. Now they need to build a Temple. The red heifer is the key to making the Temple work like it's supposed to."[29]

Whether the needed red heifer is produced from Texas, Mississippi, Europe, or Israel will be interesting to watch. While these reports are exciting and the birth of a perfect red heifer might have already occurred (or will occur soon), the search is still on for the earlier Ashes because their need is essential to the sacrifice.

The Coming Kingdom Age

Rabbi Goren believes that eight or more sacrifices of the Red Heifer (*Parah Adumah*) have taken place. Other Jewish scholars believe that as many as nine have already occurred. When the Jews find the lost Ashes of the Red Heifer, they will engage in another sacrifice, or this tenth sacrifice will be made by Messiah Himself!

The great Jewish sage, Maimonides, gives proof of this coming sacrifice. In recounting the historical record of earlier sacrifices by the high priests in his commentary to the Mishnah, the great Maimonides concludes with this climatic

---

28   Chris Mitchell (09-23-22), "Texas Red Heifers' Arrival Stirs Prophetic Excitement in Israel," *Christian Broadcasting News*, Accessed on 12/29/22, https://www1.cbn.com
29   Tzvi Joffre (09-20-22), "From Texas to Israel: Red heifers needed for Temple arrive," *The Jerusalem Post*, Accessed on 12/29/22, https://m.jpost.com

statement: "...and the tenth red heifer will be accomplished by the king, the Messiah; may he be revealed speedily, Amen. May it be God's will."

Commenting upon this section of the Mishnah, Rabbi Chaim Richman gives a compelling insight into the importance of the red heifer:

> *With this amazing statement, Maimonides recounts an ancient tradition–that the tenth red heifer is associated with the Messianic era. Does this perhaps mean that the appearance of a red heifer in these waning end times is an indication, a forerunner of the appearance of the Messiah himself, who will officiate at its preparation? If there has been no red heifer for the past two thousand years, perhaps it is because the time was not right; Israel was far from being ready. But now, we cannot help but wonder and pray: if there are now red heifers...is ours the era that will need them? With the words of Maimonides in mind what could it mean for the times we live in, to have the means of purification so close at hand?*
>
> *Are we on the threshold of the Third Temple? We are indeed moving towards our destiny; to be alive in these times is an urgent matter.* [30]

These Jewish leaders believe the coming of the Messiah is close at hand. And they believe that he will soon engage in this sacrifice of the red heifer, build his Millennial Temple and rule over the world as the Jewish Messiah.

However, with signs around the streets of Jerusalem, such as the ones proclaiming, "Prepare for the Coming of Messiah," the Jews are poised to receive and accept a coming leader who fits the description of their anticipated Messiah. Yet, these same sincere Jewish leaders will believe in the false Messiah first.

The Bible tells us that Jesus, the true Messiah of the Jews, is coming soon. He is coming to catch away the saints of

---

30   Chaim Richman, *The Mystery of the Red Heifer: Divine Promise of Purity*, 73.

God, those that believe that Jesus Christ of Nazareth is the Savior of the world, and to take these believers to heaven in the Rapture. After this event, the Jews will believe in the false Messiah, the Antichrist, who will appear on the scene at this time. His rising is mentioned in Daniel 7-9, Matthew 24, and 2 Thessalonians 2. The Antichrist (or "Beast") will commence his time as a public demagogue by confirming a peace covenant with Israel, initiating a period of judgment on Israel, called the Tribulation period. This Antichrist will rule for seven years, but in the midst of these seven years he will enter the Temple and desecrate and destroy it. At the end of his time, he will gather all the armed forces of this world to fight in the famous Battle of Armageddon. There, they will gather to fight not each other, but God Himself! Jesus will descend through the clouds, coming with ten thousand of his saints. He will speak His Word and slay all the armies of this world. Jesus will judge the Antichrist and False Prophet and send them to the lake of fire. Then, He will soon set up His reign from Jerusalem and when He comes, He will prepare the tenth sacrifice and bring with Him the Shekinah Glory of God! Jesus of Nazareth is the true Jewish Messiah and He is that prophesied Deliverer of Israel. This is the coming Branch who builds the Temple in Jerusalem.

Zechariah 6:12-15 describes the Messiah saying:

> *...Thus speaketh the Lord of hosts, saying, Behold the man whose name is the Branch; and he shall grow up out of his place, and he shall build the temple of the Lord: Even he shall build the temple of the Lord; and he shall bear the glory, and shall sit and rule upon his throne; and he shall be a priest upon his throne: and the counsel of peace shall be between them both. And the crowns shall be to Helem, and to Tobijah, and to Jedaiah, and to Hen the son of Zephaniah, for a memorial in the temple of the Lord. And they that are far off shall come and build in the temple of the Lord, and ye shall know that the Lord of hosts hath sent me unto you.*

> *And this shall come to pass, if ye will diligently obey the voice of the Lord your God.*

During the Millennial reign of Jesus, the Lord, the city of Jerusalem will no longer be a city surrounded by walls. This famous "City of Peace" will truly exist in complete serenity under the reign of God. God Himself will surround the city in the Shekinah glory cloud of fire.

Zechariah 2:4-5 says, *"And said unto him, Run, speak to this young man, saying, Jerusalem shall be inhabited as a town without walls for the multitude of men and cattle therein: For I, saith the Lord, will be a wall of fire round about, and will be the glory in the midst of her."*

Yes, the glory of God will be in the mountain of God in Jerusalem and from this mountain, Jesus will rule and reign as King of Kings and Lord of Lords.

CHAPTER FOUR

Where is The Lost Ark of The Covenant?

One of the many intriguing and beguilingly romantic things about the Middle East are the numerous stories of hidden treasure, lost cities, and secrets beyond the imagination. You have probably heard the stories of Aladdin and his magic lamp, Scheherazade and 1,001 Arabian Nights, and the royal cities of Babylon, Nineveh and Petra lost in the sands of the desert, half as old as the sands of time. Also, there is the narrative of Sinbad and his search for treasure in secret chambers—revealed by uttering "open sesame," the lost treasures of King Solomon and his mines and the legendary search for the Holy Grail. The Bible surpasses all of these intriguing tales of wonder. For in its pages are revealed the most beautiful, ancient and powerful treasure of all, the search for the golden Ark of the Covenant and its accompanying Temple Treasures.

The search for the lost Ark was recently featured in a movie, *Raiders of the Lost Ark*, which alluded to Biblical facts and modern realities of this amazing Ark of God. In it, an adventuresome archaeologist, Indiana Jones, goes through various explorations fighting off Nazis, fending against tarantulas and angry natives, warding off competitors and saving the heroine, Karen Allen, all the while securing the Ark for future research and display for a museum. The movie displays the common background of Sunday School training for audiences, shows the continued power the ark displays, and has a spectacular ending demonstrating the power of God over evil.

The History of the Ark

What is the Ark and why is it so important? The Ark is the most holy of several different vessels that God commanded

Moses to build, together with the Tabernacle (an early temple), to fulfill requirements for worship. Made of acacia wood, from the shittah (shittim) tree, this Ark was a box two and a half cubits long (three and three-quarters feet) by one and a half cubits wide and high (two and a quarter feet).

The word "ark" comes from the Latin word *arca* and it means "a chest, a box meant to hold something important." The Ark of Noah was designed to be a huge floating boat (shaped similar to an enormous box) meant to hold Noah, his family, and the representative animals of each kind in the world before the flood. The Ark of the Covenant, conversely, would be a medium size box meant to hold the Word of God, represented by the Ten Commandments, the first written scrolls of the first Five books of the Bible (the Torah), Aaron's rod that budded and a pot of manna. The anointing oil used to anoint the *Mishkan* (the Tabernacle) and its vessels, and the kings and high priests of Israel was also kept on the side of the ark.[31]

Color Image 7. A representation of the Ark of the Covenant., Ark of the Covenant Mary Harrsch (CC BY-NC-SA) worldhistory.org Public Domain

The Jews call the Ark the `Aron ("box, chest"), the distinctive term used for the lower portion of the Ark, that is, the gold-covered wooden container holding the sacred items. It is also used in compound form for the Ark with its lid, for example, `Aron Ha-Brit ("Ark of the Covenant"). The word `Aron is related to *Or*, meaning light, because the Word of God inside the Ark stood for the light of the world. Since the Ark contained the

---
31 Rambam, *Klei Hamilkdash* 1, 1-12.

stone Tablets of the Covenant (the Ten Commandments) and the Torah scroll of Moses, it was called the Ark of the Covenant and symbolized God's presence and Prophecy in Israel.

Using precise measurements for the standard cubit, the Ark would be 3'9"×2'3"×2'3". If the cubit was only five hand-breadths (15 inches) the Ark would measure 3'1.5"×1'10.5"×1'10.5" which is very unlikely. After he made a measurement of the inner gates within Warren's Gate, Rabbi Yehuda Getz concluded that a cubit equals 57.8 centimeters. If this later cubit used for the Second Temple were the same as that used for the Ark, then the measurement would be 3'7"×2'2"×2'2".

Moses received instructions for the Ark when he was given the Ten Commandments on Mt. Sinai. The Ark was layered with gold within and without and the exposed rim was also layered with a golden crown bordering the top. It had two golden rings on each side, through which were passed poles made of acacia wood layered with gold.[32]

On the top was placed a solid lid, made by pouring a slab of gold with an abundance of gold on each side, probably poured into a mold. This excess was hammered into two golden cherubim angels which stood with their wings spaced but touching in the middle; their heads tilted slightly downward. Thus, the lid, with accompanying angels, was made of one solid piece of gold.

These cherubs were supposed to have facial features like a child, one with features of a young boy and the other of a young girl. The head of each cherub was man-like or human in appearance, while the body and wings were shaped like a bird.[33] The Cherubim faced each other and expressed affection and the relationship of Almighty God with Israel, as a Father cares for his children.

---

32   Soltau, Henry, *The Holy Vessels and Furniture of the Tabernacle*, (Grand Rapids: Kregel Publishing Co., 1971)

33   Steinberg, Rabbi Shalom Dov, *The Mishkan and the Holy Garments*, (Jerusalem: Toras Chaim Institute, 1992)

Another similar golden box or "Ark" was found in the tomb of Tutankhamen, the boy Pharaoh of Egypt whose burial chambers contained immense wealth. In this tomb they found a gold-covered wooden box with a representation of their god Anubis, (which looks like a jackal), with three small idols inside. The pagan chest would contain idols while the true Ark of the Covenant would not need (or allow) an idol because the Presence of God would hover over it. Another cedarwood chest also similar to the ark was found complete with transport poles (c. 1400 B.C.)

Color Image 8, The Ark from the tomb of King Tutankhamen, of Egypt. 93189203_291 cent-dfw5-1.xx.fbcdn.net Public Domain

The "ark" of King Tut was 32 inches long with transport poles that were placed through brass rings.[34] This ark is now on display at the Cairo Museum, Cairo, Egypt.

The Jewish Ark was placed into the Jewish house of worship (first the Tabernacle, a portable structure, and later the Jewish Temple in Jerusalem). It was made to serve two purposes. First, the Ark was the throne of God and God's footstool where He dwelt between the two cherubim in the Shekinah Glory (God represented in a beautiful cloud). The Shekinah ("dwelling, resting") describes the Divine Presence, the indwelling of God, that was manifested by "dwelling" between the wings of the cherubim above the Ark (1 Chron. 13:6). It represented the presence of God with the Israelites, first in the Tabernacle and later in the First Temple.

Secondly, during the Day of Atonement, the high priest would offer a special sacrifice for the sins of the entire Israelite

---

[34] Carter, Howard, *The Tomb of Tutankhamen*, (U.S.A.: Excalibur Books, 1954)

CHAPTER FOUR

nation. He would enter the innermost holy room of the Temple and there sprinkle the blood of the sacrifice on the lid. Thus, the lid of the Ark was called the Mercy Seat because it showed the propitiation of sin, appeasing the wrath of God for the sin of the nation.

Color Image 9, The Tabernacle of Israel. Tabernacle of Moses@hoshanarabbah.org Public Domain

No one but the high priest was allowed into the innermost room, called the Holy of Holies, where the Ark dwelt. He was only allowed entrance once a year, on the Day of Atonement. The Ark was considered too holy to look upon or touch. In fact, the high priest wore bells on his robe to alert the other priests as to his movement in the Holy of Holies. He never entered without a rope around his leg, lest while in God's presence, he sinfully committed sacrilege, and died.[35] He would then be able to be pulled out by the other priests. The Ark also served as the receptacle for stone tablets containing the Ten Commandments (including the complete and broken tablets), the Law of Moses written on scrolls, Aaron's rod that budded, and a jar of manna from the wilderness journey, the latter two

---
35 Edersheim, Alfred, *The Temple: Its Ministries and Services as They Were at the Time of Christ*, (Grand Rapids: William B. Eerdmans Publishing Co., reprint 1972)

representing God's power of provision and protection.[36] After the Ark was built, Moses placed it in the Holy of Holies in the Tabernacle. (Ex. 11:21)

And no one was permitted to look inside the Ark, because you cannot look at God's written Word, the Ten Commandments, with unconfessed sin in your heart and live. That is why no one can look inside the Ark, and the men of Beth Shemesh that later found the Ark were killed when they looked inside. And you could not touch it because it represented God's holiness, and our access to God, at that time, was represented by the high priest who went to offer the blood of the sacrifice on the Day of Atonement, to atone for the blood of the individuals of the nation of Israel for a year.

This act signified and awaited a future one-time sacrifice for all people for all time, later given by Jesus Christ through His death on the cross, dying the just for the unjust (as a sinless substitute, Jesus as God incarnate in human flesh, could pay for all the sins of the world). As mentioned, the top of the Ark is called the Mercy Seat, a lid of solid gold, and it is the place where the blood was applied, signifying Jesus' bearing the wrath of God for the sin of every individual who ever lived. He was both the sacrifice and the substitute of each person who needed a pure sacrifice. And Jesus proved that He was also God in the flesh by rising again on the third day, showing that He now has the power to save all who would believe the Gospel. The former Ashkenazi Chief Rabbi Shlomo Goren explains:

> *The Ark–the 'Aron Ha-brit–includes the Ten Commandments, [i.e.,] the broken and unbroken Tablets, and the entire scroll written by Moses. It includes every item that is important for the history of the Jews, and it is the highest stage of sanctity we can have.* [37]

---

36   Ex. 16: 11-36, 25:16, Num. 16:16-26, Devarim 31:26, Bava Batra 14a.
37   Randall Price, *In Search of Temple Treasures*, (Eugene, OR: Harvest House Publishers 1994), 52.

CHAPTER FOUR

As the host of Israelites marched through the wilderness, the Levitical priests carried the Ark in procession. These caretakers carried the Ark on their shoulders and marched in the center of the nation of Israel that numbered 3 ½ to 5 million people. (Num. 2:17) Some Jewish sages believed that the Ark had special powers. It is said that lightning issued forth to consume any creature in its pathway, providing safe passage for the people through the wilderness.[38]

The next time in history we hear of the Ark is when Moses' strange request to Horeb caused Jehovah to send the Ark three days journey in advance of the people. (Num. 10:33) Again, the Ark is seen as it passed through the Jordan River before the people as it was carried on the shoulders of the priests and the waters receded for its path. (Josh. 3:11) As recorded in Joshua 6, the priests carried the Ark around the walls of Jericho and trumpets accompanied its parade. After thirteen marches, the walls of Jericho fell before the Ark by the mighty power of God.

The first abode of the Ark in Canaan was Shiloh, in Ephraim's territory. (Josh. 18:1) There it remained for several years before it was taken to Kirjath-jearim. Later, Israel took the Ark into battle with an uncircumcised heart to quell the Philistine armies. Because of Israel's sin, Jehovah delivered the Ark into the hands of the Philistines. (1 Sam. 4; Ps. 78:60-61)

While the Ark was in the Philistine territory, it was taken to the temple of the Philistine fish god Dagon. Human sacrifices were often offered to this pagan god and children were burned alive in a desperate attempt by the Philistines to secure the mercy of the gods. But the false god fell twice before the presence of the Ark and was broken up. (1 Sam. 5) The Philistine cities were smitten with plagues and over-run with mice, proving God's superior majesty above heathen gods. After retaining the Ark for seven months and enduring the plagues as judgment from the Lord, the Philistines sent the Ark back to Israel.

---
[38] Beyond the Walls (October 11, 2017), "Podcast Episode 20: Ark of the Covenant (Part 2) Biblical Mysteries," Accessed on February 6, 2023, https://audacy.com

The first two cities each experienced plagues that included mice and dysentery. As the people in the third Philistine city heard that the Ark was coming to their city, they pleaded that it not be sent to them. But the Ark was sent and that city also experienced plagues. So, the Philistines made a plan of sending the Ark back to Israel without incurring more punishment under the wrath of God. They prepared a new cart and harnessed two cows to the hitch, each of which had newborn calves. These cows had never known a yoke. On the cart they placed the Ark, together with golden gifts of mice and emerods in a separate gilded box. It would have been natural for the cows (*milch kine*) to have bolted at pulling the cart and wanted to find their calves. Yet, instead of seeking their newborn calves and without any human intervention, the cows pulled the Ark straight to the land of Israel and stopped right across the border at Beth Shemesh in Israelite territory! The Philistines took this as a sign from God that the Ark belonged to the Jews. It is evident that these cows were driven by the power of God.

At Beth Shemesh, men looked into the Ark (transgressing God's law of holiness) and God smote 50,070 men for their lack of reverence for the holiness of the Lord. (1 Sam. 6) In this passage we learn that the God's holiness is not to be overlooked or taken lightly. *"And the men of Bethshemesh said, 'Who is able to stand before this holy Lord God?...'"* (1 Sam. 6:20)

At the house of Abinadab in Kirjath-jearim, the Ark rested for the next twenty years during the reign of King David. (1 Sam. 7: 1-2) When King David moved the Ark up to Zion, he erred in placing it upon a cart because the Ark was always to be covered, never to be looked upon and only transported by the priests. While crossing a threshing floor, the oxen shook the Ark and Uzzah was killed when he reached to steady it. The fear of David through this incident caused him to move the Ark to the nearby house of Obed-Edom, the Gittite. (2 Sam. 6:10-11)

CHAPTER FOUR

After hearing a report of the great blessing on Obed-Edom because of the Ark's presence in his home for three months, King David was encouraged to move the Ark. With great ceremony and rejoicing, the Levites carried the Ark on their shoulders to the City of David, which is lower Jerusalem. Evidently, the Ark was then set up in the Tabernacle on Mount Zion in the City of David. (2 Chron. 5: 2-5) While residing there, King Solomon offered sacrifices before it. (1 Kings 3:15; 2 Sam. 11:11)

Mount Zion was originally the hill area north of Jerusalem, the Ophel, where the Tabernacle resided, the lower eastern hill of the City of David. Today's Mount Zion is the southwestern hill next to Mount Moriah, the Temple Mount, higher than the Ophel. The Ophel ("hill, mound") is the southeastern spur north of the City of David that is the oldest known part of Jerusalem. This hill at the top of the City of David is the smaller hill before you approach the Temple Mount to the north and the higher Mount Zion to the northeast. It is the section of Jebusite territory captured by King David and was the site of the Tabernacle during his days.

Through poetic usage, Mount Zion became a synonym for the city of Jerusalem and Israel itself, and spiritually as the eschatological ideal of God's chosen place on Earth. In Millennial times, Mount Zion and Mount Moriah will converge as one combined mountain as the result of an earthquake, where Jesus will reign as King of Kings and Lord of Lords.

Wanting to build a permanent Jewish Temple for worship and sacrifice, King Solomon began its construction in the fourth year of his reign on Mount Moriah. The entire Temple was finished in just less than seven years. When complete, the priests put the Ark into the Holy of Holies and drew out the staves. For the Jews, the Ark now had a permanent home. (2 Chron. 5:7-9)

Color Image 10, The First Jewish Temple with interior vessels. First-Temple-3.png, bibleodyssey.org Public Domain

At the destruction of Jerusalem, the Ark was not specifically mentioned, but the following words may be noted:

"He [the King of Babylon] ... carried out thence all the treasures of the house of Lord..." (2 Kings 24:13)

When the Temple vessels were returned to Jerusalem and restored to the rebuilt Temple under Zerubbabel, the Ark is not specifically mentioned.

Before the Babylonian captivity during the reign of good King Josiah, the prophet Jeremiah was moved to write about unusual changes to Israel that would occur during the coming millennial reign of Jesus as King:

> *And it shall come to pass, when ye be multiplied and increased in the land, in those days, saith the Lord, they shall say no more, The ark of the covenant of the Lord: neither shall it come to mind: neither shall they remember it; neither shall they visit it; neither shall that be done any more. At that time they shall call Jerusalem the throne of the Lord; and all the nations shall be gathered unto it, to the name of the Lord, to Jerusalem: neither shall they walk anymore after the imagination of their evil heart.* (Jer. 3:16-17)

When Ezekiel describes the Millennial Temple in chapters 40-48, he never mentions the Ark of the Covenant, only the inner altar of the Temple and even refers to it as an "altar of wood" indicating it was no longer overlaid with gold. (Ezek. 40-43, especially 41:22)

Suddenly there is no mention of the Ark again in Scripture. This most holy of Jewish relics is mysteriously gone! The Ark seems to have disappeared from the Jewish Temple sometime before the Babylonian invasions of 606, 595, and 586 B.C. [39]

The Importance of the Ark of the Covenant

The greatest Jewish article of worship is the Ark of the Covenant. Ever since the destruction of the Jewish Temple nearly three thousand years ago by Nebuchadnezzar, one of the greatest treasures of the ancient past has disappeared from human knowledge.

What happened to the Ark? To where did it disappear? Was it destroyed or hidden away? How could someone have viewed the Ark or touched the Ark to move it without being killed by the Lord's wrath?

If this ark was rediscovered it would have a widespread impact upon the world as one of the greatest discoveries of all time.

As Rabbi Liebel Reznick has stated:

> No other archaeological find would have a greater impact on the destiny of man. What a religious resurgence this discovery would cause. How it would cause scholars and laymen to reevaluate the past, examine the present, and speculate upon the future cannot be imagined.[40]

This discovery would be the catalyst of an amazing religious renewal and many Jewish scholars believe that its recovery would begin a spiritual revival among the Jews and other people, prompt a massive return of the Jewish people to Israel and would necessitate the rebuilding of the Temple. Other people believe that the discovery of the Ark and rebuilding of the Temple will be the way that God brings the world

---

39 "The Ark of the Covenant," *Encyclopedia Judaica*.
40 Rabbi Leibel Reznick, *The Temple Revisited* (New Jersey: Jason Aronson Inc., 1990), 146-147.

together to serve the one, true God and to see his glory in their presence.

Dr. Randall Price, respected author, archaeologist, and ancient language expert, interviewed the leader of the Temple Mount Faithful, one of the most active and militant Jewish groups involved in the process of rebuilding the Temple, about this very issue.

In his conversation with Dr. Randall Price in his Jerusalem office on January 23, 1994, Gershon Salomon said,

> We want to make all mankind again one family of God. We want to make all mankind worshippers of the One God here in Jerusalem on the holy hill, Mount Moriah–the Temple Mount. One of the important things that is connected to this great event is the Ark of the Covenant. [41]

Many claims have surfaced in the last few years as to the Ark's possible discovery and the rabbi's calculated waiting for the timing of its return to Israel. Is there any truth to these claims and what does the evidence show? To discover the Ark, we must first look at its disappearance.

To Where Did the Ark Disappear?

The Ark of the Covenant is mentioned in 2 Kings 19:15 by King Hezekiah when he prayed to the Lord for deliverance from the Assyrians. It seems likely that the Ark was removed before or during the reign of his son Manasseh, because this Manasseh set up an idolatrous image in the Holy of Holies (2 Kings 21:7). This is always referred to as the greatest desecration of the Temple under a Jewish king and with this ceasing of the Temple rituals, the Jewish priests would have had to go into hiding. Because it was their duty to safeguard the Temple, its articles and holiness, it would be unthinkable that they would not have taken the Ark and other Temple articles into hiding with them.

---

[41] Randall Price, *In Search of Temple Treasure*, Ibid., 37.

CHAPTER FOUR

Hebrew University professor Menahem Haran argues that the Ark was removed from the Temple by Manasseh.[42] However, the Bible defeats this argument because 2 Chronicles 35:3 mentions the Ark returning to the Temple after the time of Manasseh in the days of king Josiah.

Late in Manasseh's life, he repented of the evil he had done and followed after the Lord. When his grandson Josiah became king, this young king also made extensive repair to the Temple, re-instituted the priestly service and commanded the Ark to be returned to the Temple. (2 Kings 22:5-6)

It is recorded in 2 Chronicles 35:1-3:

> "Moreover, Josiah kept a passover unto the Lord in Jerusalem: and they killed the passover on the fourteenth day of the first month. And he set the priests in their charges, and encouraged them to the service of the house of the Lord. And said unto the Levites that taught all Israel, which were holy unto the Lord, Put the holy ark in the house which Solomon the Son of David king of Israel did build: it shall not be a burden upon your shoulders: serve the Lord your God, and his people Israel."

There is a difference of opinion among the Rabbis about the last part of this verse. Some Jewish authorities believe that the Ark was not only hidden in a secret chamber during the reign of Manasseh, but also later during the reign of King Josiah and was preserved by this action. Other Rabbis believe that the Ark had been destroyed by the Babylonians. However, all agreed that the priests took the Ark into hiding during the time of Josiah. It would seem plausible that if the priests could hide the Ark from their own earlier evil King Manasseh, then they would have been able to conceal it from the conquering Nebuchadnezzar, having been warned of this invasion by the prophet Jeremiah.

Jewish tradition has always maintained that the Ark has

---

42 Menahem Haran, "The Disappearance of the Ark," *Israel Exploration Journal* 13 (1963), 46-58.

been housed in a secret chamber underneath the Temple Mount since First Temple times. Evidence is also offered for support from Jewish history (both biblical and extra-biblical), the Talmud, archaeological excavations and from recent testimony of Jewish Rabbis.

The Jewish writings describe how the Ark of the Covenant, together with the Ten Commandments, Aaron's rod that budded, the pot of manna, the oil of anointing, the Tabernacle and other Temple treasures were hidden by King Josiah. The Jews believe that King Josiah, sensing the oncoming invasion of the Babylonians, ordered the Temple articles hidden in a secret underground chamber or group of chambers on the Temple Mount. King Solomon had hewed this chamber out centuries before when he also prepared hidden chambers for his own palace treasure to be safeguarded nearby from possible hostile invasions of enemy forces.

As King Solomon built the Temple, by his great wisdom from God, he foresaw its coming destruction and built a secret chamber deep within the Temple Mount to conceal the Ark in a time of danger. This kind of threat was very real, as evidenced from the Biblical account of the plundering of the Temple treasury soon after Solomon's death by the Egyptian pharaoh Shishak (1 Kings 14:25-26). And during the idolatrous rule of the kings Manasseh and Amon, who each desecrated the Temple with abominable images, the Ark was removed for safekeeping. Then it was returned to the Temple, as recorded in 2 Chronicles 35:3 in the days of King Josiah prior to the first Babylonian invasions. Speculating on where the Ark resided during this interim period, the Rabbis interpret this verse to teach that the Ark had been held in a subterranean chamber of the Temple.[43]

The great Jewish rabbinical scholar Maimonides wrote:

---
43 Mishnah. *Shekalim* 6:1

CHAPTER FOUR

> *When Solomon built the Temple, He was also aware that it would ultimately be destroyed. He constructed a chamber in which the Ark could be entombed below the Temple in deep, maze-like vaults. King Josiah commanded that the Ark be entombed in the chamber built by Solomon, as it is said (2 Chron. 35:3), "And he said to the Levites who were enlightened above all Israel, Place the Holy Ark in the Chamber built by Solomon, the son of David, King of Israel. You will no longer carry it upon your shoulders. Now, serve the LORD, your God." When it was entombed, Aaron's staff, the vial of manna, and the oil used for anointing were entombed with it. All these sacred articles did not return in the Second Temple.* [44]

Jewish scholars generally agree that the Ark was missing by the beginning of the construction of the Second Temple built by Zerubbabel. As the Jewish writings tell us:

> *"All these sacred articles did not return in the Second Temple."* [45]

However, Jewish scholars differ as to what happened next to the Ark. Some believe that the Ark always remained in the secret chamber under the Temple Mountain. Others maintain that Jeremiah the Prophet was warned by God of the coming Babylonian invasion and the impending destruction of the Temple. The Apocryphal book of Maccabees 2:1-7 records that Jeremiah hid the Ark in a secret sealed cave beneath Mount Nebo on the other side of Jordan. There it remained until the rebuilding of the Temple under Zerubbabel, when it was possibly replaced in the Temple of Jerusalem. But the priests must have removed the Ark again before the Roman invasion of Jerusalem by Pompey in A.D. 63.

The Roman Historian Tacitus tells us that when Pompey entered the Temple, he also entered the Holy of Holies and found it empty.[46] This greatly surprised him because he

---

44 *Hilchos Bias HaBechirah* 4., *Mishneh Torah*, (New York/Jerusalem: Moznaim Publ. Co., 1992)
45 *Hilchos Bias HaBechirah* 4., *Mishneh Torah*, (New York/Jerusalem: Moznaim Publ. Co., 1992)
46 Tacitus, *Historiae* 5.9.1.

thought the Jewish Temple would house great treasure, both from the impressive sight of the building, and because the Jews protested his entrance at the offering of their own lives. However, the Jews were not dying to protect the treasure of Temple, but rather its sanctity. This was because the Ark (and by it the Shekinah glory presence of God) *was once* present there, or perhaps because the Ark was thought to *be* present there somewhere *beneath* the Holy of Holies.

In the time of Jesus, all that is found in the innermost room of the Temple built by King Herod, called the Holy of Holies, is the cherubim made of olive wood and covered in gold which stood before the stone upon which the Ark had been placed.[47] This stone was traditionally the highest point of Mount Moriah where Abraham offered Isaac and where King David later saw the angelic destroyer of Jerusalem on the threshing floor of Aravnah (or Arnan) the Jebusite. It was around this flooring area in which the Temple was later built. When the Jews returned from Babylon and later rebuilt the Temple, they discovered and used the earlier Ashes of the Red Heifer for cleansing, hidden away during the invasion of Nebuchadnezzar but the Ark was never brought forth.

Did the unrest of the times encourage the Jewish religious leaders to let the Ark remain in a hidden chamber? Unrest followed under the rulership of Antiochus Epiphanes and the Ptolemies and peace was only symbolic under Roman rule. During the Roman occupation, a Roman eagle insignia was placed above the Eastern Gate of the Temple, again signaling a desecration of the Temple Mount and the Ark. But if the Ark were present beneath the Holy of Holies, it would have given adequate sanctity to the Holy Place without it being accessible to the High Priest during Yom Kippur. In the Mishnah, it records that the Ark had been removed and was not present from the time of the Second Temple.[48]

---
47 *Yoma* 5:2
48 Mishnah, *Mo'ed, Yoma,* 5.

CHAPTER FOUR

It also relates that the High Priest made his offering upon an ancient rock, called the *Even Shetiyyah* (or "Foundation Stone") which protruded from the floor of the Holy Place and was part of the highest point on Mount Moriah. The *`Even Shetiyyah* is the stone that, according to ancient Jewish sources, existed within the Holy of Holies in the Temple and upon which the Ark of the Covenant rested in First Temple times. According to tradition, this stone is identified with the rock inside the Muslim Dome of the Rock. The Arabs call this the *Sakhra* (Arabic, "rock"), which is a term for the sacred rock within the Islamic shrine on the Temple Mount, hence: *Qubbet es-Sakhra*, the "Dome of the Rock." There is no reference to the Ark in the New Testament during Second Temple times, although reference is made to other articles within the Herodian Temple. (Luke 1:9-11)

Several questions remain. Where did the Ark go? Was it hidden and forgotten? Did an earlier king plunder it? When exactly did the Ark disappear and what happened to it? Numerous theories abound as to its disappearance and possible hiding place.

There are several excavations going on at this writing and others have taken place frequently, especially within the last century. Yet could anyone actually know of the location of the Ark and discover such an old religious relic?

Dr. Dan Bahat, former official archaeologist for the City of Jerusalem tells us:

> *"I know many among us who live in this country that believe they know the secrets to the Treasures of the Temple."* [49]

---

49 Randall Price, *In Search of Temple Treasures*, Ibid., 141.

CHAPTER FIVE

𝔚𝔥𝔞𝔱 𝔥𝔞𝔭𝔭𝔢𝔫𝔢𝔡 𝔱𝔬 𝔱𝔥𝔢 𝔄𝔯𝔨?

This study examines the viable explanations of the Ark's disappearance and possible hiding places, the past expeditions and excavations in countries around the world and the current Jewish expectation of a coming Temple. To answer these questions, we must explore the conceivable stories of where the Ark might have gone.

Did Nebuchadnezzar Take the Ark to Babylon?

The first possibility usually mentioned is that the Ark was destroyed by Nebuchadnezzar in 597 B.C. or by his general, Nebuzaradan in 586 B.C. (2 Kings 24:13; 25:8-21; Jer. 39:8-10; 52:12-27)

Color Image 11, The Ishtar Gate of ancient Babylon. ishtar-gate-artists-impression-12913 worldhistory.org Public Domain

One version of this theory is that the Ark was removed along with the other Temple vessels when the Babylonians looted the Temple treasuries and transported them to Babylon, and it is still there in some location. Others believe that the Ark was either destroyed with the Temple or later destroyed in Babylon after removing its outer gold covering. This is often suggested because the destruction of the Temple implied the destruction or plunder of the Temple vessels as well.

This besieging Babylonian king was the first king to actually enter the Outer Sanctum of the Temple. Of him alone it is said that he "cut in pieces all the vessels of gold which Solomon king of Israel had made in the temple of the LORD." (2 Kings 24:13.)

The word used for "temple" in this verse is the Hebrew word "hekal" or "heichel" meaning Outer Sanctum or Holy Place of the Temple. The Holy of Holies room where the Ark was kept was called the *Kodesh HaKadashim* in Hebrew. The passage in 2 Kings 24:13 refers to "all the vessels which Solomon king of Israel had made" and must be qualified by the dual reference to "all the treasures of the house of the Lord, and the treasures of the king's house." These statements point to the Temple treasuries, not the inner sanctuary. This is further substantiated by the verse in 1 Kings 7:51 which states that the golden vessels were put in "the treasuries of the house of the Lord." These treasuries contained duplicates of most of the sacred Temple vessels, such as multiple lampstands. This means that the items being destroyed that were mentioned in the earlier passage did not come from the inner sanctuary. Isaiah had already mentioned that the Babylonian emissary Merodach-baladan was shown the inventory of these very treasuries by King Hezekiah (Isa. 39:1-5) and the next time that Jerusalem was invaded, the Babylonians immediately plundered this treasury, as predicted by the prophet in verse 6.

At this stage of the relations between Judah and Babylon, Nebuchadnezzar was only punishing the Jew's insurrection and lack of tribute payment and had not yet destroyed the Temple.

Some scholars conclude that Nebuchadnezzar never entered the Holy of Holies in the Temple but stopped his desecration of the Temple at the Holy Place or at the outer courts. It

CHAPTER FIVE

seems quite reasonable though, that if the heathen king went into the Temple area itself to plunder any treasure that he would certainly have the soldiers look through every room of the Temple for spoils. Even the act of personally going into the Temple area shows his thoroughness and lust for treasure. Nebuchadnezzar entered the Outer Sanctum of the Temple and stripped the Temple vessels of their gold, silver or bronze, thereby destroying them, and plundered the Temple treasuries (thirty-eight rooms surrounding the Temple building proper).

Even if the interpretation was accepted that Nebuchadnezzar plundered the inner parts of the Temple building, the Scripture tells us clearly that he plundered the vessels made by King Solomon. When Solomon first erected the Temple, he ordered that the building be constructed exactly three times as large as the original measurements of the Tabernacle. And, he ordered that new vessels be constructed, many larger and more elaborate and numerous than the Tabernacle vessels. However, a new Ark was not used. It was essential that the original Ark be used to continue the continuity of the Shekinah glory cloud, depicting God's presence, being always present with this Ark.

Eleven years later, the Temple had already been deprived of at least most of its inner accessories. When Nebuzaradan ransacked the Temple (in a different act of looting) and finally destroyed it, he took only the vessels of the Temple Courtyard (the bronze vessels enumerated in the list found in Babylon). He also pillaged those articles of the Temple treasuries (the gold and silver vessels mentioned therein such as the golden candlesticks of the Temple Courtyard, not of the Inner Sanctum). (2 Kings 25:13-17; Jer. 52:17-23; 1 Kings 7:48-50)

Also, if the Ark had indeed been taken it would not have been cut up for bulk gold bullion, but would have been preserved intact as a war trophy, as were lesser vessels taken from the Temple (Dan. 12:1).

It has also been suggested that the Ark was destroyed by fire in 586 B.C., when Nebuzaradan eventually trespassed and violated the Temple and set it on fire, as 2 Chronicles states that the fire "destroyed all its valuable articles." Yet, if this were true, where did the other Temple vessels come from that finally were taken to Babylon? It would more likely seem that the best vessels were taken as spoils and the smaller remains were burned with the Temple building.

If the Ark was not destroyed by the Babylonians, is it possible that they took it to Babylon as a spoil of war? The biblical narrative tells us that Nebuchadnezzar plundered the Temple before its destruction, carrying off these articles of the Temple treasuries to Babylon (2 Kings 24:13; 25:13-17; 2 Chron. 36:18). Although the text does not imply any intrusion into the inner section of the Temple sanctuary, this may have occurred.

However, the Ark was not specifically mentioned as one of the Temple vessels that was stolen, destroyed, or later returned under Zerubbabel. Certainly, the Jewish writers would have mentioned its destruction and Nebuchadnezzar have boasted of its capture if he had found and possessed it. There is no mention of *any* of the Temple treasures from the inner sanctum being captured. This lack of mention in Scripture is noteworthy because the previous capture of the Ark by the Philistines had occupied *two entire chapters* (1 Sam. 5-6). So, it would seem inconsistent that Scripture would be silent on such a dramatic event as the Ark's capture or destruction. The Ark is also not mentioned in the list found in Babylon of stolen bounty of Nebuchadnezzar, although other Temple treasure is listed in great detail.

In Ezra 1:7-11, the Bible tells us that all the vessels that were taken from Judah were later returned by the Persians. They had inventoried these items and they provided them with the list when the Israelites returned to rebuild the Temple. The contemporaries of Jehoiakim expected all the vessels taken by Nebuchadnezzar to Babylon to be miraculously returned (Jer. 27:16-28:6). Cyrus transferred these vessels to Sheshbazzar, the prince of Judah, mentioned in Ezra 1:7-11, which were also recorded in ancient records which have been discovered archaeologically. The Bible mentions 5,400 items (and the LXX records 5,469 items) but these do not match the items of the inner sanctuary by either name or by number. The original list of items taken to Babylon has been discovered and the list of items later returned was also separately found. But each list records only vessels of more minor importance and they do not mention the Ark.

Did Jewish Kings Take the Ark?

There is an opinion that earlier Jewish kings, Jehoash, Ahaz or Hezekiah, had already emptied the Temple of its contents to pay tribute to the Assyrian kings. Some people have thought that the ark was taken by King Jehoash of Israel in his battle against Judah in 785 B.C. (2 Kings 14:14) or by King Ahaz of Judah or King Hezekiah of Judah in 729 B.C. as tribute payment to the Assyrian kings. (2 Kings 18:15-16).

The purpose of Jehoash's invasion was not to capture the Temple treasure but was more in retaliation to King Amaziah of Judah. However, he did take "all the gold and the silver, and all the vessels that were found in the house of God with Obed-edom" whose family served as gatekeepers to the Temple (2 Chron. 25:24: 26:4-8). Thus, the treasure that was possessed was taken from the house of Obed-edom, not the inner sanctuary of the Temple.

The Scriptures plainly teach that Ahaz, plundered the "silver and gold that was in the house of the LORD, and in the treasures of the Kings house, and sent it for a present to the King of

Assyria" (Tiglath-pileser, the King of Assyria). (2 Kings 16:8) He also moved the altar from its place and refashioned it after the pagan altar at Damascus. (2 Kings 16:10-18) Notice, these treasures are also identified as coming from the treasuries of the "house of the Lord, and in the treasures of the King's house," not from the sanctuary of the Temple proper.

Later, Hezekiah also plundered the House of the Lord to pay tribute to the Assyrian King Sennecherib. He emptied all the treasures of silver from the Temple and King's Palace and cut off the gold from the doors and pillars of the Temple. (2 Kings 18:13-16)

In each passage of Scripture, it seems to allude to the act of plundering the treasury rooms around the Temple building and not actually the treasure of the Temple vessels inside. It tells of King Hezekiah going to pray in the area of the Temple in 2 Kings 19:14-15 relating, *"And King Hezekiah received the letter of the hand of the messengers, and read it: and Hezekiah went up into the house of the Lord, and spread it before the Lord. And Hezekiah prayed before the Lord, and said, O Lord God of Israel, which dwellest between the cherubims..."*

However, it was not possible for a king to enter the Holy of Holies and take the Ark. This passage alludes to the king praying in the Temple and mentioning that God dwells in the midst of the Cherubim. For the king to mention that God dwells between the cherubim does not mean that he literally had to be standing in the Holy of Holies. To actually go into the Holy of Holies would have meant certain death. The earlier example of King Uzziah (Hezekiah's great-grandfather) donning a priest's garment and merely entering the outer division of the Temple to burn incense on the Golden Altar, then being struck with leprosy was enough to prove that a king could not enter the place of the Ark.

Most scholars see this explanation as the actual outcome of

CHAPTER FIVE

events here, as well as those events dealing with the Kings Jehoash of Judah and Hazael of Syria mentioned in 2 Kings 12:18.

In connection with this, Menachem Haran relates how that the sin of Manasseh, mentioned in 2 Kings 21, was the greatest of all sins committed by Judean Kings.[50]

This grave sin caused the Lord to say, *"Behold, I am bringing such evil upon Jerusalem and Judah, that whosoever heareth of it, both his ears shall tingle."* (2 Kings 21:12)

This sin of Manasseh culminated in his removal of the Ark from the Temple. The writer of Kings, to emphasize his disgust, goes on to remind us that "In this house, and in Jerusalem, which I have chosen out of all tribes of Israel, will I put my name forever." (2 Kings 21:7)

Yet, Manasseh renewed pagan worship to Baal and Asherah with all its accompanying atrocities, such as "sacred prostitution" and child sacrifices, by building high places, altars, and a grove. He was involved in witchcraft by making his son pass through the fire, observing times (horoscopes), using enchantments, and dealing with familiar spirits (demons) and wizards. However, the introduction of the image of Asherah in the Temple is seen as the climactic sin of Manasseh's life.

Because the text refers to the dedication of the Temple in connection with the occasion that Solomon carried the Ark into the Inner Sanctum of the Temple, a time of holiness and blessing (1 Kings 8:16-21), the act of Manasseh is seen as the exact reversal of this dedication. The Ark of God would have to be removed to place the idol of Asherah in its place. Perhaps it was hidden at this time by the faithful priests and later moved by King Josiah. (2 Chron. 35:3)

It is interesting to note that later in Manasseh's life, he repented of his earlier abominations and faithfully followed Jehovah all the rest of his days.

---

50   Menachem Haran, *Temples and Temple Service in Ancient Israel*, (New York: Oxford University Press, 1988).

Was the Ark Lost or Stolen?

Several lesser-known theories are fascinating but do not carry much weight or validity. One theory teaches that the Ark was simply lost or misplaced. Common sense easily dispels this idea. Can you imagine the Jews of Israel losing the most sacred object of their worship? The intrinsic value of the Ark of the Covenant would be priceless. It was made of acacia wood and overlaid with gold, with its lid consisting of one solid piece of carved gold and would be worth a great sum of money today, just for its gold value.

Based upon a statement in Exodus 37:24, one rabbinical sage believed that the ark and its lid were constructed of one talent (three thousandshekels) of gold. This would mean that about twenty pounds of gold was used for its manufacture. At current modern prices (1/25/23), and with gold valued at about $1,950.40 an ounce (American), or $31,206.40 a pound, the Ark would be worth about $624,128 of gold, not including the cost of workmanship (which would be considerable).

It was also the holiest object on Earth. It is impossible to envision a Jewish priest saying, "I wonder where I left the Ark? It must be around here somewhere." The prospect of local people stealing the Ark is also very unlikely. Not only would it be considered the ultimate sacrilege for a Jew to steal such an object and potentially life threatening to even look upon or touch the Ark, but also the Temple Mount operated a twenty-four–hour rotating Temple Guard for protection of its buildings.

Is the Ark in Heaven?

Sometimes it is suggested that God took the Ark to heaven where it now resides. This view seems to have originated from traditions of the Catholic Church and has no basis in Scripture. It is similar to the many other legends that are often purported by this church that do not match Scripture and have no proof. This view is sometimes supposed by sincere people as a way that the Lord protected later generations from interpreting the ark as an idol to be worshiped. So, he hid the ark, or translated it to heaven, as he had done with the body of Moses.

The basis of this view comes from a misunderstanding or misinterpretation of Revelation 11:19 which says: *"And the temple of God was opened in heaven, and there was seen in his temple the Ark of his testament: and there were lightnings, and voices, and thunderings, and an earthquake, and great hail."*

The Ark on Earth is a duplicate of the Ark in heaven, together with the other Tabernacle and Temple vessels. John saw the *heavenly* Ark that has *always* existed in the *heavenly* Temple with God. The Ark viewed in heaven by John the Revelator is the original Ark after which the Ark of Moses was patterned, and it is the same heavenly scene that Moses saw many years earlier. References made to the archetypal Temple in Heaven and its articles are not the same as the Temple articles on Earth. For instance, the book of Revelation also mentions the Golden altar, incense, censer, harps, trumpets, bowls, ephods, and the appearance of the Tabernacle, Tent and Temple (Rev. 5:8; 7:9, 14-15; 8:2-5; 15:2, 5-7). Were all these articles translated to heaven because of their mention in Revelation? If this were true, what was the building that Nebuchadnezzar destroyed in the Babylonian invasions and what were the articles, if the original Temple building and its articles were already in Heaven? John is referring to two separate buildings and Arks.

The Apostle John makes this clear when he tells of the measuring of the Tribulation Temple on Earth in Revelation 11:1-2, and omits the outer court because it was trodden down of the Gentiles (a heavenly Temple would not have a special division for the non-chosen Gentile race). Thus, there is definitely an existing Temple on Earth during the future Tribulation Period. This Temple exists at the same time as the heavenly Temple and therefore could not be the same building. Therefore, we know conclusively that it was the heavenly Temple and Ark which John saw and described in Revelation 11:19.

Hebrews 9:21-23 confirms this belief: *"Moreover he sprinkled with blood both the tabernacle, and all the vessels of the ministry. And almost all things are by the law purged with blood; and without shedding of blood is no remission. It was therefore necessary that the pattern of things in the heavens should be purified with these; but the heavenly things themselves with better sacrifices than these."*

Consequently, the Ark on Earth is a model of the heavenly Ark of God. The Ark in heaven is the original Ark of the Lord. It was the heavenly pattern for the earthly Ark. This was the Ark which Moses saw in his vision on Mount Sinai as the Lord commanded him to build the Ark of the Covenant and the Tabernacle, with its various articles and utensils and to confuse the earthly ark with the Ark of Heaven is a grave mistake.

CHAPTER SIX

Unusual Theories of the Ark's Location

Because the Ark of the Covenant has been a part of the Jewish faith, and the Old Testament has been included in the long history of the teaching of Christianity, people from many walks of life are curious to its existence. This includes, not only reputable theories, but also some quite unusual ideas about the Ark of Moses.

What About the Vision of Masada?

One eccentric theory is mentioned by Doug Wead. His book, *Where is the Lost Ark?*, covers many traditional possibilities, but also mentions some little-known theories, which he may not personally believe. It seems that a woman had a "vision" and saw the Ark in a secret hiding place on Masada.

This is where the zealot Jews took their last stand against the Romans. This was the location of one of the desert fortresses of King Herod, which included a palace complex, ritual baths, cisterns, Roman baths, and buildings for a garrison of soldiers. This is where the most ardent Jewish fighters against the Romans made their last stand and excavators have also found many Jewish religious items and even scrolls. It is famous for the martyrdom of the Jewish fighters. and apparently, also the location of unusual visons.

Wead reports that Frida Schlaien had a dream. She claims to have encountered near-death experiences, then the story follows:

> *She found herself flying high over a strange landscape. On one side there was a large body of water, on the other side a lake. Near the lake, she saw a flat mountaintop. She then descended to the mountain. In the center she saw a wall with small stones around a hole. Soldiers were digging the hole out and eventually pulled*

out a gold box, dirt falling off the ends. "This is the Holy Ark," a voice said. The metal glowed so brightly it woke Schlaien. [51]

Schlaien later went to Israel and visited Masada. While there she recognized that this was the mountain of her dream, where she had seen Roman soldiers retrieve the ark, and then heard a voice announce it speaking in *English*. She wanted to excavate the "stone circle" of her dream, but the Israel Antiquities Department, under Avi Eytan, refused without qualified archaeologists involved who were sponsored by a specific scientific organization. (As to why, there is little wonder!)

The Israel National Parks Authority allowed Schlaien to spend three days and nights on Masada where she spent most of her time meditating. She was not allowed to dig but she did survey the exposed areas of the mountain and never saw or found an ark. So much for visions!

Color Image 12, Masada, the desert fortress of King Herod. Israel-2013-Aerial21-Masada.jpg Gadot13 CC-BY-SA-4,0 wikipedia.org Public Domain

---

51 Doug Wead, David Lewis and Hal Donaldson, *Where is the Lost Ark?* (Minneapolis: Bethany House Publishers, 1982), 122.

CHAPTER SIX

Does the Pope Have the Ark?

In 1993, J.R. Church stated that he believes the Ark was underground in vaults owned by the Vatican.[52] He also told me, as his booklet was going to press, he had met someone else who told him of seeing the Veil of the Temple or Tabernacle stored in boxes underneath the Vatican in hidden vaults.

Rev. Church met Nelson Canode, a former Benedictine monk in the Catholic Church, who claimed to have seen the container for the Ark. While working at a monastery in Subiaco, Italy, thirty miles east of Rome, the monk told Rev. Church that he was taken to a cavern four stories below ground where he claimed to have seen several containers which held the Ark and other artifacts.

Ill. 6, An overview of the Vatican and St. Peter's Basilica, basilica-di-san-pietro_1.jpg orangesmile.com Public Domain

The room also contained golden articles and some old drapes that Church believed could have been from the Tabernacle. As Canode was moving these artifacts back and forth from Subiaco to the underground vaults of the Vatican, he asked what these items were. He was told that they included the disassembled Tabernacle and the Ark.

52 Church, J.R., *The Ark of the Covenant—We Have Found It*, (Oklahoma City: Prophecy Publications, 1993)

It has never been disputed that some of the Second Temple vessels were taken to Rome after the destruction of the Jewish Temple. The Jewish historian of Roman times, Josephus, records how that Vespasian deposited some of the captured Temple articles in a specially built "peace sanctuary" that he erected to celebrate their victory and the Temple's destruction after the Jewish War. It is doubtful that any of these articles would have dated from the First Temple period. They were more probably duplicates of the Temple vessels from the Temple treasury area of the Temple Mount.

According to a seventh century record, Pope Vitalianus had the Ark and the two Tablets of the Ten Commandments in his possession in A.D. 657. There is evidence to the contrary. However, if this pope did have the Ark, history tells us that the Roman Emperor Constans II visited this pope and St. Peter's Basilica in Rome. Constans II sacked the city of many of the most valuable religious ornaments and he sent these things to Constantinople. Hence, it would seem that the Ark would have been stolen at that time and sent to Constantinople if it were ever in Rome in the first place.

The immense wealth of the Catholic Church is a well-known fact and the Vatican is famous as one of the greatest museums of the world. Not only do they have the priceless art of Michelangelo, Bernini and Raphael, there are fourteen hundred rooms of Museum pieces on display.[53] The Vatican houses the Basilica of St. Peter, numerous chapels, an immense underground cemetery and series of vaults, several universities, papal apartments, tunnels to other fortresses and properties together with many large courtyards and esplanades.

It is certainly conceivable that the Roman church or its sympathizers could have purchased or captured the Ark in earlier times and transported it to the Vatican for safekeeping. It is also known that the Vatican has hidden away many

---

53 Santini, Loretta, *Rome and Vatican*, (Narni-Terni: Plurigraf, 1975)

important Christian and historical artifacts from public view in the past. And rumors have abounded about special visitors to the Vatican who have seen Temple treasures. Moreover, some people believe that the Ark was discovered at one of the Catholic "satellite" ministries, such as an abbey or monastery, and taken from there to the underground vaults of the Vatican.

The story told by Nelson Canode might be true but even he does not claim to have actually seen the Ark or the contents of the containers. The priest who identified these articles may have been relating a rumor or tradition of the identification of these objects. And J.R. Church also later abandoned this theory in his video entitled *What Really Happened to the Ark of the Covenant*, although he still believes that the Vatican may have some related articles, such as the drapes of the Temple.[54] This theory, while possible, is pure speculation and without any real basis of evidence.

Did the Ancient Romans Take the Ark?

There are other theories distantly related to Church's view that also involve the Vatican. The Roman army invaded Jerusalem under Titus in A.D. 70 and plundered the Temple, destroyed the building, and even dismantled the Temple platform and surrounding walls. They took their spoils of war to Rome and verily depicted them in stone on the famous Arch of Titus in A.D. 81.

This included a bas-relief of the supposed Temple Menorah (the seven-branched candlestick) and other Temple articles, but curiously, the Ark is missing. The Menorah ("lamp"; pl. *menorot*) is the name used for the candelabrum, or seven-branched oil lamps, used in both the Temple and the Tabernacle.

Written records of the time do mention the Menorah and Jewish slaves, but also fail to mention the Ark. Accordingly, the Ark was probably not taken to Rome.

---

54   J. R. Church, *What Really Happened to the Ark of the Covenant* (Oklahoma City, OK: Prophecy Publications, 1993)

Ill. 7, The Arch of Titus, Rome, Italy. Arch Titus, Forum Ramanum, Rome, Italy.jpg Jebulon.CC0 en.wikipedia.org Public Domain

Part of the confusion over this point is a result of the writings of the German historian Ferdinand Gregorovius, well-known as the author of a history of the Roman Empire of the Middle Ages. This Gregorvius wrote a poem entitled "Lament of the Children of Israel in Rome" and a treatise in 1853 called "The Ghetto and the Jews in Rome."

Each of these manuscripts mentions the Ark being depicted on the Arch of Titus in Rome. The arch does show the triumphal procession of the Roman Emperor Titus carrying the spoils of the Jewish Temple through the streets of Rome. However, the Ark was not pictured in the relief on the Titus Arch. Also, the Roman historian Tacitus, in his record of spoils, does not mention the Ark.[55]

It is even doubted that the Menorah (the seven-branched candlestick) depicted on the Arch of Titus was even a menorah from the Temple building itself. This is because of the appearance of the menorah on the arch. It is well known that the Temple menorah was never fashioned with images

---
55   Tacitus, *Historiae* 5 9. 1.

CHAPTER SIX

Ill. 8, The menorah inside Titus' Arch., Menorah stjudasmaccaaeus.wordpress.com Public Domain

on it, and this can be proved from recent archaeological evidence. This would have been seen as a form of idolatry to place an image on any Temple vessel or building.

The earliest archaeological menorah drawing discovered shows the menorah with a three-legged stand, not an octagonal stand bearing images as seen on the menorah of the Roman arch. Because of the images, it is believed that this menorah on the arch must be a menorah fashioned by Herod's craftsmen as a gift to Rome. The Jewish Roman-era historian, Josephus, mentions that the Jewish priests gave Titus "two lampstands similar to those deposited in the Temple." [56]

We do know, however, that certain Temple treasure was moved to Rome as a result of the A.D. 70 invasion of Titus. The future emperor Titus, certain Roman nobles and several generals possibly kept this treasure as their personal plunder and reward. But it was exhibited in a public location.

As mentioned previously, the Temple articles were stored in a "peace sanctuary" built after the Jewish War to display their spoils of war. It is this treasure which most likely would have made its way to the Vatican. Hence, any treasure of the Temple that the Vatican may now possess is probably the remnants of the spoils of this A.D. 70 invasion, which is an astounding possibility and amazing prospect. Still, all records insist that the Ark was not in Jerusalem at the time of the invasion. It is then unlikely that the Vatican would have the lost Ark in their possession.

---

56   Josephus, *Wars of the Jews* 6.388.

Was the Ark Hidden in the Nea Church of Israel?

An additional little-known connection with the Vatican has to do with the possibility that the Ark was hidden in the underground vaults of a church of Jerusalem. In Jerusalem's Jewish Quarter of the Old City, a recent discovery of a church's remains has raised new questions.

The Nea Church (or New Church) was built in the sixth century A.D. by the emperor Justinian and consecrated to the Virgin Mary. Standing only a few decades, it was destroyed by the Jews, possibly in retaliation for the additional desecration of the Temple Mount just seventy years earlier. The Nea was one of the largest churches in all Jerusalem and included the pillars from the Temple in its construction.

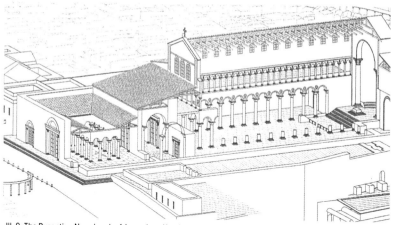

Ill. 9, The Byzantine Nea church of Jerusalem. Nea.jpg johnsanidopoulos.com Public Domain

The Byzantine rulers had not disturbed the site of the earlier Jewish Temple. But when this church was built, the enormous columns from the devastated Temple Mount were removed and incorporated into the building. You can still see, today, columns from the Jewish Temple area at the ruins of this church.

According to the introduction to his history of the Gothic War, the sixth-century Byzantine historian Procopius of Caesarea reported that the "treasures of the Jews" were carried in a

CHAPTER SIX

triumphal procession in Constantinople (Byzantium). After his victory over the Vandals, Belisarius sacked Rome and carried these vessels to Carthage in A.D. 455. Procopus relates that after the sacking of Rome the treasure was taken to Carcassone in southwestern France. The Vandal princes then transported it through Spain to North Africa.

Medieval sources also tell of the Temple treasures being deposited in the royal library of Emperor Justinian, as recorded in the sixth-century Jewish apocalyptic *War of the King Messiah*. Procopius related that a Jew had warned a high official in the emperor's court not to keep the vessels in Byzantium because they had brought defeat to the Romans and Carthaginians. So, Justinian sent a military mission to collect them and return them to Jerusalem, "placing them in one of the churches there."[57] This would logically have been at the newly constructed Nea church.

The eminent Jewish archaeological authority, Meir Ben-Dov does not agree with the truthfulness of this ancient story.

> *In our view, this story too bears some allusion to the looting of the stoa pillars from the Temple Mount. When they were removed it would appear that various vessels came to light which, of course, were removed for safekeeping to the Nea Church. The tale of the peregrinations of the Temple treasure as far as North Africa was spun in reply to a visitor who enquired about their source and the manner in which they had made their way to the Nea from the Sanctuary and the Temple Mount.*
>
> *These two curious tales were intended, therefore, to blur and conceal all trace of the pillage of the Temple Mount's ruins perpetrated by the emperor's builders.* [58]

As you can see, Ben-Dov believes that some Temple treasure was discovered during the pillaging of the ruins of the

---

57   Procopius, *War of the King Messiah*.
58   Mier Ben-Dov, *Jerusalem: Man and Stone*, (Modan Publishing House, 1990), 140.

Temple Mount when they took the pillars for the building and transported possible other vessels to the vaults of the Nea Church. Then the leadership of the government purposely began a story of misinformation as to the source of the Temple treasure. Even the treasure they might have discovered does not mention the Ark by name or any important inner sanctuary pieces.

Was the Ark Found During the Crusades?

Another view is that the Ark was found by the Crusaders and taken to somewhere in Europe, possibly Rome or any other of a profusion of major European cities. While numerous accounts attest to the vast wealth and gold the Crusaders acquired while in the Middle East, supposedly bringing back two hundred tons of golden treasure, it is not very likely that they discovered and transplanted the lost Ark. The many relics that can be viewed in various Catholic Churches and Royal Treasuries all have dubious beginnings and must be proved individually.

Color Image 13, The Holy Blood of Bruges, Belgium., Holy Blood, Bruges anBn.jpg atlasobscura.com

For instance, the blood found on lamb's wool, held in the Church of the Holy Blood, in Bruges, Belgium, was not found until the Crusader period about A.D. 1148.[59] Some people believe that this is the "miraculous blood of Christ," and it is

---

59 De Mol, J.J., *Bruges and Its Beauties*, (Bruxelles: Thill, n.d.)

CHAPTER SIX

carried through the streets ever year by a "Grail Maiden" in a public procession of the "Holy Grail." Where was this supposed blood of Christ until A.D. 1148? How do they know that the blood relic in Belgium is the correct preserved blood of Jesus of Nazareth?

There are pieces of the supposed "cross of Jesus" on display in Catholic churches and royal treasuries all over Europe, yet this cross was not discovered until the mid-fourth century. The Royal Treasury of Vienna boasts pieces of this "cross," part of Jesus' wooden manger (!) [even though we know that *stone* mangers were used in Israel in that period], the Roman "spear that struck his side," a Roman sword "of the Centurion," and bones from many apostles. But how do we know that any of these things are true? Are they the actual Biblical pieces or later fabrications? From written records alone, the historical accounts are more numerous for the "Holy Grail" and a "magical spear" than for the Ark, and even these stories are probably legends.

For instance, in the *History of the Holy Grail*, by Frederick Furnivall, the story mentions the Ark of the Covenant.

> *Joseph of Arimathea and his companions wandered away from Sarras until they came, after much journeying, to the seashore. That night, the brave Galaaz was by the grace of God conceived.*
>
> *The next day, Joseph and his company prayed before their Hebrew Ark of the Covenant, kneeling before their Hebrew or Holy Grail, weeping and requesting that they be made strong to cross the sea into that promised land where they would multiply and become the best people.* [60]

This reference seems to be a story full of symbolism. The "Ark of the Covenant" seems to have stood for the Holy Grail.

As Norma Lorre Goodrich, author of *The Holy Grail* said:

> *It is uncanny how these Grail texts imitate the Old Testament:*

---
60 Frederick Furnivall, *History of the Holy Grail*, Vol. 2, Chapter. 41.

> *Joseph for Moses, England for Israel, The English Channel for the Red Sea, English Royalty for David and Solomon's line of descent, and the Ark of the Covenant replaced by the Ark of the Grail.* [61]

Therefore, it would seem that these texts never referred to the literal Old Testament Ark of the Covenant, but only to some legendary "Holy Grail." And there is no proof that the Crusaders ever had the Ark in their possession, much less transported the Ark to Rome, France, Germany, Belgium, Spain, or even as far away as Ireland in the United Kingdom of the British Isles. All these stories are based solely upon legends and have no basis of proof.

Is the Ark in England or Ireland?

One fantastic story told about the ark is sometimes related to British-Israelism, a theological idea that is easily disproved as false. This legend teaches that the Ark was taken to the Irish isles by Ollam Fodhla (or "holy prophet") and a small band in 584 B.C.[62] The legend relates that the group landed near Ulster, where the descendants of the Tribe of Dan lived [!] The "holy prophet" who had brought the ark was the prophet Jeremiah, who subsequently buried it under a hill known today as Ollam Fodhla Cairn ("Jeremiah's Cave"). He also brought the stone that Jacob used as a pillow in Genesis 28:11 when he saw the ladder ascending to heaven with angels ascending and descending. This is claimed to be the coronation stone or the "Stone of Scone" used by the British monarchs since the time of Edward I (or Edward Longshanks). The coronation chair and stone had originally been the throne of Scotland but was taken by this English king almost a thousand years ago.

The prophet Jeremiah did leave the land of Israel and travel abroad after the Babylonian invasion, but he did not travel to Ireland. He went with several Jewish refugees to Egypt (which is in the opposite direction). This story also seems

---
61 Norma Lorre Goodrich, *The Holy Grail*, New York: (Harper Collins Publishers, 1992)
62 Dobson, Cyril C., *The Mystery of the Fate of the Ark of the Covenant*, (Haverhill, MA: Anglo-Saxon Federation of America, 1939).

CHAPTER SIX

to have borrowed several ideas from the Maccabees which tells of Jeremiah hiding the Ark on Mount Nebo which is in Jordan. The rock of Jacob is actually believed to be cut from the *Even Shetiyyah* or "foundation stone" and is from the rock under the Dome of the Rock in Jerusalem. This is a possible location of the dream of Jacob and the ladder (and the rock is actually the highest point of the mountain in that area) and many Jews believe this to be the traditional place. This rock face was possibly cut away in sections during the time of the Crusades and parts of the stone could have made their way to Europe and the British Isles. The "Stone of Scone" has always held many legends and that is the reason of its presence in the coronation chair.[63] This coronation chair has always been displayed at Westminster Abbey in London, England, while not in use at the rare coronations.

While I was there in London on a missionary tour in the summer of 1998, I was privileged to have a personal tour with the Verger of the famous coronation church. The Verger is the second in importance in the entire Westminster Abbey religious positions and is the personal escort of the Queen or other English royalty, such as Prince (now King) Charles. During our tour, Maureen showed us several unusual places inside the Abbey. We saw the crypts of the many famous composers, scientists, poets, soldiers and royalty. We saw the different chapels and the pulpit where Cranmer, Ridley and Latimer preached. And we saw the closed Jerusalem rooms where the Authorized King James Version of the English Bible was translated. However, when we came to the area where the British throne was supposed to stand, I noticed that it was missing. I asked Maureen, "Where is the Coronation Chair?" I was curious to see it and also to see the famous stone underneath. "The Throne has been temporarily moved and the Stone sent back to the kings of Scotland as a part of a political agreement," she said.

This story of the Ark in Ireland or England has no real

---
63 Mears, Kenneth, *The Crown Jewels*, (London, Historic Royal Palaces Agency, 1994)

historical basis and is only another of the peculiar ideas taught in British-Israelism, a theology hostile to the Bible and to the Jewish people.

What About Ein Gedi?

Recently, an unusual archaeological dig concerning the Ark was mentioned in the *Biblical Archaeological Review*. In this article, a group of people were looking for the lost Ark at Ein Gedi, in the Dead Sea area of Israel. Hypothetical thought, based on scanty evidence, led a Colorado-based contractor named Lawrence W. Blaser to the conclusion that the Ark was in David's Cave at Ein Gedi.[64]

Ill. 10, The Oasis of Ein Gedi near the Dead Sea, Israel. 15.-Ein-Gedi-Nature-Resrve-Hike.jpg dominiquetravels.com Public Domain

While reading the works of Ellen G. White (founder of the Seventh-Day Adventists, which is a cultic group), Blaser realized that White mentioned the Ark being hidden away in a cave before the Babylonian destruction of Jerusalem. Blaser assumed that it must be at Ein-Gedi because David, the national hero of Israel, once hid here. Discovering the nearby "Rocks of the Wild Goats," a hill which Blaser believed was an Old Testament oasis, Blaser found a nearby cave which he believed was a cave of David. His team of professional miners, who were expert in underground anomalies, made preliminary soundings of this cave, which seemed to indicate the presence of a man-made wall blocking the entrance to another cave. Excavation in

---

64 Lawrence W. Blaser, "The Ark That Wasn't There." *Biblical Archaeological Review* 9 (July/August 1983): 58-61.

this cave was fruitless because it was discovered that the wall was only a natural bedrock seal to a natural cavity. Further reflection led the archaeological team to look for a different nearby cave. The group was eventually led to a second cave, the cave of David and King Saul. Exploration and excavation of this second cave has yielded nothing to date.

Will the Real Indiana Jones Please Stand Up?

A former Christian minister, who now denies the deity of Christ and other essential Bible doctrines, claims to have found the cave or series of caves that contain the lost Ark and the Ashes of the Red Heifer. Hailing originally from Texas, Vendyl Jones believes these articles are hidden just slightly north of the area of Ein Gedi and the ruins of Qumran. Vendyl Jones has referred to himself as "Texas Jones," and makes the fantastic claim that he is the real "Indiana Jones" and that the Indiana Jones of movie fame is a fictitious character based loosely on his own life.

In 1977, Jones began digging in the Judean desert. This was motivated by his belief that he will be the one that finds the Temple treasures and ashes of the red heifer. This belief is curiously based upon his discovery of a fifteenth-century A.D. woodcut of the red heifer ceremony.

Ill. 11, Vendyl Jones and the two caves he surveyed., jones_Custom.jpg mywesternwall.net Public Domain

His own translation of the text of this woodcut reads:

> There is a Gentile, who is not an idol worshiper, a Gentile who believes in the One God, and he will find the ashes…And they will sweep every corner until they have found her.

It is Jones contention that he will be that Gentile to find the red heifer ashes. He also has frequently quoted statements by Rabbi Shlomo Goren that Gentiles will assist in the discovery of the Temple vessels and the restoration of the Temple worship. Rabbi Goren based this conclusion upon an interpretation of Zechariah 6:15.

Jones further claims that he has found the "cave of the Column that faces East" described in the Copper Scroll of the Dead Sea scrolls. They have excavated a large amount of red earth that he believes is incense from ancient times. He claims that in this cave he has found a beautiful plaster floor, Chalcolithic pottery, Roman pottery from Qumran and the flask of ancient anointing oil from the time of the Old Testament Kings. With further excavation, he maintains that the Ark and the Ashes will be found in this cave.

Vendyl Jones bases most of his hypothesis on Item 26 of the Copper Scroll which states:

> *In the inner chamber of the platform of the Double Gate, facing east, in the northern entrance, buried at three cubits, hidden there is a pitcher: in it, one scroll, under it 42 talents.*

This passage describes one cave or dwelling with a double gate or double entrance. The reference to the Ashes is certainly cryptic and debatable through the word "pitcher" or "*kalal*" (see earlier chapter on the Ashes of the Red Heifer) and it seems impossible to see any reference to the lost Ark in this Copper Scroll passage. However, Mr. Jones maintains this is conclusive proof that he will find the lost Ark and Ashes in the caves he has excavated.

Several problems arise with this theory. The Copper Scroll distinctly describes one cave or chamber with a center column that faces east. Oddly, the cave of Rev. Jones' excavation is actually two distinct caves that never meet. Yet, the Copper Scroll specifies that there is a "chamber ... of the double gate

CHAPTER SIX

[column] that faces East" which would be one cave or chamber with a double entrance. This scroll also stipulates that the cave must face east and yet neither cave in which Jones has excavated face east! Jones' caves face a more northern direction and are each on slightly different levels.

I have personally been to these caves with people who have excavated with Mr. Jones, and it seems that the plastered floor is nowhere to be found! None of the previous excavators of these caves I have talked with have seen any pottery discovered in these caves or other evidence of previous habitation. None of the objects that Jones claims to have found can be evidenced by the people I talked with who had excavated with him. They never saw any significant artifacts.

The flask of anointing oil was actually found by another nearby excavation team in a separate archaeological dig. In 1988, Hebrew University archaeologist Joseph Patrich was excavating in a cave in a region adjacent to the one in which Jones claims he found the incense. After the volunteer workers had finished the day's digging at Jones' site, some of them went to the nearby site to assist digging there. One of his workers was digging profusely with a shovel, bringing out huge heaps of soil. Then, one of Patrich's workers named Benny Ayers came afterwards and used a trowel and discovered an ancient juglet holding a liquid that Jones believes was the anointing oil of the Temple. The volunteer worker for Jones later stated that he did not find the flask of oil but stopped digging in that hole within the hour before it was discovered. He said that if he had found it while digging that he would have accidentally destroyed it before he would have known of its presence because of his vigorous digging with the shovel.

I remember meeting Vendyl Jones when I was about ten years old. He came often to Dallas, Texas, where I grew up to speak about the ashes of the red heifer. I never remember him speaking about the ark and it was never an emphasis of his earlier years in Israel. Dr. Randall Price believes that this is because the respected archaeologist Pesach Bar-Adon, who first sponsored his digs, would never have cooperated with Jones for such a sensationalist cause. The Copper Scroll does not specifically mention the Ark and that is the document upon which Jones was supposedly basing his search. And the appearance of the Indiana Jones movie has apparently generated Vendyl Jones a seemingly endless resource of volunteers and financial support.

Later, Jones' archaeological permit was revoked because he has done some previous excavation without the sponsorship of an archaeologist and he was not connected with any acceptable sponsoring institution such as a university. However, Jones did return in 1994 with about forty volunteers to renew his dig and use remote sensing equipment to determine his cave's supposed hidden chamber.

Did Indiana Jones Really Find the Ark?

As a result of the movie *Raiders of the Lost Ark*, a theory that received wide attention recently is that Pharaoh Shishak of Egypt took the Ark in the summer of 925 B.C. (According to the movie, Indiana Jones found the Ark and took it back for a museum).[65] While it is true that Shishak (Sheshonk I or Shoshenq I) did attack Israel and gain much gold and spoils, it is improbable that Shishak even came into Jerusalem (1 Kings 14:25-26).[66] The text tells us that "Shishak king of Egypt came up against Jerusalem" and that he "took away the treasures of the house of the Lord."

Numerous Bible experts affirm that Rehoboam went to meet Shishak on the outskirts of the city and offered him all the treasures from the Temple treasuries, the Kings' treasuries and the five hundred golden shields of Solomon. (The shields alone would weigh at least two tons and would be worth

---

65 *Raiders of the Lost Ark*, Paramount Pictures, 1981.
66 J. A. Montgomery, *The Book of Kings*, (Edinburgh: T&T Clark, 1951), 270.

$124,825,600 in current gold value.) Pharaoh Shishak in Egypt recorded these captured treasures but the Temple Vessels of the inner Temple are not mentioned. This would mean that he did not invade Jerusalem but only exacted tribute from the city. The Judean king had already been allied to Shishak earlier when the Pharaoh granted him political asylum at the time that Solomon had sought to assassinate him and he would have wanted to appease the Pharaoh. (1 Kings 11:34-35, 40) Before his asylum to Egypt, Rehoboam had been married to Pharoah's daughter and this helped facilitate his later living in Egypt for several years before succeeding Solomon as King in Israel. And it is why he was able to later offer the tribute to Pharoah, who he would have known personally.

The Temple of Karnak in Luxor, Egypt, records Shishak's own account of his triumphant campaigns. Nonetheless, Shishak's engraved record of the 187 conquered cities does not mention Jerusalem.

It is known that Shishak acquired great wealth while on these campaigns. When Shishak returned, he offered the riches from his Palestinian campaign as a dedicatory offering to his patron god, Amun. Centuries later, when Shishak's tomb was discovered in Tanis in 1939, his sarcophagus and mummy were covered luxuriously in gold. Afterward, Osorkon I's son, named Shoshenq II (the earlier Pharoah's grandson), had a solid silver coffin, a solid gold face mask and fabulous jewelry. Some of this gold is thought to have originally been Solomon's gold that came from the five hundred golden shields mentioned in 1 Kings 10:16-17. Thus, some scholars believe that the lavish amount of gold found with Shishak give evidence that the Ark was taken, presented to Amun, and possibly melted down for later royal use.[67]

Not only is there difficulty with this theory because Shishak probably did not enter Jerusalem in battle but rather only

---
[67] C. J. Ball Ellicott's *Commentary on the Whole Bible*, (ed. Charles John Ellicott), Vol. 3, I Kings – Esther, n.d., 70.

received tribute, but also because the treasure mentioned in the Bible came from the Temple treasuries, not the Temple proper. These were the "treasures of the Lord and the treasures of the king's house." They had been placed in the Temple treasury outside the Temple building, in a section of the Temple complex known as the House of Lebanon (1 Kings 7:1-12; 10:17). Because of the repeated use of the phrase "treasures of the king's house" we may assume that the kings also had similar storehouses of wealth (or treasuries). Because the text does not mention any specific vessels of Temple service, it seems that the captured vessels were non-ritual objects or vessels not in current use in the Temple. The treasuries also contained spoils of war taken from defeated Israelite enemies during earlier reigns (1 Kings 7:51; 2 Sam. 8:7-12). These vast treasures would have been valuable and the Temple treasures would have been dedicated as an offering to the Lord, but they would pale in comparison to the inner Temple vessels and the Ark of the Covenant.

Moreover, in 2 Chronicles 13:11, the golden menorah (candlestick) is still being used in the Temple at about 919 B.C., only five years later. Being made of solid gold and weighing ninety pounds, certainly the Egyptians would have taken it if they had been able to find it! (The Menorah would currently be worth $2,808,576 in gold value alone! Why would the Egyptians leave it behind?) We also see the Altar of Incense and the Table of Showbread still in use in the Temple. We do not see the Ark in this description, but the priests would not have been able to see the Ark's presence. Only the High Priest was allowed to enter the Holy of Holies and he only once a year on the Day of Atonement. So, it would not be unusual if the priests did not mention seeing the Ark in the same passage because they would daily see the other vessels.

There would have been little possibility that these items were newly constructed. There would have not been enough time and materials were very scarce at that period. The palace shields had been remade of brass, as mentioned in 1 Kings 14:27, so apparently gold was not very plentiful in Israel at the time. Because the ark cannot be remade, it would not reappear if Shishak took it to Egypt. Yet, the Ark did reappear in the times of Josiah (2 Chron. 35:3). Moreover, how did King Josiah move the Ark at a later time if it had already been found and deported?

One sad note is that shortly thereafter, Pharaoh Shishak died. His son, Osorkon I offered the gold from his father's treasuries, amounting to 383 tons of silver and gold to various Egyptian temples across the land during the years 924-921 B.C.[68] Thus, probably all of Solomon's wealth that was stolen by Shishak was offered to pagan deities. Also, interestingly, the Ark would not have been in Egypt even if there were an Indiana Jones character to find it.

Is the Ark Hidden at Gordon's Calvary?

One little known theory is that the Ark is hidden underground in Jerusalem, between Gordon's Calvary and the Garden Tomb.

A group of American Christian researchers believe the Ark was hidden in this western sector of Jerusalem on Mount Moriah, outside the Damascus Gate. A few years ago, an archaeological dig took place in Jeremiah's Grotto. Some of the artifacts found were shown to other archaeological experts for evaluation and dating. It was found that the coins and pottery shards dated from Roman times, the time of Christ. The group claimed to have also found the room containing the Ark and the Table of Showbread, however the Ark's existence in this chamber is in question.[69]

Could the Ark be hidden at Gordon's Calvary in Jerusalem? While it has been shown that there are many secret under-

---
68 Kitchen, K.A., "Where did Solomon's gold go?" *Bible and Spade* 7 (4): 108, 1994.
69 Video report of Wyatt Archaeological Research Organization, privately circulated.

Ill. 12, The skull face, Gordon's Calvary, Jerusalem., Gordan's Calvary A IMG_358.jpg israelinphotos.com

ground passages on Mount Moriah, such as the tomb of Queen Helena just a few blocks away (see the Ashes of the Red Heifer chapter), there is very little evidence for this theory.

An American Charismatic minister named Ron Wyatt relates,

> I broke into a chamber beneath the Calvary escarpment, north of the city wall of Jerusalem. In that chamber is the Ark of the Covenant, the Table of Showbread—that I didn't see—they were covered with animal skins, with boards, and then stone.[70]

Wyatt believes that the Ark was hidden here because of his assumption that for Jesus to fulfill the requirements for his blood to atone for the sins of the world, that his blood would have to cover the Mercy Seat of the Ark of the Covenant. He believes that when Jesus died on the cross at Calvary, that

---

70 Randall Price, *In Search of Temple Treasures*, Ibid., 155-156.

CHAPTER SIX

the accompanying earthquake opened fissures in the rock and the blood of Jesus shed ran down the cross, through the openings in the rock hill, and covered the Ark, hidden below in a chamber long before.

This theory led Wyatt to search in the area of Jeremiah's Grotto where he claims to have found a "stone case" that holds the Ark. (This stone case sounds much like the local ossuaries of the burial places.) He says that after digging for some time he broke through a chamber that held a golden table, other artifacts and the "stone case" containing the Ark. Overcome with emotion and double pneumonia, he collapsed, lying unconscious for 45 minutes. He then awakened and attempted to video and photograph the Ark with a Polaroid and 35mm camera and video camera and all photos were "mysteriously whited out."

Somehow, on another trip, Wyatt was able to borrow a colonoscope and drill a hole through the stone case. The viewing hole only allowed enough room for this colonoscope to enter and the box underneath was supposedly about an inch away, giving a total viewing circumference of just a few inches. Still, he said, "he was able to see enough to positively identify the contents of the stone case—it was the Ark!" However, it seems that only three inches of sight would be nominal in trying to determine the authenticity of the Ark's existence. Also, if the Ark and the Table of Showbread were covered with animal skins, boards and then stone, how could you tell what the objects were by looking through a colonoscope? And if you were drilling into a stone box that you believed held the ark, how would you know how far to drill without drilling through the Ark? Yet, how could you see these layers without removing the coverings and opening the covered box, or drilling to the surface of the ark? Would you want to risk drilling into the Ark or seeing it if you believed the previous photos were "mysteriously whited out" by God?

Mr. Wyatt's personal credentials are in question, both about his purported Korean War record, college education, his major fields of study and his expertise in archaeology. When investigated, it was discovered that none of what he claimed was true. He continued to explain that Dr. Jim Fleming, the founder and director of the Jerusalem Center for Biblical Studies and editorial advisor to *Biblical Archaeological Review*, was asked by Wyatt to oversee his excavation at Mount Calvary. Fleming tentatively agreed because the Jerusalem archaeologist and Hebrew University professor, Dr. Dan Bahat, had originally agreed to sponsor the dig. However, when Fleming went to the site, he grew increasingly more alarmed at the lack of professional techniques and the extraordinary claims of Wyatt. An example of this was when Fleming saw Wyatt drop a hammer down into a large crack into the mountain. Later, Wyatt told others that he had proof that the ark was hidden within the rock because he had a metal detector reading that showed metal within the rock. This was enough to cause Fleming to leave the dig. Randall Price also quoted another observer named Rev. John Woods as saying,

> I saw him [Wyatt] explaining to a group that a piece of metal embedded in the face of the Garden Tomb was part of the seal Pilate had placed upon the tomb. In fact, it was a piece of shrapnel from the war in 1967. [71]

It is true that the area of Gordon's Calvary was used as a garden in Biblical times. A garden in the Biblical sense always referred to a vineyard. Evidence of this area being such a vineyard is abundant. The area contains a winepress and some of the largest cisterns in the city. (Much water would be needed for a vineyard.) It is near the entrance to Jeremiah's Grotto and also to Zedekiah's Cave and Solomon's Quarries which contained a secret underground passage from the Temple. Consequently, the Ark would have been easy to transport to this location undetected.

---
[71] Randall Price, *In Search of Temple Treasures*, Ibid., 155-156.

CHAPTER SIX

The area was also generally associated with an ancient quarry and used as a Jewish place of stoning for capital crimes. Calvary (Golgotha) was later used as a Roman place of execution and people were killed there in various ways such as crucifixion. That is why the place fits the description of Golgotha—the Place of the Skull—in the Bible as the location of Jesus' execution outside the city walls, because skulls were scattered on the ground, as well as the hill bearing the resemblance of a skull. There were also abundant examples of Roman tombs in the area and it continued to be a place for burials. For example, some area tombs date from the Byzantine period and Stephen was stoned in a nearby area.

This evidence for the place of Jesus' execution and site of His burial and Resurrection makes it unlikely that the Ark would be buried or hidden there. It was a place of execution, death and burial and the Ark must have been kept in a ritually pure place away from a dead body or burial area. The example of the need of the Ashes of the Red Heifer for ritual cleansing is just one example of the Jews strict observance of ritual purity in regard to Temple articles. The mindful Jews would have been careful to not walk across a burial place, or even a place where a dead body has expired or laid temporarily, awaiting burial. This is exactly the kind of place the Jews would NOT have wanted to come with the Ark. They would have been careful to avoid it for purity reasons.

There is also much evidence that Jesus could have been crucified near the road at the bottom of the hill of Calvary (rather than on the hill), making it impossible for His blood to collect in underground chambers. This would be because the chambers would have been too far away from the crucifixion scene and there may have been a pit (from the Quarry, regularly used for stoning) between the road and the hill of Calvary. Thus, the blood of our Lord would have to flow *up* the hill and then through the cracks of earth made by the earthquake that accompanied His death, to finally fall through the cracked hillside to the interior on the Mercy Seat of the Ark. This theory sounds much like the earlier medieval theories of the search for the blood of Jesus on lamb's wool or of the search for the "Holy Grail." Obviously, the religious Jews from Roman times might have feared desecrating the Ark by crossing a grave while in procession with it or by hiding it in an "unclean place" such as near an execution or burial ground. Again, the idea is largely based on speculation.

CHAPTER SEVEN

The Primary Possible Locations of the Ark of the Covenant

Was There More Than One Ark?

One unusual point that must be included here is that there was probably more than one Ark. The Jerusalem Talmud clearly refers to a second Ark of the Covenant.

> A second Ark containing the Tablets broken by Moses accompanied the people to war at all times. [72]

The Jews believe that Moses himself fashioned the first Ark. The Lord had told Moses to first build the Ark and then the Tabernacle. Yet Bezaleel, together with Aholiab made the Tabernacle first and then the Ark, according to the order listed in the Scriptures. (Ex. 36-37) Moses' Ark was to be the model for the second Ark and contained the broken tablets of stone, while the Ark made by Bezaleel was much more beautifully and wonderfully fashioned. Scholars now believe that it was this Ark that was placed in the Tabernacle and later the Temple and contained the complete tablets of stone, Aaron's rod, the pot of manna and later, the complete writings of Moses (called the Torah).

The Ark of Moses was possibly hidden in a *genizah* (a sacred burial or hiding chamber) in the wilderness but seems to have made several appearances throughout Scripture. Exodus 37 tells how the Ark was made of costly materials (much gold and acacia wood) after Moses descended from Mt. Sinai with the second two tables of stone (Ex. 34:29). On the other hand, Deuteronomy 10 tells us Moses himself constructed the Ark of plain shittim wood just before he went up into the mount to receive the second set of two tables of stone. This ark was probably covered in gold, but less ornate.

---

[72] Shelakim 6

Other interesting passages include the Ark accompanying King Saul at Gibeah in 1 Samuel 14:18, while it was supposedly residing in Kirjath-jearim according to 1 Samuel 7:1.

Uriah the Hittite mentioned the Ark as being encamped with the army of Joab at the siege of Rabboth Ammon, while it was supposedly residing in the City of David (lower Jerusalem). (2 Sam. 6:2, 12; 11:11)

Another passage which refers to the existence of two Arks is found in 1 Kings 2:26. Here Solomon is banishing Abiathar from Jerusalem for his adherence to the cause of Adonijah. Solomon refuses to put Abiathar to death because he carried the Ark of the Lord before David and shared in all the sufferings that David suffered. It seems that Abiathar had accompanied David as a priest and carried the Ark of the Lord and they had suffered a continued and prolonged hardship.

The only period of David's life this story fits is before David ascended the throne, while he and Abiathar led the life of a hunted outlaw and fugitive and Abiathar encouraged David with the Word of the Lord. Yet, how could he carry the Ark if it was lodged in the house of Abinadab at Kirjath-jearim? (1 Sam. 7:1, 2 Sam. 6:3, 1 Kings 2:26) Thus, Scripture lends some weight to the possibility of two Arks.

How Many Arks Exist?

William R. Arnold mentions the possibility of three or more Arks.[73] He makes some excellent points about the existence of profane arks and the use of ephods in pagan worship. After being used by God to fight with his three hundred men against the army of the Midianites, Gideon himself fashioned a pagan ephod in later life and caused the nation of Israel to go into idolatry according to Judges 8:27. The priestly ephod was the two-piece, sleeveless linen garment of the priest, and especially of the high priest (that looked like a robe).

---
73 William R. Arnold, *Ephod and Ark*, (Cambridge Harvard University Press 1969).

His ephod was attached to the body by a woven band and joined at the shoulders by straps (Ex. 28:6-14). Because the two stones (called Urim and Thummim), used for discerning God's will, were located next to it inside the pouch of the breastplate (Ex. 28:30-31), the ephod may have been thought to possess divining powers (Judg. 8:27; 17:5; 18:14-20). Some people have erroneously thought it identified with the Ark in some passages.

Dr. Arnold makes a strong argument that this pagan ephod was more than a priestly garment. He believes it could have been a box similar to the true Ark and this pagan ark contained an idol, making this ephod or "ark" distinctly pagan. Thus, only two Arks for Jehovah were made during the Temple periods. Subsequent arks were fashioned for pagan worship and examples are found in the tombs of the Egyptian Pharaohs as well as the Biblical example of the golden box sent with the golden mice and emerods by the Philistines as they returned the Ark, as mentioned in 1 Samuel 6. The captured ark was likely Moses' ark, and the Philistine box was covered in gold. Thus, Moses' Ark was probably the battle ark covered in gold, and the Philistine box was made similar to the captured ark.

Some people believe that there were other copies of the Ark made in earlier times, such as during the Crusader period, and that's how the ark of Ethiopia and other earlier arks are usually explained. Various arks were also made for other churches in Ethiopia and several copies may exist. It is sometimes suggested that copies of the Ark were made during Temple times, though no evidence has ever surfaced to support it.

Another kind of ark called a synagogue ark was made for use in Jewish synagogues. These synagogue arks were not made like a box, but rather like an arch, pedestal or cart and were used to store and display scrolls containing Scripture or the Torah. That is why they are sometimes called Torah-arks. They are receptacles for the Torah scrolls. The Temple Ark stood for the presence of God and surely the closest we can get to his presence is through His Word.

The most likely hiding place of the Ark is one of the next four locations cited. Also, if there are two Arks, they could be hidden in distinct locations to potentially preserve at least one Ark's existence.

The Ancient Ethiopian Legend

Ethiopia is sometimes suggested as the hiding place of the Ark. Most notably, presented by Arthur E. Bloomfield,[74] the late Bible prophecy scholar, and validated by the *National Geographic*, *Saturday Evening Post*, and *Encyclopedia Britannica*, the theory is promoted by many prophecy speakers today such as Grant R. Jeffrey. According to an ancient Ethiopian legend, the *Kebra Nagast* ("Glory of the Kings"), the Queen of Sheba, who visited Solomon to survey his wealth and power, had been queen over the region of Ethiopia. While visiting Solomon in Israel, he took her as wife and she later bore a son to him named Menelik I. In time, this son came to possess the Ark.

> *And King Solomon gave unto the queen of Sheba all her desire, whatsoever she asked, beside that which Solomon gave her of his royal bounty. So she turned and went to her own country, she and her servants. (1 Kings 10:13)*

According to legend, when King Solomon gave unto the queen of Sheba "all her desire," that included bearing him a son. This son remained behind to be educated in his father's court when his mother left for Ethiopia. As a royal son of Solomon, Menelik I remained in the palace at Jerusalem and was taught by the priests of the Temple, becoming a strong follower of Jehovah.

Leo B. Roberts tells the story the Ethiopian Ark,

> *Solomon educated the lad in Jerusalem until he was nineteen*

---

[74] Bloomfield, Arthur, *Where is the Lost Ark of the Covenant and What is Its Role in Bible Prophecy?* (Minneapolis: Dimension Books, 1976).

CHAPTER SEVEN

> years old. The boy then returned to Ethiopia with a large group of Jews, taking with him the true Ark of the Covenant. Many people believe that this ark is now in some church along the northern boundary of present-day Ethiopia, near Aduwa (Adua) or Aksum; but, if it is here, it is so well guarded by the priests that no student from the Western world has been able to confirm or deny the legend.[75]

The legend relates, as Menelik was preparing to leave to return home to Ethiopia, that Solomon prepared a replica of the Ark to send with him, thus enabling Menelik to continue worshipping Jehovah in Ethiopia. But, through trickery (and with the help of a Zadokite priest), Menelik switched the Arks and left the replica in its place in the Holy of Holies. The true Ark was then taken to Ethiopia and never returned. There are several variations of this story (I discovered eight), which seemed to originate with the writing of the *Kebra Nagast* sometime in the sixth to ninth centuries A.D. and were revised in the fourteenth century.

This story is denied by several leading Jewish rabbis and by several historians. Dr. Randall Price interviewed the Chief Rabbi Shlomo Goren about this possibility in his Tel Aviv office on January 24, 1994, and he said,

> I have heard this and it is a foolish suggestion! It is a joke! The same people even say that Noah's Ark was taken to Ethiopia! The ten tribes didn't even take the Ark with them when they were exiled from Israel because they didn't govern [control] the place of the Ark. They were in Samaria and the Ark was in Jerusalem, so they couldn't get to it. So how could the Ethiopians?[76]

In this interview, Rabbi Goren also explained how impossible it would be for someone to have stolen the Ark or switched it for a replica because of the constant twenty-four-hour Temple guard in the Temple complex:

---
75 Leo B. Roberts, *National Geographic*, (September 1935).
76 Randall Price, *In Search of Temple Treasures*, Ibid., 157.

> *Nobody could make switches and nobody had free access to the Ark. whatever time of day or night it was–even on Yom Kippur when the High Priest had just a few minutes inside–they wouldn't let anyone go inside, they would kill them!* [77]

Historians also deny that the original Ark of Moses would have ever come to Ethiopia and that the *Kebra Nagast* story of Menelik and the Ark are true. While Harry Atkins was a lecturer for the Ethiopian government at the Menelik II School in Addis Ababa, he researched Ethiopian history. He contends that there was no record of the Ark being in Ethiopia until the end of the thirteenth century A.D.

Harry Atkins states:

> *At that time there was a dispute over who should be king. One of the claimants to the throne said he was a descendant of King Solomon and the Queen of Sheba. When Ykuna Amlak became king (1274-1285 A.D.), the legend of the Ark being in Ethiopia entered Ethiopian history.*[78]

The last emperor of Ethiopia, Haile Selassie, who died mysteriously in a Communist jail in 1975 as a result of the Communist coup, was believed to be a direct descendant of King Solomon through Menelik I. He was titled "King of Kings, the Lion of Judah and the Chosen of God." He claimed that the true ark was in Ethiopia and best-selling author Dr. Grant Jeffrey has interviewed his great grandson in exile in Canada whom also confirmed its presence. Prince Stephen Mengesha, the exiled great grandson of Emperor Haile Selassie, now residing in Toronto, Canada attests that the Ark resides in a hidden vault called the "Holy of Holies" at the Church of Zion of Mary in Aksum, Ethiopia and that he saw it as a child.[79]

The author of the *Sign and the Seal*, Graham Hancock,

---

77 Randall Price, *In Search of Temple Treasures*, Ibid., 158.
78 Harry Atkins. "Ark of the Covenant: Not in Ethiopia" *Biblical Archaeological Review*, (Nov./Dec. 1993), 78.
79 Jeffrey, Grant R., *Armageddon: Appointment with Destiny*, (New York: Bantam Books, 1990)

CHAPTER SEVEN

journeyed to Ethiopia to find this lost Ark. He believed that he would be permitted to see the Ark. When he arrived there, entrance to see the Ark was denied. However, Mr. Hancock did interview the personal guard of this Ark, Gebra Mikail. Hancock was also present when the people brought the "Ark" (called the *Tabot*) out of its "Holy of Holies" for an annual religious procession called the *Timkat*.

Color Image 15, The Ark of the Covenant procession, Aksum, Ethiopia, 015-Timkat-Axum-Presenting the Tabot flickr.com, Shmuel Zehavi.

The priests brought out a box-like object carried on staves. The "Ark" was completely draped in a beautiful blue cloth with the sign of the dove embroidered on the side. Graham Hancock believes this processional Ark was a copy or replica of the actual Ark because the guard for the Ark remained in his guard station at the Ark's resting place throughout the entire celebration outside the Church. He believes the actual Ark remained in the Church for safekeeping throughout the *Timkat* processional. He bases his arguments about the Ark upon the silent responses and inference he received from the Ethiopian priests.

Mr. Hancock relates his eyewitness testimony about the Ark in Ethiopia that he saw in procession by saying:

> I knew, beyond any shadow of a doubt, that what I was looking at was neither Grail nor Ark. Rather, it was in itself an emblem and a symbol...
>
> ...the sacred relic kept in the sanctuary chapel remained there—jealously guarded in the Holy of Holies. What was brought out in public procession was, therefore, merely a replica of it... that did indeed accord with the shape and dimension of the biblical Ark.[80]

Hancock was not the first to see this ark. An early thirteenth century Armenian medieval writer named Abu Salih told of seeing the Ark and the attending ceremony while in Ethiopia. He relates his experience:

> The Abyssinians [Ethiopians] possess also the Ark of the Covenant, in which are the two tables of stone, inscribed by the Finger of God with the commandments which he ordained for the children of Israel. The Ark of the Covenant is placed upon the altar, it is as high as the knee of man, and is overlaid with gold; and upon its cover there are crosses of gold; and are five precious stones upon it, one at each of the four corners, and one in the middle. The liturgy is celebrated upon the Ark four times in the year, within the palace of the king; and a canopy is spread over it when it is taken out from its own church to the church which is in the palace of the king; namely on the feast of the great Nativity, on the feast of the glorious Baptism, on the feast of the holy Resurrection, and on the feast of the illuminating Cross. And the Ark is attended and carried by a large number of Israelites descended from the family of the prophet David. [81]

It would be quite exciting if this is the actual resting-place of the Ark of the Covenant and many people attest to this possibility. If this is not the original Ark, other intriguing questions arise.

---

80 Graham Hancock, *Sign and the Seal: The Quest for the Ark of the Covenant,* (New York: Touchstone Books, 1992)
81 Graham Hancock, Ibid.

CHAPTER SEVEN

If not the original Ark of Moses, this Ark must be a very ancient copy from which a more recent copy has been fashioned. The more recent copy would be for use in the annual processional. If this Ethiopian Ark is not the original Ark, many questions arise as to its origin, age, maker and exact design as compared to the original.

Graham Hancock has alluded to an unusual possibility. He proposes that the Knights Templar may have come to Ethiopia and built the Church of Saint Mary of Zion over the Ark's current resting-place. This was the site of an earlier Byzantine church. According to this story, the Ark had been brought here from an Egyptian island named Elephantine, where it was kept for several centuries, having been moved there during the reign of Manasseh. The Ethiopian legend slowly began as a way to explain and legitimize the Ark's presence.

There was a Jewish Temple erected on the Egyptian island of Elephantine during the reign of Manasseh in the seventh century B.C. and later destroyed by Egyptian priests of the ram-god Khnum and their allies with the local Persian governor in 410 B.C. Was it built to house the Ark of the Covenant as Hancock claims? According to one Ethiopian tradition, the Ark did not arrive in Ethiopia until after 470 B.C. which would leave a two hundred-year gap in the theory that it was removed to Egypt during the reign of Manasseh and its arrival in Ethiopia. This led Hancock to the theory that the ark was taken first to Elephantine Island. The Jewish temple that stood there included animal sacrifices as part of their worship and Hancock surmises that the presence of the Ark was required to give sanctity to the land and to the sacrificial ceremony. (However, it is not clear that animal sacrifices were allowed in this temple but only incense and meal offerings, since other offerings would only be properly committed at Jerusalem). He believes the Jews claimed that God was present in their temple in Egypt in letters to Jerusalem and that the Ark guarantied this presence of God in the temple on Elephantine Island in Egypt.

The scholar Bezalel Porten, a contributor to the *Biblical Archaeological Review*, tells that he believes that Manasseh's revolt against Assyria would have led him to an alliance with Egypt and his sending a military delegation to Elephantine, because it was on the Egyptian border. The profaning of the Jewish Temple in Jerusalem would have sent Jerusalem priests fleeing for refuge and some of them may have come to Elephantine Island and built this temple to the Lord. But he denies that the Ark of the Covenant was ever taken to this location.

As Bezalel Porten stated:

> In short, Hancock's placing the Ark in the Elephantine temple as a justification for its construction does not hold up. It is possible, but the evidence is very soft. I believe the justification was the passage from Isaiah predicting the erection of a pillar to the Lord at the border of Egypt...
>
> One may wonder whether the Egyptian priests of Khnum would not have also looted or destroyed the Ark if it had been in the Elephantine temple. Hancock does not stop to ask this question...
>
> Yet, if the Ark were in Elephantine, wouldn't the Jerusalem authorities have allowed burnt offerings? Again, this question Hancock does not ask. Indeed, Hancock contends that the presence of the Ark at Elephantine provided the original authorization to offer animal sacrifices. If true, the Jerusalem authorities' refusal to allow animal sacrifice in the rebuilt temple certainly militates against Hancock's contention that the Ark was there...
>
> The notion that these fugitive priests spirited away the Ark from Jerusalem to rescue it from the clutches of Manasseh is nothing but bald speculation; it is not historical reconstruction. None of the evidence cited to support this unscholarly speculation holds up under careful scrutiny.

CHAPTER SEVEN

> *The fact that a Jewish temple was built at Elephantine may be explained by Isaiah 19:19: "In that day, there shall be an altar to the Lord inside the land of Egypt and a pillar to the Lord at its border." The Elephantine temple may have been authorized pursuant to this prophecy, but there is absolutely nothing in the Bible or anywhere else to suggest that it was built to house the Ark of the Covenant.*[82]

Another theory sometimes suggested also includes the famous Knights Templar. According to this theory, the Crusader knights took the Ark from Ethiopia back to the Holy Land and possibly even on to Europe. These religious knights saw themselves as protectors of the Temple Mount and had even renamed the Dome of the Rock with the title of "Temple of the Lord" and the Al Aqsa Mosque as the "Temple of Solomon" from which they set up their headquarters. Thus, these knights would have also seen themselves as protectors of the Ark of the Covenant and related Temple articles and would have wanted to preserve them for the future. Graham Hancock presents a strong case in proposing that the knights built many of the Coptic churches of Ethiopia because they show obvious Crusader period workmanship and architecture. If they built the churches, as Hancock brings forth, then they would have possibly built them to protect ancient relics, such as a lost Ark. Occasionally, it is even suggested that descendants of these knights still have the Ark in their possession today, somewhere in Europe. Again, these are mere fanciful speculations.

Much is made of the prophecy of Ethiopia in Isaiah 18. Some prophecy exponents see special "signs" to Ethiopia and the Ark as they relate to Jesus' Second Coming. Verse three is especially heralded:

> *All ye inhabitants of the world, and dwellers on the earth, see ye, when he lifteth up an ensign on the mountains, and when he bloweth a trumpet, here ye.*

---
[82] Bezalel Porten. "Did the Ark Stop at Elephantine?" *Biblical Archaeological Review* (May/June, 1995), pp. 54-77.

In this verse, the "ensign" is seen as the Ark, being brought to the mountains of Jerusalem when the trump of God will sound, signaling His return as all the world watches. Compare also Isaiah 11:11-12. Some writers have interpreted this to mean that the Ark of Ethiopia would be revealed in the last days and brought to Jerusalem to institute the rebuilding of the third Jewish Temple. It is even sometimes suggested that the Ark was returned to Israel from Ethiopia in 1992 with the group of Jewish exiles on the last historic flight to Israel called Operation Solomon. Dr. Randall Price mentioned a private conversation with Dr. Grant Jeffrey. Price says that Jeffrey believes there was a $42 million surplus allotment for this Operation Solomon that he thought had been sent to secure the transport of the Ark of the Covenant to Israel. However, other Ethiopian sources Price spoke with in Jerusalem said they would know of such a transaction if it had taken place and they denied that it was possible.[83]

Several problems arise in this Ethiopian theory about the Ark of the Covenant. The Queen of Sheba is usually seen as a Queen of Arabia or Yemen in southern Arabia and not of Ethiopia. No one seems to know for certain and there is no proof that the legend actually occurred. Recognized scholars have never surveyed the Ethiopian records. No one from the Western Hemisphere has ever been verified to see the Ark and the Scriptural texts are certainly open to debate. The Ark was under constant security through the Temple guards. The legend of the *Kebra Nagast* seems to be a later fabrication and the stories associated with Elephantine Island hold their own difficulties. Even the more current sources of information about the Ark being transported to Israel are people relating stories they have been told privately by persons with which it would be difficult to verify the reports.

---

[83] Randall Price. *In Search of Temple Treasures*, Ibid., 138-139, 367.

CHAPTER SEVEN

Is the Ark in Qumran by the Dead Sea?

Qumran, odd as it may seem, is also a possible resting-place of the lost Ark. Gary Collett, an American minister interested in prophecy and associated with Jerusalem Ministries International, believes that the Ark was taken and hidden there at some point before A.D. 70. Sometimes a date before 56 A.D. is given because an earthquake that year made the city uninhabitable. The famous caves of the Dead Sea Scrolls were probably sealed by the earthquake of that year, locking the contents such as the famous scrolls inside, and the city was then abandoned.

Collett believes that the community of Qumran was actually the Biblical City of Secacah. (Many trustworthy scholars such as John Marco Allegro, who did early research on the Copper Scroll, agree with this earlier name of the city, although with few other of Collett's hypotheses'.) Reputable scholars, including Allegro, believe that the Jewish sect called Essenes lived there and this group included a large group of the Zadokite priests who were the true priests from the family line of Zadok, the high priest of Solomon.

These priests had left Jerusalem and the Temple because the priesthood had become corrupt and politically tainted and the office of the high priest was sold to the highest bidder under the rulership of the Seleucids (who had been set in power originally under Alexander the Great). These true priests saw the Temple worship in Jerusalem as now corrupt and so fulfilled their worship of God through personal holiness, prayer and good works. It is believed that this "pure" priestly line became the guardian of the Temple vessels. Through the wonderful research that has been accomplished on the Copper Scroll, many of these details have now come to light. The Copper Scroll lists the hiding places of the Temple Treasure and seems to have been found with the Dead Sea Scrolls because the Essenes were the people who included part of this "pure" priestly line. According to the hiding places mentioned in the Copper Scroll, some of these Temple vessels are thought to be hidden in underground Jerusalem, in the area of Damascus and at Qumran.

Gary Collett agrees that this ruined city of Qumran was earlier called by the ancient name of Secacah, but also surmises that the Zadokites living there thought of it as a "mini-Jerusalem" or "new Holy City." By this hypothesis, he believes that *all* hidden treasure mentioned in the Copper Scroll of the Dead Sea Scrolls is really hidden at Qumran. The references to Jerusalem and Damascus are really seen as only cryptic references to different places in Secacah (or Qumran).

He arrived at this conclusion when he first noticed that the topography of Qumran bore a peculiar resemblance to the topography of the Temple Mount, including the Kidron Valley, the Mount of Olives, the Cave of Sacrifice and the Eastern Gate. Collett also noticed that Cave IV itself has sections (IV-A and B) that are carved with a likeness to the First and Second Temples. It is his belief that this is where Jeremiah once hid the Tabernacle and the Ark of the Covenant. He believes that the site was chosen because of its natural similarity to the Temple Plan. It is his opinion that the Ark was actually hidden in the small storage chamber inside the Inner Chamber of Cave IV-A or inside the now collapsed inner cave between Cave IV-A and B called Cave IV-C, then later returned to Jerusalem and placed under the Temple Mount.

Collett further identifies the area as Wadi Ha Keppah because of the natural rock formation of the small mountain that overlooks the ruins of Qumran. The word *keppa* (or *kippa*) in Hebrew can mean "vault, arch or doorway" and is also used to imply the small skullcap often worn by religious Jews. This mountain overlooking Qumran has a rounded or domed appearance similar to the *keppa*. It is Collett's contention that the term *keppa* has come down to us today through the Aramaic language in its nominative form as Qimron, which is the first-century name of Qumran, the ruined city of the Dead Sea Scrolls. This is a much more fanciful interpretation than any other scholars who have seen or interpreted the Copper Scroll or tried to determine details about the authenticity of the treasure.

Support for this theory has been proposed by Collett's interpretation of the account of 2 Maccabees 2:4-8 in which it is recorded that Jeremiah transported several Temple treasures, including the Ark of the Covenant, to Mount Nebo. In the passage, it tells us that as Jeremiah was transporting these things that he "turned and beheld the inheritance of God." While most commentators believe that the "inheritance of God" was Mount Nebo, it is Collett's contention that Jeremiah "turned around" and faced the opposite direction. Since Mount Nebo and Qumran are exactly opposite (by compass due East and West) of each other, he believes it is at the caves of Qumran where the treasures were deposited.

The Copper Scroll is one of the scrolls found in the Dead Sea area on March 14, 1952, in Cave Three. It was a special scroll, written on copper (instead of the usual leather or papyrus), listing huge amounts of hidden treasure of gold (twenty-five tons) and silver (sixty-five tons) and it mentions other hidden scrolls.[84] The scroll was actually discovered as two scrolls of copper. But when later cut open and translated, it was determined that these two scrolls were actually originally one scroll which was fastened together but broke apart in time. However, the scroll mentions another mysterious Copper Scroll that tells further details than this existing one. This other enigmatic copper scroll has never been found.

---

[84] Owen Jarus (Dec. 2, 2021), "7 Biblical Artifacts That Will Probably Never Be Found," Accessed on Feb. 5, 2023, livescience.com

Many scholars view this text as too fantastic to be accepted literally because of the huge amounts of hidden treasure. However, a few hordes of silver and copper coins were found in pots in Qumran, as well as hundreds of scrolls. For instance, in location #120 of Qumran, a hoard of 561 pieces of silver and 25 coins were found preserved in three pots. Most of the places mentioned in the Copper Scroll have never been excavated.

To discount the stories of immense hidden wealth because the amounts are enormous is not reasonable when one considers the recently discovered golden treasure of a minor Egyptian King, Tutankhamen, commonly known as King Tut. He was buried in a solid gold coffin, with a solid gold face mask inlaid with semi-precious stones and other outer gold-plated coffins fitting one inside the other. He also had a gold-plated throne and other treasures of jewels, elaborate ivory and ornate furniture.

Items 53 and 54 of the Copper Scroll are mentioned by a few people as references to the Ark of the Covenant and the Breastplate of the High Priest.

> *In the exedra of the cliff facing west, in front of the Tomb of Zadok, under the great sealing stone that is in its bottom: consecrated offerings. In the grave which is under the paving stones: 40 talents.*

In my opinion, these passages do not seem to imply the Ark of the Covenant and the Breastplate of the High Priest.

The phrase, "consecrated offerings," is believed by some to mean the Ark of the Covenant and the Breastplate of the High Priest. It would seem to be very probable that these consecrated offerings are simply a collection of tithes and offerings consecrated to God, held by the Temple priests and later hidden away. But there does not seem to be a clear description or allusion to the Ark or the Breastplate.

After carefully reading a translation of the Copper Scroll, I found at least two *possible* cryptic references to the Ark of

CHAPTER SEVEN

the Covenant. The only feasible references I could discover were Items 17 and 58.

Item 17 of the Cooper Scroll tells us:

> *In the water conduit which enters...as you go in four...cubits... 40 talents of silver in a chest.*

The listing for Item 58 reads:

> *Mount Gerizim, under the entrance of the upper pit: one chest and its contents, and 60 talents of silver.*

One of these "chests" could be the Lost Ark, but it is more probable to be a chest of offerings for the Temple. This idea that the Copper Scroll lists the lost Ark of the Covenant from the Temple is still largely speculation. Several things must be true to believe this theory. You must accept:

1. that modern Qumran is ancient Secacah,
2. that the Zadokite priests living there cryptically referred to Secacah as Jerusalem,
3. that they had the Ark of the Covenant in their possession to be able to hide it,
4. and that the cryptic messages in the Copper Scroll match specific sites at Qumran.

This series of conclusions includes much conjecture and has no real solid basis in scholarship or archaeological research.

When I first became interested in the search for the Lost Ark, I asked myself, "Where do the Orthodox Jews think the Ark is hidden?" Surely, if the Ark is the most sacred Jewish worship vessel ever in existence and was so holy that no one could look upon it or touch it, then it would seem that the Jews would have an idea as to its whereabouts. In researching Jewish sources, one always finds two predominant possibilities: the location at Mt. Nebo or the Temple Mount.

Did Jeremiah Hide the Ark on Mount Nebo?

Let us deal with Mt. Nebo first. Located in ancient Moab, which is now modern-day Jordan, Mt. Nebo is a saddle-backed mountain with two different peaks. These peaks are known as Mt. Pisgah and Mt. Nebo. There is evidence for this view in 2 Maccabees of the Apocrypha, the writings of Peter the Iberian, *Palestine Speaks* by A. F. Futterer and Volume IV of *The Legends of the Jews*. The collections of the Apocrypha, while certainly not regarded as the inspired Word of God are generally viewed as having historical value and just one of many important sources of history.

Second Maccabees 2:4-8 relates the following story:

> *The same document also tells how the prophet, following a Divine revelation, ordered that the Tent and the Ark should accompany him and how he went off to the mountain which Moses climbed to see God's inheritance. When Jeremiah arrived there, he found a room in a cave in which he put the Tent, the Ark and the Altar of Incense; then he blocked up the entrance. Some of those who followed him came up intending to mark the path, but they could not find it. When Jeremiah heard of this, he reproved them: "The place is to remain unknown until God gathers His people together again and shows them mercy. Then the Lord will disclose these things, and the glory of the Lord will be seen in the cloud, just as it appeared in the time of Moses and when Solomon prayed that the Place might be gloriously sanctified."*

According to this account, Jeremiah the prophet, being warned by the Lord of Babylon's impending invasion, took the Ark and Altar of Incense through a royal escape tunnel near the Temple to Solomon's quarries on the Temple Mount at Zedekiah's Cave, with the help of the School of the Prophets. There they retrieved the Tabernacle, which had been placed there earlier as though it were placed in a kind of *genizah* (or sacred burial place) under the Temple Mount. They then took these articles through a secret connecting cave that leads underground thirteen miles to the area of Jericho. There they traversed the Jordan River, crossed the land of Moab, climbed Mt. Nebo and hid these articles in a cave.

Before other workers had a chance to mark the place the entrance was suddenly lost, perhaps by an earthquake. Jeremiah took that for a sign that the "place shall be unknown" until the end times.

Ill. 13, The Memorial Church of Moses, Mt. Nebo, Jordan, Mount Nebo universes.art Public Domain

In 1985 on one of my trips to Israel, I toured Solomon's underground quarries (Zedekiah's Cave) where the stone for King Solomon's Temple was quarried. It is a surprisingly huge underground area and the tooling for the Temple stone is readily apparent in the walls of the quarry. King Solomon ordered that they use stone from the Temple Mount for the Temple Building. They believed that the mountain was holy, so if you were going to put God's house there, you must use holy stone, which would come from the same mountain. As we passed one curious extension of the cave in the quarry, our guide said, "This cave is thought to lead underground all the way to Jericho!" (Jericho is seventeen miles to the northwest.) On my trip in 1992, I learned that a few years earlier, two British adventurers had decided to explore this underground passageway. These men started on their journey ill-equipped, with little food and supplies. Whether they met some natural disaster, became hopelessly lost, or were attacked by someone is unknown, but these men never came out of the cave and have never been seen or heard of again.

Another exciting story about the Ark is told by Tom Crotser, founder of the Holy Ground Mission northwest of Winfield, Kansas as a part of the Institute for Restoring Ancient History International. While he lived there, he ran a construction company and led a group of 145 people who, according to Crotser, lived in a community like that formed by the Essenes in the second century B.C. This group believes that they must search to discover five objects before Christ returns. These objects are the City of Adam, the Stone of Abel, the Ten Commandment tablets, the Ark of the Covenant and the Tower of Babel. They maintain that Noah's Ark is also an important discovery. All this is based on their interpretation of Acts 3:18-21:

> But those things, which God before had shewed by the mouth of all his prophets, that Christ should suffer, he hath so fulfilled. Repent ye therefore, and be converted, that your sins may be blotted out, when the times of refreshing shall come from the presence of the Lord; And he shall send Jesus Christ, which before was preached unto you: Whom the heaven must receive until the times of restitution [restoration] of all things, which God hath spoken by the mouth of all his holy prophets since the world began.

The Institute interprets the "restitution of all things" to be these five particular objects. They claim to have found the City of Adam, the great Stone of Abel (where the second son of Adam was killed), the Tower of Babel (in Turkey?), and even Noah's Ark. Thus, only the Ark and the Tablets remain undiscovered.

While searching for the Ark on Mt. Nebo, thirty-five miles southwest of Amman, Jordan, Crotser and fellow team members, found the entrance to a cave they believe holds the lost Ark of the Covenant.

In the 1920s, A. F. Futterer, an American explorer, toured the Holy Land and searched for the Ark of the Covenant on Mt. Nebo in Jordan. He spoke fluent Arabic and traveled in Arab dress with an Arabian caravan until they happened upon Mount Nebo. On the mountain, he found a cave that he explored deeper and deeper until a concrete wall halted his search. Futterer believed that this was the burial place of Moses and it had become a cave of catacombs for other burials because of the importance of Moses. He also believed that the Ark was hidden there inside but he did not disturb the wall. However, on the wall blocking the passage, Futterer said there was an inscription written in "hieroglyphics." Because he could not read the writing, he wrote down the message and when he returned to Jerusalem sometime later, Futterer had the wording translated "by a Hebrew scholar." He reported that it was actually written in Hebrew and read: "Herein lies the golden Ark of the Covenant." Futterer also found that the numeric value of the Hebrew letters totaled 1927, which he took to mean that he would discover the Ark of the Covenant in 1927. No copy of the alleged inscription survives and no one knows who at the Hebrew University was supposed to have read it.

Antonia F. Futterer describes this "discovery" of the Ark of the Covenant:

> I believe that the Golden Ark of the Covenant, the world's greatest and valuable antique relic of all history, has been trailed to its lair (in my two years recent research work in the Holyland)—trailed to its last hiding place on Mt. Nebo where Jeremiah hid it about 2,544 years ago.
>
> I have collected convincing evidence enough to make it hard not to believe that the Ark will return to old Jerusalem. The return of the Ark would stagger the world; may change the belief of millions of

people of all nations for the better; be the greatest blow skeptics ever received; and perhaps be the greatest modern proof of the authenticity of Holy Writ. The Tablets of Sinai written about 3,525 years ago, now in the Ark, may bring to this whole world a feeling akin to Belshazzar, King of Babylon, on the night when he too saw God's "Handwriting" upon the walls of that famous city before its consummation, which made the King and all his nobles tremble with fear when this terrible warning: "Thou art weighed in the balance, and found wanting" stared them in the face.[85]

Futterer had searched for over two years for the Ark of the Covenant and was now convinced that he had found it. However, his permit to explore the Middle East, granted by the British government, was issued with the understanding that he would not attempt any digs. The government blocked his attempts over the next seven-month period to re-enter the cave he had found. Futterer also felt it was imperative for a Levite to handle the Ark once it was uncovered, and he wanted the Jews to help finance the excavation as a part of their own national pride. However, he was to return home in California empty-handed.

A close friend of Futterer's named Clinton Locy fell heir to Futterer's papers. Afterwards, Crotser met with Locy, then a retired minister in his late eighties living in Kennewick, Washington. While there, Crotser obtained a sketch made by Futterer of the blocked underground passage. Using Futterers' sketch of the passage and cave, Crotser and his team were able to find the same cave on their visit in 1980.

On their second visit to the cave (allegedly the burial place of Moses), they stayed on the mountain four days and slept in sleeping bags on location. While there, they found a depression or crevice that they believed to be the cave-opening identified in Futterer's sketch. Under cover of darkness and without a permit to excavate, they removed the tin sheet covering the

---
85   Antonia F. Futterer. *Palestine Speaks*, 1931, 536-537.

CHAPTER SEVEN

opening and proceeded into the passageway at 2:00 a.m. on October 31, 1981, the third night of their stay.

Crotser estimated this initial passageway as about six hundred feet long, four to six feet wide and about seven feet high. It led through several room-like enlargements with numerous tomb openings on both sides containing two or three levels of tombs. While they were exploring, the team with Crotser illegally broke through two walls. The walls were made of mud and rock mixed together, similar to concrete. And Crotser believed that it was obvious that someone had been there recently and plugged up the wall upon leaving. As they crawled through several tight places only four to seven feet across, the men came to a more substantial plaster or concrete wall. They peered through a crack in the wall, shining their flashlights, and saw a shiny reflection. In a soft part of the wall, the group illegally cut an opening about four feet by four feet with a hand pick. After knocking out the wall, they discovered a small room measuring ten feet by twelve feet that Crotser believes to be Moses' tomb. It is the contention of Crotser that this chamber lay precisely under the Byzantine church on the summit of the mountain and was connected to the church by a perpendicular shaft. This room also contained a large covered golden box and two wrapped figures, possibly the golden cherubim. On the side of the box were rings, through which were passed golden poles, matching the description of the Ark in Exodus 25.

The Ark found in this cave was sixty-two inches long, thirty-seven inches wide and high with front sliding doors and it looked different than Crotser's preconception. Even Crotser admitted that this golden-hued metal box did not fit his preconception of the Ark's design. "Possibly it was altered over the years," he suggests. Others argue that it must be some other piece of furniture or a replica of the original Ark. It had a brassy tinge to it, fine metal lacework and was covered with a two or three-foot blue apron on top with dried skins covering the sides.[86]

In a corner of the chamber, lying near to the Ark were two gauze-covered packages tied with leather tongs. Crotser believed that these were the golden cherubim that once sat upon the mercy seat of the Ark but he did not touch them. Interestingly, there is a tradition that the Ark was damaged and that the cherubim had been broken off earlier.

The team did not touch the Ark or attempt to move it. The Ark would have been too heavy for these four team members and quite difficult to maneuver in the tight passageway. To move the Ark would probably have upset the Vatican, who is the landowner of the surrounding area and the Jordanian government who would want to claim it as an archaeological artifact. With their flash-equipped cameras, Crotser's team claims to have taken over two hundred photographs of the Ark. Then they left the country after unsuccessfully attempting to interest the Franciscans, the palace authorities at Amman, and an archaeological professor at the University of Jordan of their finds.

Crotser had contacted several Jordanian archaeologists and had a paper that he thought authorized the expedition. A translation showed it was merely a letter from Jordan's Director of Military Security asking the Department of Antiquities to authorize Crotser to take photographs. If Crotser's group actually did some digging, the expedition should have been cleared through the Department of Antiquities. The spokesman said the Jordanian government was very angry and that the group will not be allowed back into the country. And they accuse him of breaking the law because he did not have a representative from the Department of Antiquities present. It is well known that the Jordanians do not want any Biblical

---

86 Doug Wead, David Lewis, Hal Donaldson, *Where is the Lost Ark*, (Minneapolis, MN: Bethany Book House, 1982), 90.

discoveries made in Jordan. This policy became even firmer in the summer of 1982 after the Israeli invasion of Lebanon. Hence, Crotser's vision of recovering this artifact may be lost in the red tape of bureaucracy. And other archaeological excavations have been cancelled because of the incident. The excavation at Tell Jalul was cancelled on June 5, 1982, not by the Jordanian Department of Antiquities but by the Prime Minister's office. Reliable sources, such as a University of Jordan professor of archaeology have confirmed that Crotser's expedition was a prime factor in the Jordanian decision.

The group tried to publicize their discovery and raise money for an expedition, giving interviews that were published in the major newspapers across the country. They have built a scale model of the mountain and the passageway to the chamber. This two-by-three-foot mountain model is designed for television and press photographs and it includes a representation of the accompanying ancient burial sites and Byzantine church.

The outstanding Arab-Christian evangelist, Dr. Anis Shorrosh, who was born in Nazareth, interviewed Mr. Crotser several times and eventually wrote a book about the find in Jordan in which he quotes Mr. Crotser saying,

> I believe that God allowed me and my three companions to locate the Ark in Mount Nebo in Jordan because the time has come for Israel to begin their sacrificial system and that announces the soon return of Jesus Christ.[87]

Another of the four team members named Jim Bolinger was interviewed by a *Dallas Morning News* reporter shortly after his return from Jordan. He described the Ark as "a gold-covered chest four feet high, five feet long, and four feet wide, with nine-foot golden wings of cherubim on either side of the mercy seat... a two- or three-foot apron was on top with dried

---

[87] Anis Sharrosh, *The Exciting Discovery of the Ark of the Covenant*, (Winona, MN: Justin Books, 1984), 27.

animal skins covering the ends." Because the wings were so large, possibly these were not the wings of the Cherubim that stood on the mercy seat, but rather the wings of the two huge cherubim that stood over the Ark in the Temple which each had combined wing spans of fifteen to twenty feet. The Temple Holy of Holies was forty feet wide.

Currently, they are awaiting permission to retrieve the Ark, even pursuing the help of the London banker David Rothschild, who has not responded. Knowing that the wealthy Rothschild family had been involved in numerous searches for the Ark, the team refused to publish the pictures until London banker David Rothschild would use his power, money and influence to retrieve the Ark. It is Crotser's contention that God told him to release the pictures only to banker Rothschild. Crotser says that, although Rothschild is not necessarily saved, God will put into his heart to rebuild the Temple. Although Crotser has written to him, Rothschild has not directly responded and was quoted as saying, "It's a pure joke. It doesn't have any real validity at all."

To this criticism Crotser responded,

> Some columnists don't think it's going well at all, but to me it's a healthy sign that the man would even speak out. No matter what he says, just so long as he speaks out. He can't afford to say he wants to work with us or anyone else. He's an international banker—the international banker. He's just warding off criticism from professional historians and archaeologists who are accusing us of fakery. [88]

One other interesting aspect of this story is that the Church of the Franciscan Fathers of Terra Sancta lies directly above this alleged tomb of Moses (and the supposed lost Ark) and the Roman Catholic Church owns much of Mt Nebo and Mt. Pisgah. It is Crotser's contention that the Catholic Church

---

[88] Hershall Schanks, "Tom Crotser Has Found the Ark of the Covenant—Or Has He?" *Biblical Archaeological Review* 9 (May/June 1983): 66-69.

CHAPTER SEVEN

was aware of this and specifically built the church building over the patriarch's tomb and over the Ark below resting in the mountain.

With excitement Crotser stresses,

> They're sitting on it. There's a shaft that leads right up next to the church's baptismal. You've got to believe they've known about it. [89]

This claim that the Vatican has complete knowledge of the Ark's presence is also implied by his reference to a plaque inside the monastery chapel, which apparently stated that the Ark of the Covenant was buried there somewhere at Mount Nebo. There may have been such a reference (and it would seem that the Vatican, which has vast holdings of property and articles, would know what was generally stored at each church or monastery vault). Yet, this may just have been a quote from the Maccabees writings that were displayed in the plaque. Whichever be the case, it is interesting that they happened to quote that particular passage.

Siegfried H. Horn is a prominent archaeologist who, for sixteen years, has led the Andrews University excavations at Tell Heshbon four miles northeast of Mt. Nebo. After hearing that Crotser had done excavation nearby and about his amazing claims of discovery, Horn's interest was piqued. Horn traveled to Winfield, Kansas, to meet with Crotser, see the model of the underground chamber, and view the photographic evidence to determine if Crotser had in fact seen the Ark of the Covenant. There he saw pictures of this Ark when he met with Crotser in Winfield. After viewing the slides, Horn made a sketch from memory of the box as he had viewed it. The front of the box appeared to be covered with a sheet of bronze containing a very regular pattern of small holes. Around the edges and down the middle are metal strips that form a diamond

---

89   Anis Sharrosh, Ibid., 27.

pattern. Although Horn is not certain, the diamond and the triangular shaped patterns may have been punched out of the strips. In any event, the strips are lighter yellow than the underlying metal sheet. The regularity of the patterns indicated to Horn that the metal was machine worked. Also, in the top right corner of the box, Horn noticed a distinctly modern looking nail head. Being a practiced draftsman, Horn drew a sketch from memory of the box as he had observed it and also pictures of the various details.

Once he viewed the slide photographs Horn concluded:
> *I do not know what the object is, but the pictures convinced me that it is not an ancient artifact, but of modern fabrication with machine produced decorative strips and an underlying metal sheet.*[90]

While the possibility of actually having seen the Ark and having taken over two hundred pictures of it is quite sensational, it is odd that Crotser will not make these pictures or any other evidence public. Also, if Crotser did not see the original Ark, what did he discover? It is possible that this Ark is a copy or replica. If so, again the questions are raised as to its age, origin and maker. Once again, this theory also is difficult to prove.

Is the Ark in Jerusalem?

The most widely held view by Jewish scholars is that the Ark of the Covenant was hidden on the Temple Mount in Jerusalem. It is almost the only view that is ever seriously held by rabbinical scholars.

The Mishnah tells of the Ark being hidden on the Temple Mount and even included a death warning to anyone who told its location. This secret location has been passed down through the centuries to Jewish rabbis but is not generally known to Gentiles.

---

90 "Tom Crotser Has Found the Ark of the Covenant—Or Has He?" Ibid., 66-69.

CHAPTER SEVEN

During the time of King Solomon, the platform on top of Mt. Moriah upon which the Temple and accompanying courtyards were to be placed, was hollowed out to prevent ritual impurity due to possible graves underground. Even though any possible grave would have been buried, separating it from the Temple above by earth, ritual impurity would be contracted unless there was a vacant space between the corpse and earth above it. So, under the Temple courtyard the earth was hollowed out, arches were built for support, and the top was filled-in and smoothed to prepare the Temple platform.[91]

When King Herod rebuilt the Temple platform, he almost doubled the Temple platform size and also built arches to support the upper platform, thereby, also creating a huge underground complex. There were also underground cisterns, passageways serving as entrances to the Temple Mount, *mikvahs* (specially designed bathing pools used for ritual cleansing), and a very complicated sewage and drainage system. This complex also included special escape routes such as the secret underground escape tunnel of Zedekiah, rooms for the Temple guards, the secret Royal Treasuries and special Temple Treasuries, as well as a few natural caves and possible underground burial chambers.[92]

For centuries, the Jews had excelled in underground tunneling. King Hezekiah had ordered a tunnel dug from the Gihon Spring in the Kidron Valley, to the protected Siloam pool in the Tyropoeon Valley by 702 B.C. Workers started separately on each end and dug tirelessly toward the middle by a pre-planned curved passageway, coming together within four feet of each other. The tunnel they dug was 1,750 feet long (or 533 meters). This was quite a feat in ancient times, to gain the city a protected water supply!

---

[91] *Hilchos Bias Habechiral* 5:1; *Parah* 3 and *Mishnah* 3.
[92] Meir Ben-Dov, *In the Shadow of the Temple*, (New York: Harper and Row, 1982), 20.

Color Image 16, The Wailing Wall with Wilson's Arch, Jerusalem, Israel. Author's Photo

Even today, underground tunneling is still done. Just north of the "Wailing Wall" in an underground chamber, is a magnificent stone arch, called Wilson's Arch. Vaulting from the Western Wall, the original arch once supported a bridge that spanned a deep ravine called the Tyropoeon Valley. This connected the Temple Mount to the Upper City on the west. North and west of the hall under Wilson's Arch, other long-buried and damp rooms are also being cleared and systematically explored in a three-dimensional labyrinth of construction. These areas date from the Second Temple period and afterward. Some of these rooms are between forty and sixty feet below ground level. They are located in what was the Tyropoeon Valley that has been long since filled in by debris. This explains why bedrock is so far below the ground surface in this area of the valley.

These rooms are closed to visitors, except by special permission, and are awe-inspiring. Some say the Sanhedrin, the revered court of Jewish elders, met in one especially large room known as the Masonic Hall. Although most of this room clearly dates from the Crusader period (it is cruciform in shape and crosses are carved on the walls), one lower archway appears to be made of Herodian ashlars.

CHAPTER SEVEN

Very near to this room is an underground Synagogue-like area that some people view to be the "Underground Temple." The Jews certainly hold all this area as holy, being part of the retaining wall of the Temple Mount. They pray there because this is also part of an extension of the Western Wailing Wall and is closer to the original location of the Temple on the mountain. But these Jews do not concede that any underground room is actually the embodied Jewish Temple.

There is also a six hundred-foot tunnel dug next to the buried lower courses of the Western Wall of the Temple Mount, known as the "Rabbinical Tunnel." This is a clearing of an earlier passageway.

Color Image 17, The Rabbinical Tunnel in Jerusalem. Western_Wall_Tunnels-7 israelfamilytours.com

The original intention of digging the tunnel was to clear the Western Wall and expose the majesty of the Temple Mount. This would possibly open the entire Western Wall to Jewish prayer without intruding into areas assigned to Moslem supervision. Another motive for digging the tunnel may be to get as close as possible to the Shekinah, the Spirit of God, which was believed to have dwelt in a beautiful cloud in the Holy of Holies of the Temple. One of the reasons Orthodox Jews are forbidden to walk on the Temple Mount itself is that they might inadvertently step on the site of the Holy of Holies which once housed the Ark and tablets of stone. They believe that this would desecrate this holy site. In the Rabbinical Tunnel, Orthodox Jews may get closer to this supremely holy place than anywhere else they are permitted to go.

If this Ark is hidden in underground Jerusalem, it is possible that it is buried in one of the many unexplored passageways or rooms. This feasibility leaves open the prospect that it could be buried under the illustrious Dome of the Rock.

Was the Ark Hidden Under the Dome of the Rock?

On the morning of April 19, 1911, Captain M. B. Parker and his archaeological team were discovered digging for the lost Ark in the cave of the Dome of the Rock.

Thousands rioted in protest (one report said there were over ten thousand people involved) as Parker and his team fled empty-handed, barely escaping with their lives.

The origin of the Parker Expedition of 1909-1911 takes us to Constantinople in Turkey. There, while working in a library in 1906 researching ancient history, an ancient language expert, Valter H. Juvelius, accidentally discovered a coded passage in the book of Ezekiel that described the precise location of the long-lost treasures of Solomon's Temple. (One source said the encrypted passage was in Jeremiah). Written above the text, in a coded fashion, were the clues to finding the lost, hidden treasure of the Jewish Temple. In 1906, Juvelius, the Finnish mystic, delivered a paper at the Swedish University detailing his discovery about the secret hiding place of the lost Ark. This fabulous treasure, supposedly concealed at the time of Nebuchadnezzar's conquest of Jerusalem in 586 B.C., was said to be hidden deep within the boughs of the Temple Mount in a cave connected to the city by a secret underground passageway. The cryptogram apparently contained detailed information about where this passage was and how to find the Temple treasures.

CHAPTER SEVEN

Color Image 18, The Dome of the Rock on the Temple Mount, Jerusalem. Author's Photo

Juvelius was convinced that this secret passage led from the Temple Mount (Mount Moriah), to the City of David (located on the hill of Ophel to the south of Mt. Moriah), near the area of Warren's Shaft. The Ophel ("hill, mound") hill is the southeastern spur north of the City of David that is the oldest known part of Jerusalem. It is the section of Jebusite territory captured by King David and was the site of the Tabernacle during his days, near the top of the city of David.

He was certain that if you could find the secret passage entrance on the Hill of Ophel in the City of David that it could be cleared to the Temple Mount to unearth the hidden treasure. Juvelius then tried to raise the money for an expedition to Palestine by offering a share in the treasure that he estimated would bring untold wealth. He expected the Ark of the Covenant alone would bring $200 million in an auction on the open market! But he failed to raise the capital needed for the expedition. However, Montague Brownslow Parker, the son of the Earl of Morley, heard of the search for the Temple treasure and raised $125,000 for the expedition.[93] Parker had served with distinction in the Boer War, rising to the rank of Captain in the Grenadier Guards while still in his youth and he longed

---
93 Sebag Montefiore, Simon (2011). *Jerusalem: The Biography*, (London: Phoenix, 2011), 391.

to return to a life of adventure. So, the captain raised the necessary capital, obtaining the money from such illustrious people as the Duchess of Marlborough (Consuelo Vanderbilt, who was a cousin by marriage to Winston Churchill) and the Armour family of Chicago.

Finding that all antiquities discovered in Palestine became the property of the Ottoman Empire, Parker traveled to the center of the Turkish Empire in Constantinople and immediately proceeded to bribe two high ranking Commissioners of the Turkish government. He offered to provide them fifty percent of any discovered treasure, expecting hundreds of millions in revenue![94] The Commissioners quickly and quietly agreed. Under their protection, an agent was hastily dispatched to Jerusalem to purchase all available land on the slope of Ophel.

Arriving back in England, Parker enlisted the help of several of his aristocratic friends such as Clarence Wilson, Captain R.G. Duff, and Major Foley. They purchased expensive excavation equipment and outfitted Clarence Wilson's yacht for the sea journey.

In August 1909, the expedition arrived in Palestine and the team moved into the spacious Augusta Victoria Hospice on the Mount of Olives, purchasing further materials such as tents, rifles, camp furniture, and imported provisions. They also hired a veritable army of servants, cooks, guides, bodyguards, and housemaids. They were hosted by the governor of the city, Azmey Bey Pasha, to a series of festive banquets at his official residence where they also met several local dignitaries.

Soon, the Turkish Commissioners arrived from Constantinople to supervise the search for the treasure and digging was begun in the shafts discovered earlier by Charles Warren in 1867. Juvelius was convinced that the entrance to the secret passage mentioned in the coded Biblical text might be nearby

---

[94] Silberman, Neil Parker (July-August1980). "In Search of Solomon's Lost Treasure." *Biblical Archaeological Review*, (6) 4.

CHAPTER SEVEN

and this tunnel complex was still largely unexcavated. Parker also excavated in the Virgin's Fountain, so named because it is believed that Mary had once drawn water there, but this second place was actually the northern entrance to Hezekiah's Water Tunnel. Here, Parker expected to find the entrance to a subterranean passageway that connected with a secret chamber whose northern entrance was beneath the sacred area near the Al-Aqsa Mosque.[95]

The expedition team stayed for a while at the American Colony, headed by H.G. Spafford, a former Chicago banker who had come with his wife to Israel after the tragic death of their four daughters in a shipwreck and loss of much of their fortune in the Great Chicago Fire. The Spaffords did not trust Mr. Parker, partially because his "cover story" did not sound reasonable and partly because they were digging without any qualified archaeologist as a guide and overseer. So, Parker promptly went and hired the eminent Père Vincent, a longtime resident of Jerusalem and the head of the French *Ecole Biblique et Archaeologique de St. Etienne*. The entire tunnel of Hezekiah was cleared and other shafts were discovered and explored, yet each shaft always seemed to lead *away* from the Temple Mountain and their goal of hidden treasure instead of leading *toward* the Temple Mountain, as the coded passage had told. Extensive detailing of their excavations and accomplishments were recorded in *Underground Jerusalem: Discoveries on the Hill of Ophel* by Père Vincent, the Dominican father and Jerusalem's most respected archaeological authority.

Because of difficult weather conditions, Parker stopped the excavations in November 1909 and returned to England, where he hired several engineers who had recently completed the London Subway and bought several pieces of expensive machinery for the next season of excavation.

---

95   Addison, Graham (2011). *Raiders of the Hidden Ark: The story of the Parker expedition to Jerusalem*, (Edgecumbe Press), 230-233.

After failing to discover any "secret passageway" the Turkish government officials grew weary of waiting for their immense golden treasure, whether by honest means or not. So, the officials shortened their allotted time of excavation and gave them only eleven more months to discover their treasure. The local people had been alarmed when Parker first began to dig because of the secrecy and because they initially did not follow any proper archaeological techniques while exploring. And they also feared that the team were digging in the tombs of David and Solomon and were disturbing the site. Meanwhile, the Baron Edmund de Rothschild had purchased adjoining land on the Ophel and applied for permission for his own archaeologist to excavate there, evidently realizing Parker's actual intentions.

Parker moved to a rented house close to the excavation site and began the search in earnest, working his excavation teams day and night by torchlight to clear the passageway. After clearing away the subterranean water system, discovering Bronze Age burial caves and traces of ancient fortifications, Parker realized that even if he did find the secret passage in time, that they would be unable to clear the entire distance to the Temple Mount.

The teams were given two more weeks before they were kicked out of the country. In desperation, Parker resolved to search on the Temple Mount. He had become close friends with Azmey Bey, the Mayor (or Turkish Pasha) of Jerusalem. Parker offered the mayor and other leading officials such as the Sheikh Khalil, the hereditary guardian of the Dome of the Rock, (and according to some sources, he also paid the commander of the city garrison) handsome bribes amounting to $25,000 each! This would allow these "Westerners" entrance to the Temple Mount to secretly excavate for the treasure.

Disguising themselves in Arab dress, Parker and a small group of excavators made their way to the Temple Mount under cover of darkness. First, they excavated in the southeast corner of the Temple Mount in the underground complex known today as Solomon's Stables. It is now understood that King Herod, not King Solomon, probably built these chambers, since many changes to the mountain and great enlargements to the Temple Platform took place under Herod's reign. And the area was only later used as stables during the Crusader period. Parker's group dug in this area for seven nights and sadly found nothing. Then, on the night of April 17, 1911, Parker and his men secretly entered the Dome of the Rock.

The Dome (mistakenly called the Mosque of Omar) is built over a sacred rock (called *Even Shetiyyah* in Hebrew, meaning "foundation stone") that is thought to be the rock upon which Abraham was to offer his son Isaac. It is also traditionally the place where Jacob had his dream of a ladder ascending to heaven. Again, this was the threshing floor area of Arnan that King David purchased as the ground for the future Temple (2 Sam. 24: 21-25; 2 Chron. 3:1). Of most eminent importance, this is the place where King Solomon built the first Jewish Temple and the presence of God resided here over the Ark of the Covenant. And it is also where Mohammed is conjectured

Ill. 14, Inside the cave called the "Well of Souls" Jerusalem dome of the rock2 1880.jpg Public Domain

to have ascended to heaven on his horse Borek, supposedly leaving the hoof-prints of the horse in the rock as he went.

Underneath this rock is a series of caves called the "Well of Souls" or "Well of Spirits," also called Bir al-Arwah. Curiously, the underground temple in Egypt where the fictitious character Indiana Jones discovers the lost Ark is also called the "Well of Souls," but the real location is in Jerusalem.

Some Jews believe the creation of the World began from this stone and that Heaven is directly above. They also believe that the Garden of Eden began in Israel and spanned across the modern Arabian Desert to the Persian Gulf, including all this vast Middle East area. Muslims believe that the Garden of Eden began in Babylon and traversed to the land of Israel and the Mediterranean Sea. The Muslims also believe that this "Well of Souls" leads directly down to the pits of Hell, is filled with all sorts of demons and that anyone who enters its depths never comes back alive. And they point to markings in the rock, claiming that these are the hoofprints left behind, when the horse of Mohammed named Borek jumped with him astride to Heaven.

However, it is known that the Crusaders repossessed this Dome and returned it to its original use as a Christian church. While the Crusaders occupied the building, they removed the top of this rock, selling the cut-away stone to churches all over Europe. Accordingly, these "hoofprints" would have been on the original rock surface, not the current surface of the stone. To see them today would mean that the "hoofprints" would have to have been impressed through six feet of solid rock!

Although the rock itself is very large, the cave below is actually smaller than anticipated. Hidden in the marble floor of the first cave is a shaft leading to a very large cave or series of two other caves below ground. Parker and his men broke through this floor and let themselves down to the cave below. Here, in a large, deep passageway several hundred yards below the

CHAPTER SEVEN

sacred rock, they discovered a basin with a plastered interior that plainly showed marks of the different levels of liquid that had stood in it. This chamber was possibly a cistern or retainer for the blood of the sacrifices of the Temple and could have been included as part of the vast drainage system built for the Temple area.

Before the Englishmen had a chance to explore the caves fully, an attendant of the Shrine discovered the team. This attendant was unable to sleep at his home because several people had come to his residence, so he had come to the Dome Shrine a little after midnight to sleep on the carpeted floor. All the other guards are thought to have been paid-off and were not there on guard duty. He was apparently the only one who came, probably because he had not been advised or paid-off since it was not his normal night to serve guard duty. Suddenly, he was awakened by curious noises coming from the cave (which he surmised might be demons). He picked up a torch and started to nervously descend into the "Well of Souls." There he noticed the marble floor of the first cave had been broken and that the men had let themselves down by ropes. Then he searched for intruders through the second cave and the third cave. As he drew nearer, he heard strange voices speaking another language (i.e., English) and the sounds grew steadily louder. Suddenly, he rounded a corner and was so horrified to find the light-skinned, English Gentiles exploring there that he thought they were ghosts and ran out screaming at the top of his lungs!

He soon realized that these intruders were not ghosts but light-skinned Englishmen, but he was too scared to go back down there alone. So, he ran through the streets screaming the news that the Christians have stolen the Crown and Ring of Solomon, the Ark of the Covenant and Ten Commandments and the Sword of Mohammed! At that time, if you were English, European, or American residing in Palestine it was assumed that you were Christian and not Muslim. So, the "Christians" (Anglo or Caucasian people) were accused of this theft.

According to another variation of this story, this Muslim guard discovered Captain Parker and his team in the early morning hours as he saw the workers dumping baskets of rubble near the Dome of the Rock. He was horrified at their sacrilege of the site and then alerted their presence to the Muslims.

Parker and his panic-stricken men quickly gathered their tools and ran out of the cave. They knew that it was illegal for a non-Muslim to be on the Mountain, which was holy to both Muslim and Jew, and that they might be beheaded or at least imprisoned by the Arabs if caught. So, they fled to their awaiting yacht in Jaffa. There, news of the uproar in Jerusalem had preceded them by telegraph and the customs officials immediately detained them.

The Muslims, upon hearing that Parker's men had supposedly taken the sacred treasures such as the Crown and Ring of Solomon, the Ark of the Covenant and Ten Commandments and the Sword of Mohammed, rioted in the most Anti-Christian uprising of the century threatening widespread massacre! An angry crowd had mobbed the entrance to the government citadel.

The Turkish governor of the city, fearing for his own life at the hands of the crowd, ordered his troops to quell the disturbance. Before his soldiers had a chance to take up positions at the Temple Mount, the furious mob seized Sheikh Khalil. The mayor Azmey Bey himself was mobbed, spat upon and called "a pig" for his suspected complicity in the incident. The soldiers were not able to control the growing mobs, and by nightfall, rioting and mayhem had spread to all parts of the city. The Muslim populace literally ran through the streets of Jerusalem with swords drawn, striking at anything that appeared, and killing many people.

CHAPTER SEVEN

Parker spoke to the customs officials in Jaffa and explained that he did not know anything about the matter. The officials wanted to detain the Englishmen until they received further instructions from Constantinople, but Parker knew that he must escape at once.

He was a gracious, diplomatic, and shrewd man, and soon he had persuaded the customs officials, who had repeatedly searched their baggage with no results, to come to his yacht to further discuss the matter. Their luggage was detained as the men were allowed to row out of the dock and board their yacht in the harbor. Next, the customs officials began to come in their own vessel to meet with Parker. But before the customs officials could row out to the yacht, Parker ordered his crew to weigh anchor and steam out to open sea. They had escaped with only the clothes on their backs, but they were still alive!

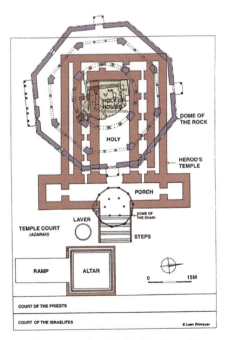

Ill. 15, Ritmeyer location of the Ark at the Dome of the Rock, Jerusalem. TemplePlan-Coltn.jpg

Was the Ark of the Covenant at the Dome of the Rock Location?

The Ark may have stood on the location of the *Even Shetiyyah* (the Foundation Stone) at the site of the current Dome of the Rock in the earlier days of the Temple. There are four main views as to where the Temple might have stood on the Temple Mount. The Northern location is in line with the Dome of Spirits and the Golden Gate. This would place the Temple door in line with the Eastern Gate.

The Southern location lies in front of the Al-Aqsa with the Al-Kas [i.e., the washing fountain] serving as the Holy of Holies. The Aqsa ("Arabic, "the farther") is the term used for the farther mosque in the Koran.[96] It probably originally indicated a mosque located in the northern corner of Mecca, but the tradition and location was later moved to Jerusalem, hence the Al-Aqsa Mosque. It is thought to give the Muslims a connection to Jerusalem. Originally, the Muslims were not associated with Jerusalem, and the story of Mohammed riding a horse to heaven was a later story. Some people believe it was deliberately fabricated to give the Muslims a connection to Jerusalem and the Temple Mount and to legitimize the Muslim presence there.

The center position with the Dome of the Rock serving as the Holy of Holies is another view. And the center site with the Dome of the Rock serving as the High Altar is the final possibility.

The official rabbi of the Temple Mount area, Rabbi Mayer Yehuda Getz, believes that the Dome of the Rock is the site of the Great Altar with the Holy of Holies located 210 feet forward from the rock. Rabbi Leibel Reznick also agrees with this location and gives a strong argument in his book *The Holy Temple Revisited*. However, the most interesting study is the view that the Ark might have stood on the Foundation Stone under the site of the Dome of the Rock.[97]

Leen Ritmeyer advanced the evidence for this concept in an article for *Biblical Archaeological Review*, as well as his website.[98] He believed that this was the right location for two reasons.

The Dome of the Rock now occupies the highest point on the Temple Mountain in the Temple Mount Complex. And this location matches the description given by the Mishnah for the

---

[96] *Surah* 17
[97] Leen Ritmeyer, "The Ark of the Covenant: Where It Stood in Solomon's Temple," *Biblical Archaeological Review*, (Jan./Feb. 1996): 46-53
[98] Leen Ritmeyer, "Here in this carved-out place, stood the Ark of the Covenant," *Ritmeyer Archeological Design*, Accessed on Dec. 27, 2022, https://ritmeyer.com

Temple. The largest open space on the Temple Mount was on the south, the second on the east, the third on the north, and the least on the west.[99] He also identified the square courtyard that the Temple stood upon as being a five hundred royal cubit section on the Mount. The only place the Temple might have stood, according to these calculations, would have been in the location of the Dome of the Rock. He then asked himself, could he identify where the Ark of the Covenant stood?[100]

By examining the Temple Mount itself and doing extensive measurements, comparing them to other measurements and to the historical record of the Temple Mount, he was able to determine where the Temple stood. Thus, he would have known where the Holy of Holies was and in the center of that area, he found a depression of the Rock that measured 4'4"×2'7". He believes that this is the very location for the placement of the Ark of the Covenant which was 3'9"×2'3".

Where Else on the Temple Mount Might the Treasure Be Hidden?

Most Jewish scholars agree that the Temple treasure and Ark of the Covenant were hidden on the Temple Mount. Some scholars believe that it is hidden under the Dome of the Rock in the "Well of Souls," but most experts look for the Ark in another location.

King Solomon built hidden chambers underground to house the Temple Treasury and he also built underground chambers for the Royal Treasury to be hidden nearby. According to the Mishnah and various Jewish authorities, the Holy Ark was hidden by King Josiah in a secret passageway of the Temple complex. [101]

While the Temple Mount has been inaccessible for archaeological excavation because of almost two thousand years of

---

99   *Middot* 2.1
100   Leen Ritmeyer "The Ark of the Covenant: Where It Stood in Solomon's Temple." *Biblical Archaeological Review* (Jan./Feb. 1996): 46-53
101   *Shekalim* 6:1

constant foreign occupation, the writings in the Mishnah have preserved the Orthodox rabbis unyielding confidence in the Ark's existence beneath the Temple platform.

Charles Wilson explored chambers under the Temple Mount in the Nineteenth Century.

Wilson described it thus:

> Cut into the rock at the eastern end is a low doorway that leads to a flight of steps. The steps ascend toward the south, then sharply eastward. This eastward passage is covered by semicircular vaulting, and at the end are the remains of another doorway. A few feet beyond the doorway the opening is blocked by earth.[102]

Although the Ark could be hidden in one of these chambers, it is difficult to speculate as to when it might be possible to explore them. Whether Muslims or Jews have explored them in the past is difficult to determine.

Supposedly the Muslims are not particularly interested in these underground chambers and also consider them too sacred to explore. However, each time an existing structure or stone formation is identified by archaeological journals as remains of the Temple platform, they are promptly covered over by the Muslim caretakers. Next we will examine the continued search for the Ark.

When looking into the facts of events around the Temple Mount, it is vital to have first-hand information. The renowned Bible scholar, author, and researcher Dr. Randall Price is one of the prime sources of information about the Ark and the Temple. He served as the public voice for the Christian television ministry "Day of Discovery," and therefore has developed a relationship with and interviewed all of the significant people in Israel over several years. He also served as an official licensed tour guide for Israel, has

---

[102] Charles Wilson, *Ordinance Survey of Jerusalem*, (London, 1865)

made over 150 trips there, and was a professor at Liberty University in Lynchburg, Virginia, for many years. His many books and videos are one of the primary sources of the facts about many Temple Mount details. Consequently, this book refers to his key interviews.

Digging for the Ark

The Jews recently discovered Warren's Gate (a lost passageway leading to the Temple Mount) while exploring the Rabbinical Tunnel.[103] In July of 1981, Rabbi Meir Yehuda Getz, the chief rabbi of the Western Wall and all holy places in Israel, was in the process of building a new synagogue behind the Western Wall that would face the Temple Mount. The Jews were attempting to get as close as possible to the area of the Holy of Holies on the Temple Mount to pray. As one of Getz workers was knocking out a stone to affix a Torah cabinet, they accidentally discovered Warren's Gate and the open area behind it. In explaining this discovery, Rabbi Getz tells why he believes that this opening will lead to the chamber of the Ark:

> *After we traced the leaking water to its source, we discovered this large opening [Warren's Gate] 25 meters long, 30 meters high, and 8 meters wide. I believed it was from the First Temple. When we found this entrance gate, I ordered the wall to be opened and we discovered a giant hall shaped like Wilson's Arch, but with exit tunnels running in different directions. The length of this hall was about 75 feet. There were some stairs that we descended for about 30 feet; however, at the bottom everything was full of water and mud. When we pumped this away, I found an insect. This insect verified that this place was opposite the Holy of Holies because it is recorded in the Mishnah tractate Yoma that if the priest was found unclean, and therefore unable to get out of the Holy of Holies, he should release an insect that would go under the veil. I have discovered that insect!* [104]

---
103 Warren, Charles, *Underground Jerusalem*, (London, 1876)
104 Randall Price, *In Search of Temple Treasures*, Ibid., 164-165.

It was Rabbi Getz's contention that this large, vaulted room was from the First Temple period. But Rabbi Goren thought of the discovery in a more historical context and gave a thorough explanation:

> *When King Solomon built the Temple, he built the Western Wall as a frame...Between this frame and the actual wall of the Temple there was a stone filling to fill the gap in between. We discovered that underneath this frame all the stones are connected with the frame of the Temple. When our workers first entered the gate, they thought that these kinds of rooms might have been built by the Turks for just collecting water, but then they saw an arch... and a beautiful hall-way. This big vault that we saw was one of the main entrances to the Temple, probably the Second Temple.*[105]

It was now evident to the rabbis that they could enter the secret priestly passageways hidden for two thousand years and so they assembled a select group of ten men to further excavate this underground area. This team included students of the Ateret Cohanim Yeshivah who began clearing the great hall that once served as a cistern to the Temple Mount. While observing this area, Ze'ev Bar-Tov, the treasurer of the Temple Mount Faithful organization said, "It looked just like a big, cleaned apartment–not like most digs; it was very clean!" After doing further exploration, they discovered a shaft, which they believe leads to the Holy of Holies area of the Temple. After finding a passageway behind this hall that led to the northeast, the team began to work on this area.[106]

Rabbi Getz describes the location of this passage:

> *From the place where the insect was discovered, we saw several openings. One entrance was toward the gate. It was closed but we opened it. From there, we saw a wall that was later built and was about nine to twelve feet away from the warning wall*

---

105 Randall Price, *In Search of Temple Treasures*, Ibid., 165.
106 Zimmerman, Michael A., "Tunnel Exposes New Areas of the Temple Mount" *Biblical Archaeological Review*, VII: 3, (May/June 1981): 34

of the Western Wall, which itself was only fifteen feet from the Holy of Holies.[107]

As the Jewish team continued their digging toward the direction of the Temple, they believed that they were excavating straight toward the area of the Holy of Holies. In describing this difficult task, Chief Rabbi Goren tells of the impassioned work done by these rabbis and student priests:

> We decided together with Rabbi Getz to start digging beneath the Temple Mount in the direction which, according to my measurements [taken in 1967 after the Six-Day War], we had to go in order to reach the Holy of Holies. It took us a long time–a year and a half–and it was very hard work. We found chambers half-filled with water and there were swamps and such that we had to drain. I had hoped that if we had enough time–another year and a half–we would have been able to reach the surface of the Holy of Holies beneath the Temple Mount.[108]

Later, Rabbi Goren revised his earlier interview, showing greater reservation in expressing how close he actually came to the proximity of the presumed chamber of the Ark:

> I imagined that I was there when I had dug in about 50 yards in a straight line from the place where the chamber of the Ark was. But it was still very deep–maybe 100 meters. If Charles Warren dug over 100 meters and he didn't get to the end [the bedrock], what can one say about the Temple, its foundation, and the chambers beneath it! I believe that the Ark is somewhere beneath the Temple and the problem now is one of digging down a hundred meters.[109]

This work had been done in great secret. News of excavations in this area would have surely upset the Muslims population nearby. Although underground, the Muslims would believe

---
107   Randall Price, *In Search of Temple Treasures*, Ibid., 165-166.
108   Randall Price, *In Search of Temple Treasures*, Ibid., 166.
109   Randall Price, *In Search of Temple Treasures*, Ibid., 167.

that a Jewish presence near their holy sites would desecrate them, all the while forgetting that these sites are also very holy to the Jews. This excavation beneath the Temple Mount in the tunnel had been a carefully guarded secret for years. Rabbi Getz mentioned this to Randall Price in 1991 when he said, "It has been ten years since its discovery and it is still a secret." Rabbi Goren continued in this line of thought, relating:

> *This work was very secret. Nobody on the outside knew what we were doing inside. No news of our dig had been revealed to any journalist; we did not reveal the story to anyone. We had a budget and only a few people–about ten–were engaged in the work, but they took a vow not to tell anything about their work.*[110]

However, news eventually leaked to the media and this public exposure put an immediate end to the work. When news reached the Muslim Wakf (the Muslim Temple Mount security) that the Jews were about to uncover the Ark, they stopped the excavation by sending a Muslim mob to attack the diggers.

In describing the motives for the attack, Rabbi Chaim Richman of the Temple Institute says:

> *They were afraid that if the Jews found these objects it would be the surest sign of all of a Jewish presence on the Temple Mount–that it wasn't some sort of mystical tradition. They were afraid that if these things were uncovered that we would rebuild the Temple. It is part of an orchestrated effort to destroy and eradicate any semblance of Jewish presence around the Temple Mount.*[111]

As they were digging in this vicinity, the Muslims rioted and attacked the unsuspecting Jews who were hard at work in the passage. A fight ensued between Muslim and Jew and the Jews were quickly overwhelmed. The border police claim that they had to intervene to keep Getz, Goren, and the other workers

---

110 Randall Price, *In Search of Temple Treasures*, Ibid., 167.
111 Randall Price, *In Search of Temple Treasures*, Ibid., 168.

from being killed, although there is good evidence that they left the Jews there to die and the Jews brought their own men with guns to save their people from being killed. (This is another reason for the secrecy. The Jews were well aware of how dangerous it might be for them to dig for the foundations of the Temple, the lost Temple vessels or make any effort to rebuild their Temple. Yet, the Jews were so determined that fear of fighting or even death could not stop them.) After the police had arrested the students of the Yeshiva the riot was stopped. But another Arab riot occurred later at that site. That was followed by a general strike called by the Muslim Council to protest the search for the Ark.

It is Rabbi Goren's belief that the entire riot scenario was part of a political plot to close his diggings in deference to Arab sensitivities following the Camp David peace accord between Israel and Egypt. While telling this account to Price, Rabbi Goren said, "This is the original story that no one else knows, not even Rabbi Getz."

> *One day a journalist who was a good friend of mine came up to me and told me that he knew what we were doing beneath the Temple Mount. I asked him to promise not to reveal it to the media and he promised me that he wouldn't, provided no other journalist found out. However, several months later he told me that a television journalist had learned of our secret and he was going to broadcast it on television. Because my friend wanted to be the first to announce it, he said that his promise was no longer valid. I begged him not to do it, saying he would destroy the entire work. He went ahead and announced on the radio that we were digging beneath the Temple Mount to get the direction of the Holy of Holies in order to find the Ark.*[112]

Gershon Salomon, the leader of the Temple Mount Faithful, also took part in the excavation and he tells what happened inside the tunnel.

---
112   Randall Price, *In Search of Temple Treasures*, Ibid., 168-169.

> *We had just discovered another wall which blocked our continuance into the tunnel. I remember that the workers, along with Rabbi Getz, started to break down this wall, since beyond this point Rabbi Getz conjectured it continued to the place under the floors where the Ark of the Covenant, the Menorah, and the other vessels were. We were so very close! But at this moment the Arabs started to demonstrate against our activities...* [113]

Rabbi Goren tells his version of the story by telling of his encounter with government officials who sought to close the project:

> *After he [the newsman] announced it, the Arabs got together on the Temple Mount and prepared to open the entrances on the Temple Mount to go down inside the tunnels and prevent our work. But while they [the Arabs] were still talking about it, Joseph Berg, the Minister of the Interior and of the police, suddenly came to my office and said that he would like to prevent the Arabs from going down to stop our work. He promised to put police at every entrance on the Temple Mount and to put an iron chain on the openings of these entrances so that no one could go down. But I didn't trust him. I knew that Berg would, if he could, hand over the Temple Mount to the Arabs—the Wakf. So, I asked him to sign an agreement, which he did, but before he had even left the building on the elevator, I got a call from the Western Wall, saying, "Did you know that there is a fight at the Wall with your people where they are digging? There are hundreds of Arabs that have gone into the chambers and there could be bloodshed!" I knew then that Berg had concocted the story of his offer of help to camouflage his real intention of opening the entrances to the Arabs and telling them to go down to get us.*
>
> *When I arrived at the Wall there were hundreds of police—even the chief of police was there–and I was happy they were there because I thought they [the Arabs] would not be able to do anything. I asked them to come with me to see what was going*

---

113   Randall Price, *In Search of Temple Treasures*, Ibid., 169.

CHAPTER SEVEN

> on inside the dig. Some of the top officers followed me, but when I reached the place there were hundreds of Arabs inside—coming in from both sides and crying and shouting. ...I went to get the police to arrest the Arabs and take them out, but when I turned all the officers had disappeared. When I came outside of the tunnel to the Wall there were no police to be found. There are always police at the Wall to protect the people–to be on the safe side. But this time there were none! I became afraid because we were alone, so I called Berg at his office and told him that he had betrayed me! I asked him to send police to protect us because otherwise we would be killed. When the police still could not be found, I called him again and told him he would be held responsible and that I was going to mobilize the boys of the Yeshiva Ha-Kotel and my Yeshiva Ha-Idrah and they were going down with pistols—with weapons—and there will be bloodshed! So, I called General Ariel Sharon, the defense minister, and told him the story and said if you do not send soldiers to evacuate the Arabs from the chambers, there will be bloodshed. But he said that he had foreign guests and could not do anything.
>
> Finally, I called to the boys from the Yeshivot and a few hundred came with weapons. Meanwhile a cry came from Rabbi Getz's wife: "They are killing my husband!" At that moment, the police appeared from where they were apparently hidden on the Temple Mount. The radio had reported that three Arabs had been killed and many wounded in the riot, but it was a lie! It was simply an excuse for the police to exercise authority over us and to close our dig. The police arrested the boys from our Yeshivah and put them in prison. They did nothing to the Arabs. Then they gave orders to immediately erect a new wall over the entrance to the tunnel and to close the chambers to prevent any Jewish access. As a result, we lost all connection with the chamber which we were digging that led to the Ark.[114]

The police put up a wall at the entrance three meters wide (nine feet), made of steel and concrete. The government's

---
114   Randall Price, *In Search of Temple Treasures*, Ibid., 169-171.

Ministry of Religious Affairs later reinforced the original closure with a steel and plaster wall. It was later covered with a natural rock surface in 1992 because the smooth plaster finish drew too many questions from tourists. While in Israel in 1993, I inquired of Jewish rabbis at the Wailing Wall about the possibility of current digging in the Warren's Gate passageway and was told digging had not resumed.

Rabbi Goren was to attend an official send-off for then current Prime Minister Menachem Begin as he went to the United States to meet with President Reagan. At the airport, Goren again confronted Berg in Begin's presence about his organized efforts and complicity in closing down the Temple area digs. And Goren said that he gave them an ultimatum that his boys be released from prison within the hour–and they complied!

Rabbi Shlomo Goren describes this thrilling discovery:

> "I started digging just beneath the Temple Mount from outside, just a few years ago. We were very close to the place on the Temple Mount, where the Holy of Holies was located. We were very close, beneath the Holy of Holies. We believe that the Holy Ark made by Moses, and the table from the Temple, and the Candelabra made by Moses, along with other very important items, are hidden very deep underneath the Holy of the Holies. We started digging and we came close to the place; we were not more than thirty or forty yards away. Unfortunately, we were so close that the Arabs started rioting and attacked us, and the government became afraid. They stopped us, and built a wall to prevent further entrance."[115]

The Jewish rabbis still insist that they know the exact location of the Ark under the Temple Mount. And Rabbi Getz admits that the Israeli government also knows the location of the Ark but it is too politically sensitive to discuss publicly. The Rabbis believe that the government is working toward

---
115   Thomas Ice, Randall Prince. *Ready to Rebuild*, Ibid., 145.

a peace agreement that will give away Israel's land, demean and damage their sovereignty as a nation and especially work against the Jewish prospects of rebuilding a Temple by giving the Arabs more sovereignty over the Temple Mount. They believe the government is going against God's will and because of their frustration, have decided to go public with their story about the search for the Ark. The Muslim Arabs have currently begun to build another Mosque on the Temple Mount in the area of Solomon's Stables (with the government looking the other way). They have done extensive remodeling of the Temple Mount with bulldozers, destroying archaeological details, and yet the government is attempting to stop the Jews from having a prayer area on the Temple Mount itself.

Certain rabbis in Israel, such as Rabbi Nahman Kahane of the Institute for Talmudic Commentaries, doubt that Goren and Getz know the true location of the Ark. But Rabbis Yisrael Ariel and Chaim Richman of the Temple Institute are convinced the story is certainly true. Yet, even though Randall Price believed that Goren and Getz were telling him honest accounts of the events that transpired while they were digging for the ark, he also believed that they told him only as much information as they wanted him to know.

Randall Price believes that the story is suppressed for many reasons. Some of the rabbis are not always pleased with how their words are used and their stories are told. For instance, being Orthodox Jews, they would not want to be seen as promoting the coming of Jesus Christ (because we believers in Jesus understand that the soon return of Christ is associated with the rebuilding of the Temple and all its related events). Some rabbis did not want to talk with me while I was in Israel because they believe the Ark is too holy to discuss with people from a secular background. It is the contention of many rabbis that the advent of Messiah and the Third

Temple are related to the Ark and to bring it out early might be premature for their Messiah's timing. The rabbis are also experiencing tremendous opposition from the government and the religious sector and they may be careful about what they want portrayed in the public.

Getz and Goren maintained that the government wanted the digging stopped because of the Camp David peace accord with Egyptian Anwar Sadat and they used Police Chief Berg to accomplish their aims. Gershon Salomon gave his synopsis:

> *Joseph Berg gave the order by decision of the government of Israel to close the gate to not incite the Arabs and to stop their demonstrations. It was not because of the orthodox Jews; they were not involved; and none of them could say to the government to stop us [that is, none of them had the clout]. When the government of Israel wanted to do something, she did it, and so to say today that this [the closing of the gate] is because of the orthodox Jews is to rewrite history.*[116]

The Muslim Wakf also opposed the excavation by Goren and Getz. They ordered the digging stopped, orchestrated the riot, and sealed off the entrance at their side. As Rabbi Getz said, "The Muslims were against the idea that we do any kind of digging in general. They said that it [the Temple Mount] is theirs." Soon after the incident, Gershon Salomon presented an appeal to the Supreme Court of Israel to keep the gate open, but it was closed because of Arab demonstrations and for fear of further Arab reactions and violence.

Why Do the Muslim Arabs Not Retrieve the Ark?

Sometimes it is wondered why the Muslim Arabs do not get the Ark? It is known that of the thirty-six cisterns and other underground chambers on the Temple Mount that twenty-five of them are still in use. The Muslims used cistern #4 to attack Rabbi Getz and his workers in 1981. The Wakf also

---
116 Randall Price, *In Search of Temple Treasures*, Ibid., 177.

claims that the Jews were never in Israel in ancient times, that they never used the Temple Mount and that all archaeological remains are Islamic or pre-Islamic, but certainly not Jewish. They have occasionally discovered remains of the Temple, other Jewish synagogues, Christian churches, and other Jewish and Christian evidence and all these remains are promptly destroyed, removed, or covered over as reported in the *Biblical Archaeological Review*. So why would they want to find evidence of something that they deny existed?

Gershon Salomon has also suggested that the Muslims know of the many legends of the demons that guard the area beneath the Dome of the Rock as the "Well of Souls" or "Well of Spirits [or Demons]." While they know of the stories of hidden treasures below in the cave or chambers of the area, they also know that the earlier people such as the Mamelukes, Arabs, Muslims and Turks were afraid to venture too deep inside. They have heard many stories of people who tried to reach these chambers, but tradition says they immediately died strange and mysterious deaths. The rabbis might also be careful about what they say to restrict a Gentile desecration of the underground site. Rabbi Goren also related, "Frankly, I do not want the Arabs to know the exact location of the Ark. They may dig and destroy evidences."

Eyewitness to the Discovery of the Ark

Was the Ark actually seen by anyone? It is difficult to determine the full truth of what happened. Some stories claim that the excavators made their way to the very chamber of the Ark and saw the Ark itself. Yet, Rabbi Getz's calculations determined that the Holy of Holies was still about ninety-six feet away from their last location of excavation. Rabbi Goren still maintained that the Ark was much deeper within the area of the Holy of Holies. He stated that you would have to dig not a few meters, but about a hundred and fifty meters to reach the secret room.

Asked again about whether he had been to the very chamber of the Ark, Rabbi Getz replied:

> *We know where it is, but we did not discover it. According to the rabbinical writings it is called the Gear He'Etzem ("Chalk of the Bone") and is located deep within the ground. I wanted to go through the tunnels and reach this area, since I knew the direction–I might be off only fifteen to eighteen feet–but it is impossible to reach because it is deep under the water which flooded the tunnels.* [117]

In giving his assessment about the Ark's discovery and the possibility of recovering it and bringing it out to be viewed publicly, Gershon Salomon responded:

> *I did not hear anyone say that they had found it. What I heard is what Rabbi Getz said very clearly in those early days: "We are at an important point in history. After twenty-five hundred years we are marching to the place of the Ark of the Covenant, and we must do it quickly!" He was wonderful, and he was determined to do it!*[118]

Whatever the truth of the finding of the Ark, it seems evident that the Jewish rabbis are not telling all they know about the story. And they could make preparations to bring out the Ark sometime in the near future to facilitate rebuilding the Temple. It seems that they are determined that the Temple will be rebuilt, and this will require the Ark of the Covenant.

Not just a copy of the Ark, but the original Ark of Moses that contains the Ten Commandments written on stone must be found. The Jews know where it is but are just waiting for the right timing or possibly a sign from God to bring the Ark to public light. They believe that this sign may be the event that brings the Messiah to power.

---

117 Randall Price, *In Search of Temple Treasures*, Ibid., 184.
118 Randall Price, *In Search of Temple Treasures*, Ibid., 184.

Rabbi Yehuda Getz concludes:

> I will give everything in my life to get to the Ark, to get to the tablets inside the Ark ...If I could have found the Ark of the Covenant, it would have been a sign that Messiah was on my side...The time will come when we will enter.[119]

Reflections on the Ark's Discovery and the Coming Temple

Truly, soon the Ark will be found, and the rebuilding of the Temple will occur. We stand at the very threshold of that momentous day. According to ultra-conservative Jewish thought, the discovery of the Ark of the Covenant would be the ultimate factor in forcing Israel to rebuild the Temple. Many times, observers of the Jews who are looking for the Ark and Ashes are impressed and sometimes obsessed with the idea of looking for treasure, such as the gold of the Ark, or additional offerings of coins and articles that might be hidden with the Ark. However, for the observant Jews, finding the Ashes of the Red Heifer and finding the Ark of the Covenant is not just a search for treasure, in the physical sense of riches, but more of a spiritual treasure which enables and opens the door for a soon coming rebuilt Jewish Temple.

Rabbi Hacohen, founder of the School of the Levites, recently stated:

> If we find the ark, it will force us to build the Temple. After all the first Temple was built to house the Ark of the Covenant. If we find the ark, what would we do with it? We couldn't store it in the Prime Minister's basement. It would demand the rebuilding of the temple. However, if we find the ark or not, we are going to build the temple of Almighty God on the Har Habayit, the Temple Mountain.[120]

Matiyahu Dan Hacohen is not the only rabbi who looks for

---

119   Randall Price, *In Search of Temple Treasures*, Ibid., 185.
120   Randall Price, *In Search of Temple Treasures*, Ibid., 185.

the soon coming Temple. This sentiment is evident in many Jewish circles. While dedicating a recent 1992 edition of the Mishnah Torah, Rabbi Touger relates:

> As the text was being composed, we would frequently tell each other: "Work faster. At any moment, Moshiach (Messiah) may come and rebuild the Temple. Who knows how the book will sell then!" May He come speedily in our days and reveal the "Sanctuary of the Lord established by your hands," the Third Temple (Ezekiel's Temple.) May we all merit to serve God there.[121]

John Ankerberg interviewed Gershon Salomon, leader and founder of the Temple Mount Faithful, one of the most diligent groups working to rebuild the Temple, for his Christian television series "The John Ankerberg Show." In this interview, given in May 1993, Salomon gave an overview of his belief about the coming Third Temple and the discovery of the Ark of the Covenant, stating:

> *I have no doubt that you and I shall see the Ark of the Covenant in the middle of the Third Temple on the Temple Mount in Jerusalem, very soon—in our life.*

> *The Ark of the Covenant cannot be put in a museum, nor in a synagogue, but only in one place, the Temple. We know that the generation of the destruction of the First Temple hid the Ark of the Covenant for the time of the Third Temple, the last and eternal Temple. The bringing of the Ark of the Covenant and all the holy vessels to the Third Temple will be by the will of God. We shall see it whether or not we want to see it because God has already decided it. And if God decided it, it is as good as fulfilled. We shall be the generation of the complete redemption—we shall see again as a reality the Ark of the Covenant here on the hill of God, and nations and peoples will come from all the world to see the glory of God.[122]*

---

121   Rabbi Touger. 1992 edition of the Mishnah Torah, preface.
122   Randall Price, *In Search of Temple Treasures*, Ibid., 313, 185.

CHAPTER EIGHT

Thus, the driving force to find the Ashes of the Red Heifer and the Ark of the Covenant is to rebuild the Temple. That is the ultimate goal of the Jews at work in this area. The days are eminent when the Ark of the Covenant and the Ashes of the Red Heifer will be found. The rebuilding of the Temple will quickly follow which leads us to the coming of the Lord and the end of this world as we know it. Are you prepared for that day? Are you ready for the end of the world? End-time events are quickly falling into place. Prophecies are being fulfilled. The end is very near. Arc you ready to meet God? How will you fare when you stand before Him in Judgment?

CHAPTER EIGHT

Peace in the Middle East

Peace—the most elusive dream of the Middle East. Kings have searched for it, diplomats have negotiated for it, and countless lives have been given all in a desperate and timeless pursuit of that culminating goal of peace. And yet, is peace really possible in the Middle East? In the minds of many people, peace is just around the corner.

The Mid-East Peace Agreement

In October of 1993, Israel began negotiations for a first-time peace agreement with their constant enemy and sworn opponent, the Palestinian Liberation Organization. On May 4, 1994, the peace agreement was signed, although both sides requested further negotiations.[123] This contract, negotiated in part by the United States of America, was one of the most surprising pacts of the Century. Many people around the world were ecstatic at the possibility of lasting peace and yet there were many doubts by both Jews and Arabs.

Doubts among the Jews are not without justification. The foundation of the PLO has been to literally annihilate the Jewish race. "We will drive them into the sea!" has been their rallying cry.[124] Each section of their organizational charter outlines their intention to eradicate the Jewish people at all costs. Total destruction of the nation of Israel and total eradication of the Jewish race has been their theme. And now they are talking of peaceful self-rule among the Jews!

The Arabs are also suspicious of their own leadership, having been committed to fighting for so long and now turning to

---
[123] This Day in History May 04, "Yitzhak Rabin and Yasser Arafat sign accord for Palestinian self-rule," Accessed on Dec. 9, 2022, History.com
[124] Elder of Ziyon, "Did Arab States Really Promise to Push Jews into the Sea?" Accessed on December 9, 2022, algemeiner.com

talk of peace. Much violence has resulted among the Arabs against themselves and yet the question still remains, will peace ever come to the Middle East? To find the answer to real and lasting peace there is only one source of truth, the Word of God. God gives us the answers through the words of prophets heard down through the centuries. Let us examine the end-time events as given in the Bible.

The Dead Come to Life

Ezekiel 37:21-28 reveals some very illuminating facts. The earlier part of the chapter is the famous story of the valley of dry bones. Ezekiel has been transported through the Spirit of God to a valley full of dry bones. A vast army has died and all that remains is a great array of skeletal bones. Ezekiel was commanded to prophesy to these bones that they might live again. So, he began to prophesy and all the bones regathered themselves, stood up on their feet, sinew and flesh came upon them, and they began to breathe! This great valley of dry bones had become a living, breathing army! And they are a picture of how God will raise up the nation of Israel in the last days.

This amazing vision is a picture of future events. Behold the Word of the Lord:

> *Then said he unto me, Son of man, these bones are the whole house of Israel: behold, they say, Our bones are dried, and our hope is lost: we are cut off for our parts.*
>
> *Therefore prophesy and say unto them, Thus saith the Lord GOD; Behold, O my people, I will open your graves, and cause you to come up out of your graves, and bring you into the land of Israel.*
>
> *And ye shall know that I am the LORD, when I have opened your graves, O my people, and brought you up out of your graves,*
>
> *And shall put my spirit in you, and ye shall live, and I shall place you in your own land: then shall ye know that I the Lord have spoken it, and performed it, saith the LORD (Ezek. 37:11–14).*

CHAPTER EIGHT

The Regathering of Israel

In this revealing passage of Scripture, the Lord tells us how He would regather Israel as one nation "in the land of Israel" in the last days. God then elaborates in further detail about this end-time regathering in the enlightening chapter.

Ezekiel 37 continues:

> And say unto them, Thus saith the Lord GOD;
> Behold, I will take the children of Israel from among the heathen, whither they be gone, and will gather them on every side, and bring them into their own land:
> And I will make them one nation in the land upon the mountains of Israel; and one king shall be king to them all: and they shall be no more two nations, neither shall they be divided into two kingdoms any more at all (Ezek. 37:21–22).

Speaking through the prophet Ezekiel, God foretells the regathering of Israel in their own land under a solitary ruler. In the Old Testament, the nation of Israel had split into two separate kingdoms under the sons of Solomon, Jeroboam and Rehoboam, and were afterward known as Israel (the northern ten tribes), and Judah (Judah, Benjamin, and the Levitical priests who also returned to Judah). Israel had been taken away in the Assyrian invasion in 722 B.C., and Judah was exiled in the Babylonian invasions of 605, 597, and 586 B.C., later returning in 536 B.C. under King Darius. There, they had endured the rulership of the Macedonian Greeks, the Ptolemy Greeks, the Seleucid Greeks, a short independence under the Maccabees, and then Roman rule until they were dispersed in 70 A.D. and again in 135 A.D. Since that time, Jews had lived with their own culture and faith in countries all over the world, always yearning to return to their own land, and even praying to worship again in a rebuilt Jewish Temple.

Even before the turn of the Century, Jews were already gathering together under Zionism to immigrate to Palestine.

The Balfour Declaration, placing Palestine under British rule, gave more leniency to Jews to return to their land.[125] After the horrific Holocaust of Nazi Germany, Jews were fleeing to any place of refuge, especially to the U.S. and trying to return to their historic homeland. In 1948, the United Nations (under pressure from the United States of America) declared Israel as a free, independent nation under self-rule.[126] Since that time, Israel has been a unified, democratic nation and has even recaptured the "mountains of Israel" in 1967. "The mountains of Israel" refer specifically to the West Bank, whose ownership is debated today, but which the Bible clearly says will be inhabited and controlled by Israel in the last days. The Bible plainly has ceded that land to Israel, which includes the controversial Golan Heights, part of Lebanon, and the entire Western Bank.[127] God had said that He would make them one nation again when they returned and that they would inhabit the mountains of Israel.

Ezekiel 37 continues:

> *Neither shall they defile themselves any more with their idols, nor with their detestable things, nor with any of their transgressions: but I will save them out of all their dwellingplaces, wherein they have sinned, and will cleanse them: so shall they be my people, and I will be their God.*
>
> *And David my servant shall be king over them; and they all shall have one shepherd: they shall also walk in my judgments, and observe my statutes, and do them.*
>
> *And they shall dwell in the land that I have given unto Jacob my servant, wherein your fathers have dwelt; and they shall dwell therein, even they, and their children, and their children's children for ever: and my servant David shall be their prince for ever (Ezek. 37:23–25).*

---

125   Hurewitz, J. C., *The Middle East and North Africa in World Politics: A Documentary Record—British-French supremacy*, 1914-1945, (Yale University Press, 1979), 106.
126   "1947: The international Community says YES to the establishment of Israel," Accessed on Dec. 13, 2022, mfa.gov.il
127   Genesis 15; Exodus 23; Numbers 34; Ezekiel 47; 1 Kings 8:65; 1 Chronicles 13:5; 2 Chronicles 7:8.

This prophetic passage explains how Israel will ultimately turn from idolatry and unbelief and return to serving the Lord with their whole heart. It also foretells the coming Prince of Peace, the Messiah who will sit and rule upon the throne of his father David. But this passage also mentions a little noticed prophecy: that David would again sit and rule over Israel in their future Millennium. Jesus will be the ruler over all of the world, as King of Kings and Lord of Lords (Rev. 19), but David would be resurrected and rule again over the people of Israel, ruling under his Lord, Jesus Christ, King of the Earth. (This event is explained in detail later in the book.)

The Coming Messiah

In Luke 1:31-32 the angel Gabriel tells Mary that the baby Jesus will be the final Prince to come:

> *And, behold, thou shalt conceive in thy womb, and bring forth a son, and shalt call his name JESUS.*
>
> *He shall be great, and shall be called the Son of the Highest: and the Lord God shall give unto him the throne of his father David.*

Jesus fulfilled this prophecy as the coming Messiah and Jewish Prince and He will one day, bodily and visibly, sit and rule upon the throne of his father David. At this coming Kingdom Age, often referred to as the Millennium (when God rules this world for a thousand years), Jesus will literally be King of Kings and Lord of Lords and he will rule a combined Kingdom of justice and righteousness. The seat of this government will be in Jerusalem, and the people of Israel will forever reside in their Promised Land.

God's Covenant of Peace

Ezekiel 37 concludes:

> *Moreover I will make a covenant of peace with them;*
> *it shall be an everlasting covenant with them:*
> *and I will place them, and multiply them, and will set my*
> *sanctuary in the midst of them for evermore.*

> *My tabernacle also shall be with them:*
> *yea, I will be their God, and they shall be my people.*
>
> *And the heathen shall know that I the Lord do sanctify Israel, when my sanctuary shall be in the midst of them for evermore (Ezek. 37:26-28).*

Ezekiel concludes that Israel will make a covenant of peace in the last days. It is one of the great signs of the Kingdom of God. And yet who makes this covenant of peace with Israel? Is it the Palestinian Liberation Organization? Is it the United States of America or Russia? Is it the Antichrist?

Verse 21 has the answer: "And say unto them, Thus saith the Lord. ..." Yes, only God Himself will ever make a lasting covenant of peace for Israel. The prophet Jeremiah tells us, "They have healed also the hurt of the daughter of my people slightly, saying, Peace, peace; when there is no peace" (Jeremiah 6:14), meaning many people have promised lasting peace to Israel but there was no real peace. Only Jesus of Nazareth, the great Prince of Peace, can institute true peace for Israel. There will only be real peace in the land when God Himself brings that peace and establishes His Kingdom on this Earth.

God's Sanctuary in the Land

Another sign of this coming Kingdom of God is the placement of the sanctuary of God in the land. This means there will be a rebuilding of the House of God, namely the Temple. Not only will there be a rebuilding of the Temple in that day, there also will be the setting up of the Tabernacle. Note the passage in Ezekiel 37, "My tabernacle also shall be with them."

We conclude from this passage of Ezekiel that the Old Testament Tabernacle must be found again and this implies that the original furniture of Moses will be found and utilized inside. However, the climactic comment to this entire passage tells us that the Temple must be rebuilt.

CHAPTER EIGHT

And the heathen shall know that I the Lord do sanctify Israel, when my sanctuary shall be in the midst of them for evermore.

Here, the Lord proclaims that the entire heathen world will know that the Lord revives Israel, God is ruling through Israel, and David is again on the throne, but the ultimate factor is when His Temple is reestablished in Jerusalem.

Peace in the Temple

The Temple built by Zerubbabel was begun with a foundation laid in 538 B.C., restarted in 520 B.C.[128] and completed in Jerusalem in 516 B.C., and yet God mentions another coming future Temple. Here peace is again mentioned in connection with the rebuilding of the coming Temple.

Zechariah 6:12-13 tells us:

> *And speak unto him, saying, Thus speaketh the LORD of hosts, saying, Behold the man whose name is The BRANCH; and he shall grow up out of his place, and he shall build the temple of the LORD:*
>
> *Even he shall build the temple of the LORD; and he shall bear the glory, and shall sit and rule upon his throne; and he shall be a priest upon his throne: and the counsel of peace shall be between them both.*

In this passage of scripture Zechariah tells us of the coming of the Branch. This is one of many titles for the coming Messiah of the Jews, the Anointed of God, to rule over His Kingdom. This passage also tells how Messiah will build the Temple, will sit upon a throne, and be a priest upon his throne. This means that this Kingdom will have Messiah as the King as well as the "priest" or "pastor" (the religious leader) of the world. And this Messiah will establish a counsel of peace between them both. That means that there will be peace between government and religious faith. Everyone worldwide will come to the Temple

---
128 Janet E. Tollington, *Tradition and Innovation in Haggai and Zechariah 1-8* (Sheffield, England: Sheffield Academic Press, 1993), 132.

at Jerusalem to serve the Lord as Savior and King. This will be the only true and lasting peace of the world!

Peace will not come through the work of diplomats or kings. Peace will not come though philosophers or religious leaders. Peace will not come through social welfare programs or international détente. Peace will only come when the world turns to Jesus, the Savior and King of glory! Only God will make an everlasting covenant of peace!

Peace is coming to the Middle East and to the world. It is more than just a dream, more than a fairy tale. It is the future of the universe. There will be "peace on Earth, good will toward men."

CHAPTER NINE
Will the Jewish Temple Be Rebuilt?

There is no doubt that the rebuilding of the Temple of God is a controversial issue today among several groups of people, including the Jews and Arabs. We know that there are a group of Israelis interested in soon rebuilding the Jewish Temple in Jerusalem. The subject is a favorite among students of Bible prophecy, and many people view this action as the climactic event that precedes the very coming of Messiah!

What Does the Bible Say?

Does the Bible teach that there will be a new Jewish Temple rebuilt?

Zechariah 8:9 says,

> *Thus saith the LORD of hosts; Let your hands be strong, ye that hear in these days these words by the mouth of the prophets, which were in the day that the foundation of the house of the LORD of hosts was laid, that the temple might be built.*

Zechariah 1:16 tells us,

> *Therefore thus saith the LORD; I am returned to Jerusalem with mercies: my house shall be built in it, saith the LORD of hosts, and a line shall be stretched forth upon Jerusalem.*

Zechariah 6:12-13 proclaims,

> *And speak unto him, saying, Thus speaketh the LORD of hosts, saying, Behold the man whose name is The BRANCH; and he shall grow up out of his place, and he shall build the temple of the LORD:*
> *Even he shall build the temple of the LORD; and he shall bear the glory, and shall sit and rule upon his throne; and he shall be a priest upon his throne: and the counsel of peace shall be between them both.*

Other Biblical references, such as Daniel 9:26-27 and Ezekiel 43:5-10, detail the circumstances of rebuilding the Temple and Temple activities.

Thus, the evidence from the Bible is conclusive that there will be another Temple built in Jerusalem. The topic is much like the Second Coming of our Lord Jesus. We may not know when the event will happen but there is no doubt from the Bible that each of these things: the Second Coming of Jesus and the rebuilding of the Temple is a sure event that is shortly to come to pass. In fact, often these two occurrences are coupled together and viewed as happening at the same time.

The Second Coming of the LORD

Listen to the words of Jesus:

> *Let not your heart be troubled: Ye believe in God, believe also in me.*
>
> *In my Father's house are many mansions: if it were not so, I would have told you. I go to prepare a place for you.*
>
> *And if I go and prepare a place for you, I will come again, and receive you unto myself; that where I am, there ye may be also (John 14:1-3).*

Here, Jesus has told us that He would go away to heaven, but He also prophesies that "I will come again." That means that Jesus will return one day to this world.

The Liberal Objection

Some liberal Bible interpreters have tried to claim that Jesus will never come back literally. To make such a statement, one of two things must be true:

1. Jesus must not have told us the truth about His Second Coming, or
2. These liberal interpreters must not believe the Word of God.

The Bible is very specific in telling us that God cannot lie: *"In hope of eternal life, which God, that cannot lie, promised before the world began" (Titus 1:2).*

CHAPTER NINE

Jesus was not lying about His Second Coming. He was certainly not capable of lying, for God cannot sin (Hebrews 6:18). Thus, when Jesus referred to His Second Coming, He was telling the literal truth about His future and His return.

When referring to the liberal, Bible-denying interpreters, we must remember these commentators doubt various miracles of the Bible and often doubt the Bible itself! If the Bible is not literally true, then you must trust the interpretations of men. These men would have you believe their words and not believe the Holy Scriptures. Yet, how can you believe the words of men over the Word of the living God? There is no truth but in the Scriptures: "... thy Word is truth." Simply stated, I would rather believe God than men.

Jesus is coming again! Jesus said He was coming back, and the Bible is very clear in stating that Jesus will come again.

The Manner of Jesus' Coming

What about the manner of His coming? How will Jesus come to this Earth again? The Bible gives the believer exacting details.

Several ideas have been introduced by Bible commentators about the possible interpretations and the method of His coming. They are generally reduced to three concepts:

1. ***Jesus is not coming back in any form.*** This view is presented by Albert Schweitzer, represented as believing Jesus was deluded into thinking of Himself as a Messiah who would set up a future Kingdom through His disciples. Because Jesus was frustrated in His concepts, He decided to die, and the cross killed any future hope of a Kingdom of God in future history.[129] This view denies the deity of Jesus Christ as well as belief in the Bible as God's Word; it is a non-Christian view of Jesus.

    In the Supra History theory of Barth-Brummer, eschatology

---

[129] Alva J. McClain, *The Greatness of the Kingdom* (Winona Lake, IN: BHM Books, 1959), 13.

(the doctrine of the last things) does not refer to a chronology of things on Earth, but to eternity only. There is no future of Jesus or the Kingdom on Earth because everything mentioned in Scripture is beyond time, and only in eternity. They irrationally present Scripture to fit whatever they teach. "They have no compunction about rearranging the Biblical material or throwing out portions or regarding its history in part mythical" and "they appear at times to make a virtue out of obscurity and irrationality."[130]

This view denies any logical, historical, and grammatical interpretation of the Bible, but relies on using Bible verses in a "pick-and-choose" fashion to make it say whatever preconceived idea the person is presenting. It uses Eisegesis in interpretation (Reading an interpretation into the text), instead of Exegesis (Gleaning the meaning from the text). Jesus, and all teachers of the Bible in Biblical times, consistently used exegesis in Bible interpretation. Thus, because the Bible said Moses wrote the Pentateuch, then it was taught that Moses wrote the Pentateuch. The Bible was taught using exegesis, interpreting the Bible in a normal, logical, consistent way following normal historical/grammatical considerations in its context.

2. **Jesus is not coming back literally.** The passages about the Second Coming are to be interpreted allegorically. Thus, the "spirit" of Jesus is coming to this world through a liberal Christian social order and this "spirit" will usher in the Kingdom of Peace. In this world in which we currently live, we do not see this mystical "spirit" of Jesus (a "spirit" of love) moving across this world. The proponents of this theory of promoting a Christian social order generally see the world growing into a state of non-violence, sinlessness, and an ultimate utopian society through peaceful influence. They would see all forms of a social Kingdom,

---
[130] Alva J. McClain, *The Greatness of the Kingdom*, Ibid., 15

even those promoted by a non-Christian religion such as the degraded religion of India practiced by Gandhi pointing to one way of peace, or by aggressive, warring communism promoted by Russia and China as another way of peace, each serving as another part of the advancement of this "Christian Socialism" bringing about "social reconstruction."[131] Nations worldwide would all lay down their weapons, and evil in all forms would be nonexistent as the entire world fell into a unified state of love!

It is quite obvious that the world is not growing into an ultimate utopian society. More wars have been fought since the Great War of World War I and the following World War II than any other time in history. There are more crimes, racial violence, murders, diseases, famines, and atrocities against society today than at any other time. No, the world is not getting better; it is sliding headfirst into the pits of Hell, racing with breakneck speed for Armageddon!

What about the allegorical interpretations? The Bible has made several unusual prophecies that seem miraculous to even conceive. Yet, again and again, the trustworthiness of the Bible has been vindicated. Just a few recently fulfilled prophecies include:

1. The regathering of the nation of Israel.
2. The repossession of the land of Palestine.
3. The desert vegetation blossoming like a rose.
4. The preservation of the Jewish people and their culture.
5. The reintroduction of the dead language of Hebrew.
6. The consistent military rise of Israel.
7. The miraculous deliverance of Israel from enemies.
8. The gradual and continued returning to the faith of Jehovah.

---

[131] Alva J. McClain, *The Greatness of the Kingdom*, Ibid., 11.

All these prophecies require a literal fulfillment, and all have been fulfilled. Why would we doubt the literal fulfillment of further prophecies? God's Word is true, and it will always come to pass, literally and finally.

3. **Jesus is coming back, bodily and visibly, to this world.** The passages of Scripture are to be interpreted literally and will result in a future Kingdom when God Himself reigns in this world. The debate then ensues as to which passages are literal, and how to interpret them.

To find the manner of Christ's coming, let us consult the Word of God.

In the first chapter of Acts, Jesus has gathered with His early church on the hillside of the Mount of Olives. He had finished His ministry on Earth, providing redemption for all men, and He now was delivering His last sermon. Jesus gave the early church the Great Commission, sending Christians to spread the gospel to every living creature around the world. Then He ascended back to heaven.

Acts 1:9-11 gives us the scenario:

And when he had spoken these things, while they beheld, he was taken up; and a cloud received him out of their sight.

And while they looked stedfastly toward heaven as he went up, behold, two men stood by them in white apparel;

Which also said, Ye men of Galilee, why stand ye gazing up into heaven? this same Jesus, which is taken up from you into heaven, shall so come in like manner as ye have seen him go into heaven.

How is Jesus to return to this Earth? The Bible specifies that this "same Jesus," not another Jesus or someone like Jesus (not another Messiah), but "this same Jesus, which is taken up from you into heaven, shall so come. ..."

CHAPTER NINE

The alternate possibility of another messiah such as Rabbi Schneerson, David Koresh, Sun Young Moon (who is not even Jewish), or another messiah of history, such as Bar Kokhba, is smashed by the literal interpretation of the Bible. Only Jesus of Nazareth resurrected in a glorified body can be "this same Jesus."

What is the manner of His coming? Acts 1:11 tells us, "This same Jesus ... shall so come in like manner as ye have seen him go into heaven." Jesus is coming back in the same way that He left. In His ascension to heaven, Jesus stood on the Mount of Olives and stepped on a cloud, and the cloud received Him out of their sight. One day, Jesus is coming again to this Mount of Olives, and He is coming in the clouds (Zech. 14:4).

For the Lord himself shall descend from heaven with a shout, with the voice of the archangel, and with the trump of God: and the dead in Christ shall rise first:

Then we which are alive and remain shall be caught up together with them in the clouds, to meet the Lord in the air: and so shall we ever be with the Lord (1 Thess. 4:16-17).

Behold, he cometh with clouds; and every eye shall see him, and they also which pierced him: and all kindreds of the earth shall wail because of him. Even so, Amen (Rev. 1:7).

Jesus left in the clouds and He is coming back in the clouds, both in the Rapture and at Armageddon. He is coming back literally, bodily and visibly, to rule this world as King of Kings and Lord of Lords and He will rule literally from Jerusalem sitting upon the throne of His father David.[132]

We know that Jesus is coming back again. We know how Jesus is coming back and we even know where His return will be. The only thing we do not know is when it will happen. So, it is with the rebuilding of the Temple. We know the Temple will

---
[132] Walvoord, John F., *The Rapture Question* (Grand Rapids, MI: Academic Books of Zondervan Publishers, 1979)

be rebuilt, we know how it will function, and we even know future events to occur inside. The only thing we do not know is when it will be rebuilt.

When Will the Temple Be Rebuilt?

Many Bible scholars believe that the Temple will be rebuilt before the Rapture of the saints. Other Bible researchers believe that the Jewish Temple may be built after the Rapture, but by the middle of the Tribulation Period. With our modern technology, we know that men can build enormous skyscraper towers in just six months. So, it is conceivable that the Temple could be erected very quickly, once all obstacles were removed. The Bible tells us that the Antichrist will enter the Temple in the middle of the seven-year Tribulation Period, so the Temple must be rebuilt by that time.[133] When looking at its soon rebuilding, several clues are coming to light.

There is a debate among the Orthodox Jews about the actual timing and process of rebuilding the Temple. Some Jews believe that when Messiah comes that He will bring the Temple with Him from heaven and establish His Kingdom on Earth. Other Jews believe that the Temple must be rebuilt, and when all the house of Israel returns to the Lord with their whole heart, then Messiah will come to take possession of His Kingdom. These Jews perceive the rebuilding of the Temple as the establishment of the Messianic Kingdom and its rebuilding as a precursor to His return. Yet, which view is correct according to the Bible? Must the Temple be rebuilt for Messiah to return, or will He return and bring the Temple with Him? The amazing thing is that both views are correct because the Bible teaches that there must be two future Temples built in Jerusalem!

The Bible is very clear that in the last days, in a time period called the Tribulation Period, the Antichrist will enter the Temple to desecrate and destroy it.

---
133 Matthew 24:15

CHAPTER NINE

The Seventieth Week of Daniel

This time period is called the Tribulation Period or the Time of Jacob's Trouble because of the distress, persecution, and judgment upon Israel and the entire world. In Daniel, this period is named the "Seventieth Week" and is described as the culminating time of the end of the world.

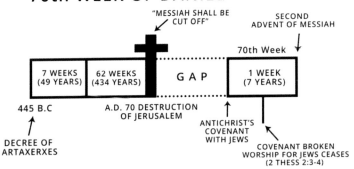

Ill. 16, The Seventy Weeks of Daniel Chart. 70th Week of Daniel Studyandobey.com

Daniel was given a prophecy about the end of the world where he divided the time periods into seventy weeks, each week standing for a period of seven years (Dan. 9:24). It is usually believed that Daniel described each of these years as three hundred sixty days long, using lunar years rather than solar years.[134] This is concluded by comparing the years in Revelation 11:3 where the three and one-half year Great Tribulation is given as twelve hundred and sixty days (three and one-half years times three hundred sixty days per year).

Daniel had told us that there would be sixty-nine weeks, or four hundred eighty-three years. But after these sixty-nine weeks that the Messiah would be "cut off" for a time, signifying a pause in time. After this pause in time, sometime in the future the "Seventieth Week" would commence and the Antichrist will desecrate the Temple. This is during the last week of seven years called the Tribulation Period.

---

134   Combs, James O. *Mysteries in the Book of Daniel* (Springfield, MO: Tribune Publishers, 1996).

And after threescore and two weeks shall Messiah be cut off, but not for himself: and the people of the prince that shall come shall destroy the city and the sanctuary; and the end thereof shall be with a flood, and unto the end of the war desolations are determined.

And he shall confirm the covenant with many for one week: and in the midst of the week he shall cause the sacrifice and the oblation to cease, and for the overspreading of abominations he shall make it desolate, even until the consummation, and that determined shall be poured upon the desolate (Dan. 9:26-27).

In this passage of Scripture, Messiah is "cut off," speaking of his first coming. Then later the Antichrist comes to power and destroys the city of Jerusalem and the Temple, committing an "abomination of desolation." Verse 27 explains in further detail that Antichrist will make a covenant of peace with Israel. Yet, in the midst of that "week" (three and one-half years into the seven-year period) that Antichrist will break that peace covenant. This is the time that he enters the Temple to desecrate and destroy it. The prophet Daniel is quite precise in foretelling this future "seventy weeks." Given 490 sets of 360-day years, Daniel tells us to the day how long it would be before Messiah comes! Using this calculation, the first sixty-nine years of weeks is 483 sets of 360-day years which would be 173,880 days.[135] This leaves the seventieth week to be future.

The original day that this prophesy would commence was given in Nehemiah 2:1 where Artaxerxes gives permission to Nehemiah to rebuild the Jewish capital. This decree was given "in the month of Nisan, in the twentieth year of Artaxerxes," a time marking the first day of a New Year. This would correspond to our modern time of March 14, 445 B.C. The first "seven weeks" was completed when Israel finished

---

[135] Countryside Baptist Church, Lake Mary, FL, Daniel's Seventy Weeks – Daniel 9:20-27, Accessed on Dec. 13, 2022, countrysidebaptist.com

CHAPTER NINE

rebuilding the city of Jerusalem in 396 B.C.[136]

The next "sixty-two weeks" then began and continued until "Messiah was cut off, but not for himself." Messiah was cut off or denied by Israel during the beginning of His Passion Week. Jesus was formally presented to Israel as King at His triumphal entry in Jerusalem. Great masses had gathered to greet Jesus as He entered the city, shouting, "Hosanna: Blessed is the King of Israel that cometh in the name of the Lord." However, this is the same time that the religious leaders began the plot of betrayal with traitorous Judas Iscariot. This day was April 6, A.D. 32, exactly 173,880 days after March 14, 445 B.C. Thus, the Word of God was fulfilled to the exact day![137]

David Reagan gives an alternate view using solar/lunar years as in the Jewish calendar, of the beginning of the seventy years starting at the decree given to Ezra by Artaxerxes in 457 B.C. (Ezra 7:11-26), a decree to rebuild the city, appoint judges and magistrates, and to teach the law. This leads to the first forty-nine years ending in 408 B.C., when Nehemiah completed his own work on the city, and the 483 years ending in A.D. 27, the last Jewish jubilee spent in Israel, when Jesus read about the Messiah fulfilling the essence of the Jubilee by reading Isaiah 61 in Luke 4:21, as He was beginning His ministry. After His three and a half-year ministry, this would place the crucifixion in the spring of A.D. 31, when Passover fell on Wednesday. Jesus was crucified that morning and buried that evening. The next day was a High Sabbath. On Friday after the High Sabbath, the women bought the spices and then rested on the regular Sabbath (Saturday) before going to the tomb on Sunday morning.[138]

We have seen how that the first "sixty-nine weeks" have transpired and that the Messiah was "cut off" at the end of

---
136 Sir Robert Anderson, *The Coming Prince* (London: Hodder and Stroughton, 1909), 121–123.
137 David Jeremiah, Decoding Daniel's Seventy-Weeks Prophecy, Accessed on December 9, 2022, https://davidjeremiah.blog
138 David R. Reagan (July 7, 2014), Daniel's 70 Weeks of Years, Accessed on January 31, 2023, https://raptureready.com

this time. We also have mentioned a pause in the prophecy of an unspecified length. This pause has continued for about two thousand years, but the prophecy will resume when Antichrist comes to power, marking the beginning of the "seventieth week." At the middle of this period, the Scriptures teach that Antichrist will defile the Temple. The Bible tells us a great detail about the desecration of the Temple by Antichrist.

The Temple Is Desecrated

In Daniel, we have seen that the Antichrist breaks his peace covenant with Israel and commits the "abomination of desolation," followed by the destruction of the city and sanctuary.

Second Thessalonians 2:3-4 tells us:

> *... That man of sin be revealed, the son of perdition;*
>
> *Who opposeth and exalteth himself above all that is called God, or that is worshipped; so that he as God sitteth in the temple of God, shewing himself that he is God.*

The Apostle Paul has told us that this Antichrist will enter the Temple and claim that he is God. He will set up his own image (or idolatrous statue) in the Temple and seat himself there as "God" reigning in the midst of the Tribulation, commanding all people to worship him.[139]

Matthew 24:15-22 expounds:

> *When ye therefore shall see the abomination of desolation, spoken of by Daniel the prophet, stand in the holy place, (whoso readeth, let him understand:)*
>
> *Then let them which be in Judea flee into the mountains:*
>
> *Let him which is on the housetop not come down to take any thing out of his house:*
>
> *Neither let him which is in the field return back to take his clothes. And woe unto them that are with child, and to them that give suck in those days!*

---

139 Revelation 13

CHAPTER NINE

> *But pray ye that your flight be not in the winter, neither on the sabbath day:*
> *For then shall be great tribulation, such as was not since the beginning of the world to this time, no, nor ever shall be.*
> *And except those days should be shortened, there should no flesh be saved: but for the elect's sake those days shall be shortened.*

Jesus told His followers that the abomination of desolation is a sign to the Jews. When this abomination is seen in the holy place, then all Israel will flee into the mountains. There will not be time to return to home or to work for any forgotten articles. The time will be difficult to those people with small children, and especially difficult if it falls in the winter or on the Sabbath day, because observant Jews are only allowed to travel a short distance on the Sabbath. This judgment of God, called the Great Tribulation, will be so severe that if God in mercy did not shorten these times, no person in the world would be left alive!

The entire seventieth week of Daniel is called the Tribulation Period, but because of the intense persecution of the Jewish people, and because of the intensified wrath of God on the Earth, this second half of the week is called the Great Tribulation.

Many scholars believe that the abomination of desolation is a time when the Antichrist will desecrate the Temple with the profane sacrifice of a sow (a female pig, considered an unclean animal).[140] He will thrust the Ark of the Covenant out of the Temple and put his own image in its place and set up his throne in the Holy Place, bidding all men to worship him. At this time, the Jews will realize that this is not their Christ (their Jewish Messiah) but is "Anti-Christ" because he is "Anti-God." Having rendered ultimate insult upon the Jewish people and undergoing their repulsion, he then orders the

---
140 Lust, Johan, "Cult and Sacrifice in Daniel: The Talmud and the Abomination of Desolation." in Collins, John Joseph; Flint, Peter W. (eds.), *The Book of Daniel: Composition and Reception, Vol. 2* (BRILL, 2001), 682.

execution of the Jewish people. Already, John the Revelator has told us of Antichrist's intense persecution of the true Christian believers who refuse to follow him.[141] Now, the Jews endure that same brutal injustice. The Bible says that they will flee into the mountains.[142]

The Jews Flee to Petra

It has long been believed that the Jews will flee to the lost desert city of Petra, also called Bozrah, in the Bible. In this mountainous region of Jordan, the sandstone city is accessible only by traversing a long, steep, narrow canyon by horseback or jeep. The canyon is so narrow that in some places a Jeep can barely pass and the top of the canyon walls often press together.

This is the lost city of the Edomites (the Idumeans), a red-rose city half as old as the sands of time.[143] Esau, the brother of Jacob and son of Isaac, founded this city centuries ago. Jacob was later renamed Israel by the Lord and was the father of the twelve tribes of Israel. His brother Esau also had many sons and founded the civilization of the Edomites. This is the city that refused passage to Moses and the children of Israel during their journey from Egypt.

Later, Paul spent three years here after his salvation and baptism to be taught by the Lord (Gal. 1:17-18). The Bible mentions that Paul stayed in Arabia and this region was commonly known as Arabia Petrea, and so it is logical that Paul would have stayed in its principal city of Petra.

This was the capital city of King Aretas, who is mentioned by Paul in 2 Corinthians 11:32. Aretas IV Philopatris was the king of the Nabataeans from about 9 B.C. to A.D. 40. His daughter, Phasaelis, was married and divorced from Herod Antipas.

---

141 Revelation 6:9-11
142 Matthew 24:16
143 About Petra – Visit Petra, Accessed on December 9, 2022, https://visitpetra.jo

CHAPTER NINE

Color Image 19, The Treasury of Petra, Jordan. Al_Khazneh_Petra.jpg en.m.wikipedia.org

Herod then married his stepbrother's wife, Herodias. It was opposition to this marriage that led to the beheading of John the Baptist. The ornate multistory carving called the Treasury (Arabic, "Al-Khazneh"), the first view you encounter when entering the city, is believed to be Aretas IV's mausoleum. The name "Treasury" comes from the assumption of the Arabs that the top center carving of a vase must contain hidden treasure. Because it is almost impossible to climb, the Arabs used the center vase for rifle target practice for years, as they did much of the façade, marring the pristine nature of the city when first discovered.

At Petra is found huge ruins, underground dwellings, and tombs large enough to house at least one hundred thousand people in its twenty square miles. This will be the ruined city to which the remnant of Jews flees to escape the wrath of the Antichrist.

The Battle of Armageddon

At the end of this terrible Great Tribulation, the Antichrist will try the most desperate and blasphemous of all acts. He will gather the great armies of the world together at the Valley of Megiddo, called Armageddon, to kill the Jewish people and to fight against God Himself.

Antichrist will be planning to first attack the Jews in Jerusalem, and then wipe out the remaining Jews in Petra. As he is preparing his armies for attack, an earthquake occurs and divides Jerusalem into three parts. Since Antichrist cannot get to the Jews because of the separated city of Jerusalem, he turns his armies to go to kill the Jews who are hiding at Petra. At that stupendous moment of the attack, Jesus appears to fight in the famous Battle of Armageddon.

This is the King of Glory, the strong Victor, mighty in battle is He! Several events happen at this decisive moment in history. There are actually several battles, so these events can be more accurately referred to as the Campaign of Armageddon.

The setting is described for us in the nineteenth chapter of Revelation.

> *And I saw heaven opened, and behold a white horse; and he that sat upon him was called Faithful and True, and in righteousness he doth judge and make war.*
>
> *His eyes were as a flame of fire, and on his head were many*

> *crowns; and he had a name written, that no man knew, but he himself.*
>
> *And he was clothed with a vesture dipped in blood: and his name is called The Word of God.*
>
> *And the armies which were in heaven followed him upon white horses, clothed in fine linen, white and clean.*
>
> *And out of his mouth goeth a sharp sword, that with it he should smite the nations: and he shall rule them with a rod of iron: and he treadeth the winepress of the fierceness and wrath of Almighty God.*
>
> *And he hath on his vesture and on his thigh a name written, KING OF KINGS, AND LORD OF LORDS (Rev. 19:11-16).*

Jesus will descend from heaven with ten thousand of his saints to fight against this great demagogue and his armies. The Antichrist will have the audacity to fight against God, and the Lord will soundly defeat him. As the armies in the vast Valley of Megiddo raise their weapons to fight against God, Jesus just speaks the Word and overcomes them.

Color Image 20, The Jezreel Valley of Megiddo, Israel. precipice-jezreel-valley.jpg travelujah.com Public Domain

All the saints will be with Jesus descending from heaven to watch the great array. These saints are not coming down to fight in the conflict. King Jesus does not need our help. He, alone, will fight in the battle against Satan's forces. We are coming with Jesus to witness the vast array of the battle.

Jesus will speak His Word and slay the armies of this world. This spoken Word will be like a sharp, two-edged sword, literally cutting the bodies of the soldiers in half. That is why the Bible describes the blood of the slain being so deep that it rises to the height of the horse's bridal because of the utter destruction of these armies.

Before Jesus will descend to Jerusalem, first He will destroy Antichrist's government at political Babylon, and then destroy the armies in the Valley of Megiddo at the Battle of Armageddon. The Jews will have fled from the Antichrist, but he has assembled a vast army to finally annihilate the Jewish people. A great earthquake has divided Jerusalem into three parts, and Antichrist cannot get to the Jews in the city.[144] So, he turns to kill the Jews in hiding at Petra. As he goes to Petra, the land of the Edomites, to where God's chosen people will be in hiding, the Jewish people realize that all hope of rescue is lost. This is the end of their existence. Then is the fulfillment of Romans 11:26-27 where all Israel is saved in one day.[145]

The people of Israel will see Jesus appear in the clouds arrayed in the shekinah glory of God and they will realize individually and as a nation that this is Jesus of Nazareth coming back. There has always been a believing remnant of Jews who believed in Jesus as Savior. Now, all of the unbelieving Jews who have a hardened heart will experience a sudden loss of this hardness as it melts away. They "shall look upon me whom they have pierced (a reference to Jesus' crucifixion) and they

---

144   Zechariah 13:8
145   Isaiah 66:8

shall mourn."[146] They will mourn because they will realize that they also were involved as a people, just as the Romans and all the unbelieving world, in the crucifixion of their Savior. Then, they will repent and believe and be spiritually saved from sin and given eternal life. Israel will return to Jehovah and believe in Jesus as their Savior at this moment in time. This is the meaning of Matthew 23:39, "For I say unto you, Ye shall not see me henceforth, till ye shall say, Blessed is he that cometh in the name of the Lord." The unbelieving nation will not see or return unto the Lord until they see Him coming in glory to save them as a nation, and then they will believe in Jesus as a nation.

Jesus will go there to rescue them from the armies of the Antichrist and bring them into their own land in Israel. Jesus loves the Jewish people and he will not let them be extinguished as a nation. Isaiah 63:1-4 gives us a picture of the victorious Savior returning from Petra (the city of Bozrah in the land of Edom), still wearing His battle raiment stained with the blood of His enemies.

Behold, the Word of the Lord:

> *Who is this that cometh from Edom, With dyed garments from Bozrah? This that is glorious in his apparel, Travelling in the greatness of his strength? I that speak in righteousness, mighty to save.*
>
> *Wherefore art thou red in thine apparel, And thy garments like him that treadeth in the winefat?*
>
> *I have trodden the winepress alone; And of the people there was none with me: For I will tread them in mine anger, And trample them in my fury; And their blood shall be sprinkled upon my garments, And I will stain all my raiment.*
>
> *For the day of vengeance is in mine heart, And the year of my redeemed is come.*

---

146   Zechariah 12:10

Jesus Descends to Earth

Zechariah 14:2-3 tells us about the Battle of Armageddon. In this passage, he tells of His coming to fight in Jerusalem, and to rescue the Jews who have been cut off by an earthquake. The Antichrist had gathered his vast army in the Valley of Armageddon and has attacked the city and attempted to take the city of Jerusalem, to ravage the women and to kill the people, but an earthquake has divided the city and he cannot get to the Jews. Jesus next comes to fight the Antichrist and his forces and to rescue the Jewish people.

> *For I will gather all nations against Jerusalem to battle; And the city shall be taken, and the houses rifled, and the women ravished; And half of the city shall go forth into captivity, And the residue of the people shall not be cut off from the city.*
>
> *Then shall the LORD go forth, and fight against those nations, As when he fought in the day of battle.*

Then God continues His description in Zechariah 14:4-5. Here, he describes the earthquake that will divide the mountain and that results of Christ's coming.

> *And his feet shall stand in that day upon the mount of Olives, Which is before Jerusalem on the east, And the mount of Olives shall cleave in the midst thereof toward the east and toward the west, And there shall be a very great valley; And half of the mountain shall remove toward the north, And half of it toward the south.*
>
> *And ye shall flee to the valley of the mountains; For the valley of the mountains shall reach unto Azal: Yea, ye shall flee, like a ye fled from before the earthquake in the days of Uzziah king of Judah: and the LORD my God shall come, And all the saints with thee.*

This great mountain will divide in half as He descends to Earth. Jesus will then descend to the Mount of Olives in

Jerusalem. He will cross over the Kidron Valley and ascend Mount Moriah, entering through the Eastern Gate, which opened as a result of an earthquake that split the Olivet Mount. There He will set up His millennial reign and usher in the Kingdom Age. From this mount, the entire world will come to worship Jesus as Savior and Lord.

Christ Will Establish His Throne

Jesus will redeem His beloved Israel and claim Jerusalem as the seat of His throne. He will repossess the land and establish His eternal reign. This will accomplish the final fulfillment of the prophecy of Jesus in Luke 1:32-33, given to the virgin Mary.

> *He shall be great, and shall be called the Son of the Highest: and the LORD God shall give unto him the throne of his father David:*
>
> *And he shall reign over the house of Jacob for ever;*
> *and of his kingdom there shall be no end.*

For centuries the Jews have known that they would one day repossess the land, live in peace and prosperity, and God Himself would be their Priest and King. The Bible is full of prophecies about the coming Kingdom of God on this Earth. King David prophesied about this coming Kingdom in Psalm 24. The entrance of Messiah into Jerusalem as he enters through the Eastern Gate to inaugurate his Kingdom is given in one of the most beautiful sonnets of poetry ever penned.

> *The earth is the LORD's and the fulness thereof;*
> *The world, and they that dwell therein.*
>
> *For he hath founded it upon the seas,*
> *And established it upon the floods.*
>
> *Who shall ascend into the hill of the LORD?*
> *Or who shall stand in his holy place?*
>
> *He that hath clean hands, and a pure heart;*

Who hath not lifted up his soul unto vanity,
Nor sworn deceitfully.

He shall receive the blessing from the LORD,
And righteousness from the God of his salvation.

This is the generation of them that seek him,
That seek thy face, O Jacob. Selah.

Lift up your heads, O ye gates;
And be ye lift up, ye everlasting doors;
And the King of glory shall come in.

Who is this King of glory? The LORD strong and mighty,
The LORD mighty in battle.

Lift up your heads, O ye gates; even lift them up,
    ye everlasting doors;
And the King of glory shall come in.

Who is this King of glory?
The LORD of hosts, he is the King of glory.
Selah.

CHAPTER TEN

Temple Preparations Today

One of the most interesting and politically explosive issues today is the rebuilding of the Jewish Temple. Today, in Jerusalem, Israel, there are two Jewish groups, the Temple Institute and the Temple Mount Faithful, as well as many other interested parties which are actively pursuing the prospect of rebuilding the Jewish Temple.

Jewish Priesthood Schools

Two different religious schools, the Ateret Cohanim, a yeshiva for the education and training of Temple priests,[147] and the Institute for Talmudic Commentaries, an organization for research into the Temple and priesthood under the auspices of the Young Israeli Synagogue, are involved in training for the Temple priesthood.

These schools provide extensive research and training on the Biblical, Talmudic and Midrashic laws of the office of the priesthood, a genealogy of qualified priests, training on proper cutting and burning of the sacrifices and their accompanying rituals and liturgies, and specifications on rebuilding the Temple, Temple vessels, and instruments of music.

While traveling in Israel, I visited the site of both "priesthood" schools, and saw vessels and clothing reproduced for the Temple in the Temple Institute Museum. Many of the articles and requirements for rebuilding the Temple are already in place at this very moment!

David Aaron was my tour guide on my first visit to Israel in 1985. He was a student at one of these priesthood schools, learning the exact manner of cutting the sacrifices and how to fulfill other duties of the priesthood.

---

[147] "Returning, Reclaiming, and Rebuilding a United Jerusalem," Accessed on December 9, 2022, ateretcohanim.org

While on my 1992 preaching tour of the Holy Land, I was thrilled to visit the Temple Institute Museum which displays many articles already prepared for Temple worship. These Levitical Jews have already replicated with exacting detail the garments of the priests, the high priest's golden crown, many instruments of worship, and various utensils and pieces of furniture for the Temple.[148] These articles include the seven-branched candlestick (the Menorah), the silver trumpets, the vessel for ashes (the Mizrak), and the incense chalice.

Color Image 21, The articles of the Temple Institute. Temple Institute Postcard templeinstitute.org

The Jews are very careful to reproduce or manufacture these articles to Levitical law, even matching the precise weave of the linen for the priestly garments. They have also discovered the very source of the color of purple for the garments, and have found that the ancient Jews used a worm that, when crushed, produced the desired color needed.

The Orthodox Jews have researched the manner in which the early Jews made the metal objects for use in the Temple, and how each item of the Tabernacle, and later, the Temple was constructed. These faithful people have researched the manner of crafting the Old Testament harps and trumpets and they are meticulously and beautifully created.

---

148   The Temple Institute, Accessed on Dec. 9, 2022, temple.org

CHAPTER TEN

Playing the Temple Instruments

While visiting Israel for the fourth time, I toured the Harrari harp factory, accompanied by a U.S. Embassy official.[149] While there, I played each of two different types of harps made for Temple worship as well as a thirty-six-inch long solid silver trumpet and a smaller trumpet.

The harps were beautifully fashioned and possessed a thrilling tone. One triangular harp was similar to our modern folk harp and sounded much like music of the Western Hemisphere because it utilized a major scale.

The other lyre-shaped ten-string harp sounded oriental because it used an oriental set of notes on the scale. The Temple trumpet was a long straight trumpet with a flared bell made of solid silver.

Color Image 22, A harp from the Harrari harp factory of Israel. Harrari harps and trumpets harrariharps.com

---

149 King David Harps, Harrari Harps Jerusalem, Accessed on Dec. 9, 2022, harrariharps.com

Although visually stirring, the horn was difficult to play and did not sound as rich and refined as our modern trumpet, being fashioned in an ancient manner. The smaller trumpet was also very impressive, but retained the sound of a trumpet of antiquity. Later, I found that very few Westerners had ever been allowed to play certain of these instruments.

Laying the Temple Foundation Stone

The Temple Mount Faithful have already quarried the foundation stone for the rebuilding of the Temple. These Jews are very serious about their goals of rebuilding the Temple and renewing sacrificial worship in Jerusalem.

On October 8, 1990, they attempted to lay the foundation stone for the Temple on the Temple Mount.[150] After quarrying the stone with ancient tools, they brought the huge stone to the Western "Wailing" Wall of Jerusalem.

With much pomp and ceremony, a large crowd of Jews, led by the Temple Mount Faithful, ascended the ramp in the Tyropoeon Valley that leads to the top of the Temple Mount. It was their intention to march onto the Temple Mount to lay the foundation stone for the literal rebuilding of the Jewish Temple, to try to begin the process for a new Temple.

The Jerusalem police had already been notified of the explosive situation and were on hand to oversee the ceremony but had already informed the Jewish group that they would not be allowed on the Temple Mount itself. So this began as a peaceful demonstration where the Jews would not be able to ascend the Temple Mount but only reenact ceremonies and make their intentions known. In this unusual land, the sacred seat of Islam, Judaism, and Christianity, the local authorities often make concessions to try to appease one faith without trying to oppress another religion.

---

150 Inbari, Motti. *Jewish fundamentalism and the Temple Mount: Who will build the Third Temple?* (SUNY Press), 79-80.

CHAPTER TEN

However, the Muslim Arabs were very fearful of the situation and distrustful of the government. This was the second annual demonstration by the Temple Mount Faithful, and the Arabs had already prepared a retaliation. Almost immediately, the Arabs rushed to the western side of the Temple Mount and began to throw stones on the Jews praying below at their holy "Wailing Wall."

Often these stones were portrayed in the media as being very small rocks, but many of these stones were, in fact, large boulders that were hurled onto the Jews praying several stories below. There are no natural boulders on the smooth surface of the Temple Mount; the Arabs brought them to attack the Jews. At the same time, the Arabs went to their loudspeakers that call them to prayer and started broadcasting, "Kill all of the Jews! Kill all of the Jews!"[151]

Reports tell that several hundred Arabs stormed the Temple Mount in riot and protest of the Jewish ceremony. (One report said that several thousand Arabs were involved in the rioting.) Whatever the actual number, there was a very large group of Arabs present. The small band of police on the Temple Mount was immediately overrun, barely escaping with their lives, and were holed up in a small building on the Temple Mount itself. Below, large groups of police and military were called in to quell the disturbance.[152]

These military personnel followed standard procedure in disbursing a riot by first issuing threats. When these went unheeded, they followed by shooting tear gas into the crowd, then shooting over the heads of the crowd. Unsuccessful with that, they next fired rubber bullets at the mob.

After that action failed to quiet the crowd, the military finally resorted to using live ammunition. As the riot cleared, many

---
151   "1990 Temple Mount riots," Accessed on January 23, 2023, military-history.fandom.com
152   "The Middle East; 19 Arabs Killed in Battle with Jerusalem Police," NYT, Oct. 9, 1990. Accessed on Dec. 9, 2022, nytimes.com

Jews and Arabs lay injured and seventeen Arabs had been slain.

This sad commentary is given to portray the great extremes the Jews are willing to endure and the determination they possess to rebuild their Temple at all costs. It is quite clear that certain Orthodox Jews are willing to fight and to endure bloodshed to accomplish the rebuilding, and that the Arabs are equally as determined that the Mount not be disturbed.

In the mind of many Jews in Israel today, it is very close to the time that the Messiah will return and the Jewish Temple will be rebuilt and they are actively preparing for the rebuilding in every detail.

Finding the Holy of Holies

Recent digging from an underground extension of the Western "Wailing" Wall has uncovered a tunnel that many people believe leads to the Holy of Holies on the Temple Mount. On the western side of the Temple Mount, at the corner of the Wailing Wall, inside of Robinson's Arch, the Jews have been opening a passageway to the extreme end of the Western Wall.

Inside the Rabbinical tunnel they have recently rediscovered an archway first discovered by the British explorer Charles Warren. The Gate Bab Al-Mat'hara, renamed Warren's Gate, is an underground passage leading directly on the Temple Mount to where the Temple itself once stood. This is probably an earlier entrance to the Temple, used by the priests of Herod's time. With further exploration, this would establish the exact location of the past Jewish temples and would give the precise location for the placement of a future Temple.

Why Rebuild the Temple?

One question that might come to mind is, "If Jewish worship has continued for two thousand years, why do the Jews need to rebuild the Temple?"

CHAPTER TEN

There are three reasons:

1. The Temple Mount has always been the most sacred place of Jewish worship in the world, and since its destruction, Orthodox Jews have always prayed to one day rebuild it.

2. Many Orthodox Jews see rebuilding the Temple as the concluding requirement for the coming of Messiah and the establishment of the Kingdom Age with His triumphal reign in Israel.

3. The Temple was actually built as the "House of God," and the Shekinah-glory cloud (God manifest in a beautiful cloud) there resided. Thus, to rebuild the Temple would bring God back in a literal, physical form in their midst.

The Jews have rabbinical commands for rebuilding the Temple. Listed in the Hilchos Bais HaBechirah (the Laws of God's Chosen House) of the Mishnah Torah are specific commands about the rebuilding:

1. They are to build a sanctuary.
2. They are to build an altar with stone that is not hewn.
3. They are not to ascend to the altar on steps but on a ramp.
4. They must fear and reverence the Temple.
5. They must guard the Temple completely.
6. They must never cease watching over the Temple.

The Jews have prayed for centuries to rebuild; to pray on this Mount has been their heartfelt cry. As soon as the Temple Mount was recaptured in Jerusalem, the Jews started expressing a desire to pray on this holy site once again.

Even during the recapture in the War of 1967, the Jewish

general Shlomo Goren, later Chief Rabbi of Israel, measured the Temple Mount to determine the exact location of the earlier Temple. These measurements define the area to rebuild another Temple by telling them specifically where the past Temples stood. By comparing these measurements with archaeological details, they can determine with exacting precision the location of the Temple, its altar, and its respective buildings.

A Peaceful Goal

The Orthodox Jews want to accomplish their goals by peaceful means. There is no sympathy or cooperation with terrorists or individuals for any violent action. They are establishing organizations to accomplish these directives in a quiet, orderly fashion.

An early Temple organization, the Society of Faithful Men, has worked to enable the Jews to soon rebuild the Temple. Established in 1979, this group has pursued many different avenues to develop and coordinate the organizational structure to soon rebuild.

Guardians of the Sanctuary

On October 14, 1983, this Orthodox group announced the institution of the Shmirat Hamikdash (Guardians of the Sanctuary), a new world international organization designed to organize and oversee a computerized compilation of all qualified priests. This group has researched the genealogies of each Levitical family to establish the priest's qualifications and listed the Levites and Cohanim who can serve in Temple functions. They have found a certain genome in DNA which identifies someone as a part of the Jewish priestly family, or Cohanim. They have advertised to gain Jewish involvement worldwide and have stored the names of those Jews who are qualified and willing to serve.

This organization is also involved in maintaining the sanctity of the Temple Mount, and they work to ensure that no Jew enters the Temple Mount. Although some rabbinical leaders claim to know the exact location of the Holy of Holies from the earlier Temple, the Jews are restricted from entering by rabbinate order to not desecrate the Temple Mount by inadvertently stepping on the Holy of Holies.

The goals of this society are as follows:
1. To publish and distribute literature.
2. To hasten the establishment of the Temple.
3. To call for an annual conference for all the priesthood, the Levites and Cohanim.
4. To set up branches worldwide to help collate information and verify the identity of the priesthood.
5. To build a center in Jerusalem for the priesthood. Mikva'ot (ceremonial cleansing baths by immersion) will be provided.

Many Rebuilding Developments

Many new books and articles are being written by Rabbinical leaders regarding the placement and specifications of the Temple and the requirements of the priesthood.

There is an interesting argument continuing today on the placement of the Temple proper. Archaeological digs have been transpiring for several years in the Rabbinical tunnel inside of Robinson's Arch to find the location of the respective Temple buildings.

Any archaeological evidence uncovered on the Temple Mount is always observed and pursued. However, the Arabs do not want any excavations or research done on the Temple Mount and promptly cover over any discovered evidence.

There have been many third Temple models and pictures

TREASURE AND THE COMING TEMPLE OF GOD

produced and museums established. For instance, a current picture of the Temple Mount has been reproduced without the enclosed Islamic buildings (the El Aqsa Mosque and Dome of the Rock Shrine) and includes a superimposed picture of the rebuilt Temple over the modern city of Jerusalem.

There is a model of the third Temple at the Atara L'yoshna Temple Model Museum in Jerusalem as well as the various articles on display at the Temple Treasures of the Temple Institute.

Ill. 17—The Jewish Temple superimposed over the modern Temple Mount. Superimposed Temple default.jpg contentdm.lib.byu.edu

Discovering the Oil of Anointing

A recent discovery in the Qumran area of the Dead Sea was the existence of an ancient flask of oil. Reported in *Biblical Archaeological Review*, this ancient flask of oil was of an extinct variety of the balsaph tree. In an ancient clay pottery flask, dated to the time of the Old Testament kings, archaeologists discovered the "oil of anointing" of the type used to anoint Old Testament kings such as David.[153]

A controversial researcher, Vendyl Jones, first took credit for the find but it was soon realized to be the discovery of others.

---
153 Joseph Patrich, "Hideouts in the Judean Wilderness," *Biblical Archaeological Review*, 15:5 (Sept/Oct 1989).

His research team had finished their daily work and gone to assist another nearby archaeological dig. In the section in which one of his workers was excavating, the flask was found. However, by the worker's own admission, Mr. Jones' assistant had stopped over an hour earlier from digging. Another worker came in from the nearby team and used the trowel method to dig, eventually finding the flask.

This find is very exciting. If this is actually the "oil of anointing" used in Old Testament times, then Israel once again could anoint a high priest, a future king, or a future Messiah! Will this flask be used to anoint the Antichrist as the king and Messiah of Israel? Only time will tell.

The Search for the Lost Ark and Ashes

The search for the lost Ark of the Covenant and the Ashes of the Red Heifer are the last requirements for the rebuilding of the Temple.

It is true that the Orthodox Jews believe that they must find these lost Ashes to cleanse the Temple mount and priests. And they believe they must have the lost Ark of Moses to place in the Temple.

In the previous chapters about the Ark, the possible whereabouts of the lost Ashes is given and twenty-one different possible locations of the lost Ark are explored. The Jews are very close to regaining the lost Ark and Ashes. They know where these articles are hidden and will soon gather them to the Temple Mount.

The day is fast approaching when the building of the Temple will commence. Can you imagine the excitement of the Jews as they anticipate the rebuilding? How close we are to the Second Coming of the Lord and the possibility of Jewish worship in a future Temple on the Temple Mount. We may soon see the fulfillment of the Jewish prayer, "Next year in Jerusalem!"

CHAPTER ELEVEN
The History of the Temple

The Jewish Temple, once described by an ancient author as the most beautiful building in the world, was unique among all ancient sanctuaries.[154] Although not the largest of the ancient edifices, or even the most elaborate in carvings, it was truly the most important. Some scholars, although seeing some similarity to the ancient Phoenician temples, believe that the Jewish House of God was the greatest of all influences for other temple worship to ever exist!

The Tabernacle in the Wilderness

The Temple had its origin when God first commanded Moses to build the Tabernacle in Exodus 25-26. This Tabernacle (Mishkan, "dwelling"), a forerunner of the Temple, was the first temporary and portable sanctuary ever built, in ancient times.[155] It was to be the dwelling of God's presence.

It consisted of a large rectangular building with portable walls and was roofed by four layers of tents. This Tabernacle was divided into two rooms: the Holy Place which was thirty feet by fifteen feet, and the Holy of Holies which was fifteen feet square, totaling forty-five feet by fifteen feet.

Surrounding the Tabernacle was a rectangular outer courtyard comprising one hundred fifty feet in length and seventy-five feet in width, with one doorway on the east side. Inside the courtyard was the brazen laver (used for ritual washing) and the brazen altar (used for burning sacrifices).

When entering the Tabernacle, one passed between the five entrance columns and outer veiled door to the Holy Place. On the left was the large Menorah (a seven-branched candlestick), on the right was the Table of Showbread (containing one loaf of bread for each of the twelve tribes of Israel), and at the end of the

---
154 Talmud, Bava Batra 4a
155 Kiene, Paul F., *The Tabernacle of God in the Wilderness of Sinai* (Grand Rapids, MI: Lamplighter Books, 1977).

room in the center, the continuously burning Altar of Incense.

Once a year, on the Day of Atonement, the high priest of Israel would pass through the inner veiled door to the Holy of Holies to sprinkle the blood of the sacrificial lamb on the Ark of the Covenant. This room contained the Ark of the Covenant (a golden box with a special golden lid, endowed with two exquisite cherub angels extending their wings over the lid to cover the Mercy Seat of God). Each of the subsequent Temples utilized the same basic floor plan and furniture. These buildings were patterned after the heavenly Temple and Temple objects that Moses saw in heaven when he received the Ten Commandments from God.

After the possession of Canaan by Israel, this Tabernacle resided in Shiloh. Maimonides tells us,

> *Once they entered the Land of Israel. They established the Tabernacle in Gilgal (where it stood) for the 14 years until they conquered and divided the land. From there they went to Shiloh, where a stone house was built, and it was covered with the Tabernacle curtains—as opposed to a solid roof. For 369 years the sanctuary stood in Shiloh. On the death of Eli, it was destroyed, whereupon they came and built a sanctuary at Nob. On the death of Samuel, it was destroyed, whereupon they came and built a sanctuary at Gibeon. From Gibeon they came to the Temple in Jerusalem. The length of time of the Tabernacle in Nob and Gibeon was 57 years.*[156]

Later, the prophet Jeremiah prophesies that if Israel did not repent and return to the Lord, that the Jewish Temple would be destroyed just as the earlier sanctuary had been demolished in Shiloh (Jer. 7:12-14). But how could the Tabernacle be repeatedly erected if it was destroyed by the Philistines when they captured the Ark in battle? Because the curtains, the roof, and other portable parts of the Tabernacle survived. It seems that the Philistines came and destroyed the stone walls

---
156 Mishna Torah, *Hilkhot Beit ha-Behirah* 1:2

of the temporary sanctuary after the removal of the portable Tabernacle, but not the Tabernacle itself.[157]

The Tabernacle was later moved to Nob. Nob was a priestly town in the vicinity of Jerusalem. David went there to meet the priest Ahimelech, who fed David and his men with bread from the Table of Showbread and gave David the sword of Goliath (1 Sam. 21:9). King Saul was informed by his shepherd Doeg, who saw David and his men go to Nob. He came and had Doeg the Edomite massacre all eighty-five priests, their entire families including women and children, and all the oxen, donkeys and sheep because the Jewish people refused to kill the priests and their families (1 Sam. 22:16-19), Then the Tabernacle was moved to nearby Gibeon, a Levitical city on the north side of Jerusalem (1 Sam. 4:1-22; 1 Chron. 21:29). And finally, it was moved to Mount Zion in Jerusalem for Temple worship, until it was probably placed in a special genizah (a burial or hiding place of sacred objects) under the Temple Mount in Solomon's quarries.[158] Numerous theories abound as to its current whereabouts, usually citing underground Jerusalem, Qumran, Mount Nebo in Jordan, or the Vatican as possible hiding places.

The Tabernacle and the Temple are known as the tent of meeting, tabernacle of Jehovah, tabernacle of testimony, tent of the testimony, sanctuary of Jehovah, house of God, house of Jehovah, temple of Jehovah, sanctuary of this world, tent of communion, sanctuary of God, sanctuary of testimony, and holy temple of God.

The Temple of Solomon

The first of the Temples was built by King Solomon on Mount Moriah in Jerusalem. King David had purchased the threshing floor of Arnan the Jebusite as the future location and he wanted to begin building the Temple.

---

157 Akiva Males, "Reconstructing the Destruction of the Tabernacle at Shiloh," *Jewish Bible Quarterly*, 44:1 (January – March 2016)
158 TB Sotah 9a, Rashi in his Commentary on 2 Chronicles 5:5.

It is possible that King David had already begun its building as a wooden Temple, encouraged at first by Nathan.[159] But later Nathan was sent by the Lord to warn David against building. The Lord restrained him because David was a man of war (2 Sam. 7:5-13; 1 Chron. 17:3-6.)

So, David assembled one hundred thousand talents of gold (worth about 2.6 billion dollars), a million talents of silver (worth about 2 billion dollars) and quarried many tons of stone, bronze, and iron beyond measure. He also brought cedar wood from Lebanon (1 Chron. 22:14-15) as well as organized an elaborate array of workmen and craftsmen.

Solomon started work on the temple in the month Iyar (Ziv in the Bible) in the fourth year of Solomon's reign, 2928 A.M. (957 B.C., four hundred eighty years after Israel's exodus from Egypt). The Temple was completed in the month of Marcheshvan (Bul in the Bible) of 2935 A.M. (950 B.C.), the eleventh year of Solomon's reign, in a little less than seven years.

Solomon's Temple Measurements

The Temple included a front porch called a portico and was surrounded by a courtyard with several gates.

The Portico (porch) was multistoried:
> Length: 20 cubits (40 ft.-12 m.) (north to south)
> Width: 10 cubits (20 ft.-6 m.) (east to west)
> Height: 30 cubits (60 ft.-18 m.)
> Height including top floors: 120 cubits (240 ft.-72 m.)

The Holy Place (middle room called "Hechal"):
> Length: 40 cubits (80 ft.-24 m.) (east to west)
> Width: 20 cubits (40 ft.-12 m.) (north to south)
> Height: 30 cubits (60 ft.-18 m.)

---

159 Fereday, W. W., *Solomon and His Temple* (Kilmarnock: John Ritchie Limited, 1941)

CHAPTER ELEVEN

Ill. 18—The Temple of Solomon, built in 950 B.C. 3.jpg templeinstitute.org

The Holy of Holies (end room of the Temple):
- Length: 20 cubits (40 ft.-12 m.)
- Width: 20 cubits (40 ft.-12 m.)
- Height: 30 cubits (60 ft.-18 m.)

The Temple was surrounded by three stories of small rooms called galleries. These thirty-eight galleries were used to store the treasures and utensils of the Temple.[160]

The Holy of Holies

On the floor of the Holy of Holies (which was twenty cubits square), were placed two cherubim made of olive wood overlaid with gold. "... And they stood on their feet, their faces were inwards." (2 Chron. 3:13) The height of each cherub was ten cubits (twenty feet or six meters). One stood to the north of the Ark of the Covenant and one stood to the south.

"Five cubits was the length of one wing of the cherub, and five cubits the length of the other wing of the cherub; it was ten cubits from the tip of one wing to the tip of the other."

---

160 Haran, Menachem, *Temples and Temple-Service in Ancient Israel* (New York: Oxford University Press, 1988)

(1 Kings 6:24) Each cherub touched with one of its wings touching the northern wall and southern wall respectively, their other wings jointly providing a kind of canopy for the Ark which was placed underneath. The length of the four wings as they spread out was twenty cubits wide and they filled the entire width of the Holy of Holies.

It seemed to be a miracle that the angels could be placed into the Temple, their wing width filling the width of the room without providing room for their body. However, I believe that the cherub's wings swelled out of their body and then circled over their head, there touching to spread out to the remaining interior.

When Solomon's Temple was built, it was designed to be a permanent structure, not just a temporary Tabernacle. The Temple included the original furniture of the Tabernacle, but it also included ten additional candelabra (menorot) and ten additional tables of showbread positioned around the original table of showbread and original Menorah of Moses.[161]

This Temple was glorious, overlaid inside and out with gold and silver, utilizing cedar wood floors (except for the Holy of Holies), with elaborate carvings, doorways, and fixtures throughout.

However, eventually because of the idolatry of Israel, the Temple fell into various stages of disrepair and even disuse and later was cleansed and reused under various revivals (such as under King Josiah).

Jewish Temple Terms

When studying about the Jewish Temple, its buildings and precinct, several Hebrew terms will often occur. The *Azarah* (Hebrew, "enclosure") is the term for the sacred precinct of the Jerusalem Temple or its outer court, and it includes the entire Temple Mount platform. The *Soreg* (Hebrew, "partition") was

---
161 1 Kings 7:49; TB Menahot 98b.

the partition dividing the inner court of the Jews from the outer court of the Gentiles in the Second Temple precinct. A sign was placed on this partition warning Gentiles not to enter on pain of death. This caution sign has been discovered and is able to be seen while visiting the excavations of the Temple Mount from the Second Temple Period in Jerusalem.

The Temple building itself was divided into three parts: namely, the porch, the main sanctuary, and the innermost room. The *Ulam* (Hebrew, from Akkadian ellamu, "front porch") was the first division of the Temple, namely, the forecourt or main entrance porch.

The *Hechal* (Hebrew, originally from Sumerian e-gal, "great house," and Assyrian ekallu, "palace, temple") was the second division of the Temple, namely, the main room or sanctuary. And the *Devir* (Hebrew, "sanctuary" though derived from a word meaning "the back part of the room") was the third division of the Temple, namely the innermost chamber, the Holy of Holies, where the Ark of the Covenant was housed.

The Temple Is Attacked

As judgment for Israel's idolatry, God allowed Pharaoh Shishak of Egypt to attack Israel and he plundered Jerusalem in 925 B.C. He plundered the gold of Jerusalem, including the three hundred shields of gold from King Solomon's palace (weighing more than two tons), and took other gold from the Temple including the golden walls. He probably did not plunder the Temple vessels and furniture which were most likely hidden. His son, Pharaoh Osorkon I, offered this and other plundered gold and silver, amounting to at least 383 tons, to Egyptian gods in 921 B.C. This is the final story of what happened to much of the lost gold of King Solomon.

Israel's own kings sometimes contributed to the loss of the Temple and its vessels. The Southern king, Ahaz, stripped the Temple of a portion of silver and gold, broke up part of the Temple furniture and utensils, and removed the bronze oxen from the Brazen Sea for currency to pay tribute to the Assyrian king, Tiglath-Pileser III (2 Kings 16:7-9, 17, 18; 2 Chron. 28:21, 24).

In 605 B.C. the Babylonian king Nebuchadnezzar attacked Israel, capturing King Jehoiakim and the royal family, as well as thousands of others (including Daniel) as slaves who were taken to Babylon. In 597 B.C., another invasion and deportation included removing the remaining treasure of the Temple (and the prophet Ezekiel) (2 Kings 24:13; Ezek. 9:1-8; 10:18, 19). The final destruction of the city took place in the third Babylonian invasion in 586 B.C. and included burning the Temple, the palace complex and all the houses of the city (2 Kings 25:8-9; 2 Chron. 36:18-19).

Rebuilding the Temple Under Cyrus

Cyrus, the Persian king, gave permission for about fifty thousand Jews to return to Jerusalem to rebuild the Temple in 538 B.C. under the leadership of Zerubbabel. With the help of Phoenician workmen, like those who had helped Solomon in building the first Temple, they began laying the foundation for the second Temple to be built after the fashion of the first Temple (Ezra 3:7-10). The Temple vessels were returned, an altar was constructed, sacrifices were begun. and the observance of the Biblical feasts restored.

However, Samaritans in the Northern Kingdom brought such strong opposition that work was halted for fifteen years. King Darius decreed that work start again for the rebuilding and prescribed local taxes from even the Samaritans to finance the construction, which was completed in 515 B.C

The Turbulent Reign of Antiochus Epiphanes

For several years, worship continued in the Temple unrestrained. The land was ruled by the Persians and later by Alexander the

Great (who was Macedonian-Greek), the Egyptian Greeks (the Ptolemy Dynasty), and finally by Syrian Greeks (the Seleucids). Under the reign of the Seleucids in 196 B.C., Antiochus IV, called "Epiphanes" (meaning "the illustrious"), or "Epimanes" (the "madman"), invaded Jerusalem and captured the Temple. He was sometimes called this second name quietly (or it was "whispered") because of the terrible things he did to the Jews and to the Temple.

There he defiled the Temple with pagan idols and impure sacrifices, even sacrificing a sow (considered an unclean animal) on the altar and spreading the various parts of the sacrifice all over the Temple Mount in an effort to defile the Temple and insult the Jews.

Antiochus the "madman" is often seen prophetically as a picture of the Antichrist (in the same manner as Hitler, Mussolini, and others) and this act he committed is sometimes referred to as the "abomination of desolation," again foreshadowing the Antichrist.

This Antiochus performed various persecutions on the Jewish people and also built a fortress called the Acra on the south side, between the City of David and the Temple Mount, to quell any Jewish uprisings.

The Maccabean Revolt

A priestly family named Maccabees, who later became the Hasmonean Dynasty, rose up and led a successful rebellion, recapturing the city and regaining the Temple in 141 B.C., thereby restoring freedom of worship. During this time, the Temple was renovated, a new altar was built, and the defiled one dismantled and stored under the Temple Mount.

The Mount was refortified with a new defense called Baris located on the northeast corner, the Acra fortress was dismantled, and the Temple Mount platform was extended toward the City of David. This extension included two new underground entrances and a bridge built over the Tyropoeon Valley to the west to connect the upper city, including Mount Zion, to the Temple Mount. They also established walls and an arcade around the Temple platform to enlarge the area and better defend it.

The Temple Mount Proper

The Temple Mount location was Mount Moriah, which stood to the north of David's and Solomon's Palace. There a large platform for the temple complex was erected on multiple arches, with open space below to the bedrock ensuring an additional measure of purity. It was a rectangular platform, holding the Temple proper, as well as multiple additional buildings, such as the Royal Stoa, (a Basilica used as a shopping area), and areas for schools, housing, sacrificial functions, and a variety of other features. The platform of Solomon was enlarged several times, and eventually included an additional raised platform where the Temple stood, and where the Dome of the Rock stands today. For an in-depth look at each stage of the Temple enlargement in different time periods, see the extensive research done by Leen Ritmeyer.[162]

The Roman Invasion

About 64 B.C., the Romans under Pompey assumed Israel as a province and thus began various stages of peaceful leniency and stormy persecution of the Jews. During this Roman period, an Idumean named Herod the Great ruled over Israel as a puppet king for Rome, as did his sons afterward.

Herod Remodels the Temple

Herod the Great completely remodeled the Temple Mount, almost doubling the size of the Temple platform, enlarging the Baris fortress into the Roman Antonia fortress, and

---
[162] Leen Ritmeyer, "Temple Mount." Ritmeyer Archaeological Design, Accessed on December 27, 2022, https://ritmeyer.com

included more underground entrances and grand exterior stairways to the Temple mount.

A large water basin, the Pool of Israel, was added, the walls raised or extended and raised, and an Arcade or Stoa was added all the way around the Temple Mount. Four huge porticos (large halls) were also added.

Color Image 23—The Temple of Herod. 888uzmf88e6j61.jpg reddit.com

The Royal Basilica, largest of all Temple buildings, was built on the south side and was probably used as a shopping mall. This Basilica included Supreme Court chambers for the Sanhedrin (the Jewish Judicial Court). The Temple building proper was completely dismantled, enlarged, remodeled, and rebuilt on a grand scale with marble walls and a golden crown at its summit. And the Nicanor Gate in front of the Temple proper was a huge gate with seventy-five-foot-tall silver lintels and copper doors; it was called the Beautiful Gate.

This was the Temple of the time of Jesus of Nazareth, where He taught the learned doctors, preached from the steps and porches, overturned the money-changers tables, performed many miracles of God, and offered the Passover sacrifice on at least three different occasions.

The Second Temple Destroyed

In A.D. 70, under the rule of Herod Agrippa II, the Second Temple was destroyed by the Roman emperor Vespasian and his son, the Roman general Titus Flavius. This was part of a series of battles fought across the land of Israel (which included the famous siege of Masada) as an attempt to put down the First Rebellion of the Jews to Roman rule.

During the destruction of Jerusalem, as in the earlier Babylonian siege, the Temple was burned and then dismantled, the city was burned, many Jews were taken away as slaves, and the Temple Mount was at least partially dismantled. One reason the Temple Mount was dismantled was that the Romans wanted to get the gold that melted from the walls into the ground below.

However, Josephus relates how that Pangar, a Roman military dux, explained to Vespasian why he left the Western Wall intact.

Preserving the Western Wall

Pangar said, "For your glory did I leave the Western Wall intact; otherwise, no creature would know what you have destroyed. Now they will appreciate what kind of fortified walls, unequaled anywhere, you have overcome."

Vespasian was not very well pleased with this idea of forgoing final destruction of the city, and he ordered

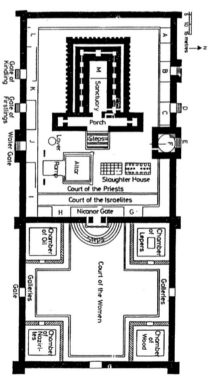

Ill. 19—The floor plan of Herod's Temple
Image5VC.jpeg emp.byui.edu Public Domain

Pangar to throw himself off a high pinnacle in Rome, claiming that if he lived, it would have been the gods will that he not utterly destroy Jerusalem. Pangar did not survive.[163]

Thus, at least part of the Temple Mount and surrounding walls (such as the Western "Wailing" Wall) was left in place. And it is amazing to now view these Herodian Temple Mount stones, averaging many tons each, and to realize the astounding buildings that must have once there stood.

Soon tensions between the Jews and the Romans began to ease under the ascension to the throne of the Roman emperor Publius Aelius Hadrian in A.D. 117. Jews took hope in soon realizing a new Temple to Jehovah. Hadrian was not initially hostile to the Jews, and soon official contact was made between Judean Jews and the Roman government and permission was given to rebuild the Temple.

The Bar Kokhba Revolt

However, in A.D. 129, serious hostilities to Hadrian broke out as he changed in his attitude toward the Jews and began to transform the city into a Roman colony, even renaming the city Aelia Capitolina. A second revolt ensued in A.D. 132 under the Jewish leader Simon ben Koseba and eventually was larger and much more difficult to overcome than the First Revolt. In fact, it has been noted that if the Jews had been a little more organized and cooperative among themselves, they could have easily defeated any Roman army. The Jews, at this time, were one-fourth the size of the Roman Empire in population.

Shimon (Simeon) ben Koseba was soon proclaimed the Messiah by the eminent Talmudic Rabbi Akiva and renamed Bar Kokhba, the Son of the Star, basing his name upon Numbers 24:17, "There shall come a Star out of Jacob." He began his reign as a prince, established a new calendar from

---
163 Josephus, *The War of the Jews*, 3.168.6; Midrash Lamentations Rabbah 1:5, 31.

his first year of reign, and issued coins with the new calendar year. These coins included an engraving of the Temple and Ark of the Covenant and the name of the high priest.

The Temple of Bar Kokhba

Rabbi Leibel Reznick believes that Bar Kokhba rebuilt a Temple in Jerusalem (as the Messiah would do). It must be in this Temple that Rabbi Gamaliel entered after the destruction of the Temple of Herod. Gamaliel mentioned entering into a Jewish Temple and offering his Passover sacrifice.[164]

Ill. 20—Cave Eleven of the Dead Sea Scroll caves, Author's photo.

Thus, the Temple building proper was completed, although the surrounding courtyard was never reconstructed. Another source believes the Temple building was never built; they only built an altar for performing the sacrifices. But letters found in Qumran show he enforced Temple tithes.[165]

Interesting light on this Temple has been revealed by archaeologist Yigael Yadin. Dr. Yadin was one of the experts of the Dead Sea Scrolls. These scrolls were ancient manuscripts of Biblical and religious literature found in various caves of the Dead Sea area of Israel. In Cave Eleven, researchers found several additional scrolls.

---

164   Leibel Reznick, *The Holy Temple Revisited* (Jason Aronson, Inc., 1985), 153; Pesachim 74a
165   Bar Kokhba, Accessed on Jan. 31, 2023, encyclopedia.com

CHAPTER ELEVEN

One of the discovered scrolls came to be known as the Temple Scroll because it described the details of a future Jewish Temple. This proves a detailed plan for another future Temple existed in Israel before the fall of the Temple of Herod. This may have become the Bar Kokhba Temple.

The Size of the Temple Mount Platform

One unusual, related subject is the Temple Platform. The size of the elevated platform in the midst of the Temple Mount has often puzzled scholars. It is too small for the entire Temple and surrounding courtyards, but too large for just the Temple itself.

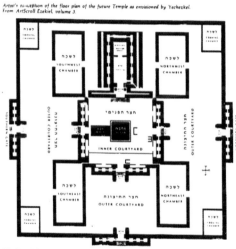

Ill. 21, A floor plan of the Temple Scroll Temple. ArtScroll, Yechezkel, Ezekiel, Moshe Eisemann

The Haram "(Arabic, "enclosure") is the present upper platform upon which the Dome of the Rock is built, and which is thought to approximate the earlier Herodian Temple platform. The full title used by the Muslims for the larger, complete Herod Platform is al-Haram al-Sharif ("The Noble Enclosure").

It also does not match the relevant mathematical proportions of the Dome of the Rock. It seems elusive as to why it was built to its current proportions. However, it does seem to fit the exact size and shape of the Messianic Third Temple described in the book of Ezekiel, if the sizes given in Scripture for the reed are interpreted as equaling a cubit of nineteen inches! Thus, the Jews may have rebuilt a Temple in the time of Bar Kokhba following the plans found in the Temple Scroll.

Bar Kokhba reigned as the Messiah-king in Jerusalem for two and a half years. In A.D. 135, his reign ended when the Roman emperor Hadrian captured Jerusalem and probably destroyed the Bar Kokhba Temple. The Romans would have attempted to eradicate any stronghold the Jews held to Jerusalem. They even made it illegal, upon penalty of death, for a Jew to be found in Jerusalem or its outer regions. Also, the Romans built a temple of Jupiter, dedicated to the pagan worship of Juno, Jupiter, and Minerva on the Temple Mount.

The Roman Pagan Temple

The Roman pagan temple was possibly built on the east side of the Temple Mount, partially including the famous Eastern Gate. The exact reason the Eastern Gate was built on a large scale since the time of Solomon has long remained a mystery. It seems that the gate was never in alignment with the Temple proper, yet was built in a grand style, even from antiquity.

The Gate is made in a double gate fashion; it is called the Gate of Mercy and the Golden Gate. Scholars now believe that this was the Throne Room of King David and possibly of King Solomon. It could have also been used as a Judicial chamber at another time. And it could have been a gate for bridegrooms and mourners. The gate is currently being used for a Muslim school, resting on the foundations of the earlier throne room and Roman building.

There were definitely Roman structures built in the area of the Eastern Gate. A Roman gate inscription is still visible today near this ancient place, Today's American consulate states that a Roman "holy place" stood on the Temple Mount. An equestrian statue of Hadrian was also raised on this mount to overlook the ruins of the Temple. Thomas Ice and Randall Price present evidence that the Eastern Gate area was used to display the equestrian statue and was not the location of the Roman pagan Temple. This Roman temple was instead built to the north of the destroyed Jewish Temple.[166] This is the more common view held today.

This pagan temple soon fell into disuse because the Gentile Christians were already worshipping in secret under threat of persecution, the Jewish Christians fled to upper Galilee and Syria, and most other Jews were moved at this time to Tiberias in upper Galilee or to Rome. All that remained in Jerusalem, for the most part, were a Roman garrison of soldiers and a few other native people.

The Coming of Constantine

In A.D. 324, Emperor Constantine converted to Christianity (at least outwardly) and Jerusalem became a holy Christian city. His mother, Helena, built many churches across Jerusalem and Israel, and the pagan temple on the Temple Mount was torn down, leaving the mountain bare. Eventually, the Christians used the location as a place of refuge. Using this mount as a place of refuge would possibly have been an attempt by the Christians to show contempt for the pagan Roman religions, but it has also sometimes been interpreted by Jews as an attempt to insult and desecrate their holy Temple site.

In A.D. 363 a new emperor, Julian, renounced Christianity and was called "The Apostate." Under Julian, full rights were granted to the Jews including permission to restore the Temple. Interestingly, an earthquake and fire destroyed the supplies which had been quickly gathered to rebuild the Temple and Julian was killed within a year, resulting in a new emperor, Jovian, who was loyal to Christianity. It seems that the time had not yet come for the rebuilding and for the return of the Messiah. The Persians captured Jerusalem in A.D. 614 with the help of the Jews, and permission was once again given to rebuild the Temple but was withdrawn under pressure from the Christians.

---

166 Ice, Thomas and Price, Randall, *Ready to Rebuild*, Ibid., 78.

Building the Dome of the Rock

In A.D. 629, Heraclius, the Byzantine emperor, recaptured Jerusalem. In that year, an octagonal church was started by the Byzantine Christians on the site of the central rock on the Temple platform. Different theories abound as to why it was built.

It is generally agreed that the church was not completely finished, and work was halted when the Muslims recaptured the Holyland in A.D. 637. At what stage the work was halted is a little difficult to determine.

It is my belief that the entire outer structure was finished (including the golden dome and internal walls and facing) and the church was in the process of finishing the interior decorative facade of the ceiling, walls, and floors.

We know that the Dome of the Rock is the only Muslim octagonal structure existing in the entire world, and that this was specifically a Byzantine style of church building. The other Byzantine churches with this style of building in Jerusalem alone are abundant, examples being the Church of the Holy Sepulcher, the Church of Mount Zion, and similar churches of the time period throughout Israel, such as churches in Bethlehem, Capernaum, as well as throughout the Byzantine Empire.

The original finishings have been changed several times. Many rulers changed the interior decorative tiles, and the original golden dome was eventually removed and melted down to pay tribute to a past Caliph. The current domed roof was replaced with $1.4 million in gold in 1992.

Crosses Adorn the Dome of the Rock

On my fourth trip to Israel, while speaking to my guide I said, "I have heard that this Dome of the Rock used to be a church and that it also displayed several crosses. Where were the crosses?"

He told me that, like many churches, it had many crosses displayed throughout its interior. The top of the dome used to be crested with a cross, and he showed me several places inside (now covered over with other decoration often insulting to Christianity) where crosses were painted or fashioned to the walls.

The El Aqsa Mosque

The existing El Aqsa Mosque was also a Byzantine church or basilica built by the Emperor Julian. Often these Byzantine churches were built over the site of earlier apostolic churches and so the origin of the church itself is difficult to date. This may also be one of the earliest church sites.

Color Image 24, The El Aqsa Mosque, Jerusalem, Israel., Author's Photo

Moreover, the floor plan of the El Aqsa is similar to other Byzantine churches in Jerusalem (such as the Nea Church, the Church of the Holy Sepulcher, and the Church of Gethsemane) and to other churches in the previous Byzantine Empire.

The existing Dome of the Rock was finished (by only adding interior decoration) in A.D. 691 by King Abd al-Malik ibn Marwan, the famous Caliph of the House of Ummayad.

Although a shrine and not a mosque, it is sometimes mistakenly called the "Mosque of Omar" after Umar ibn al-Khattab, the Saracen Caliph of Islam, who conquered the country for the Muslims. After locating and cleaning up the mount, he first held Muslin prayers there. His actual mosque is nearby.

The El Aqsa Mosque is credited to Caliph Abd al Malik who built it (or remodeled an earlier building) two years after the Dome of the Rock. Its construction is variously also credited to his son, Caliph al Walid II, in A.D. 705-715.[167]

The Mosque was originally built as a church in ancient times and the arched doorways pictured here were built by the Crusaders while it again operated as a church. It is today called the El Aqsa, meaning the "far corner," the farthest stronghold of Islam from Mecca. In modern times the King of Jordan was shot by a deranged assassin at this entrance.

The Coming of the Crusaders

During the Crusader years(A.D. 1099–1187), the Dome of the Rock (or the El Aqsa Mosque) was again used as a Christian church. The El Aqsa Mosque was extensively remodeled and renamed "Solomon's Temple." It was used as the religious center for the Crusader order of the Knights Templar. The entire front of the structure is specifically built in a Crusader style, especially the large gate-like entrances. (Compare it with various churches throughout Europe, such as the Lazarus Church, of Nuremburg, Germany.)

The Dome of the Rock was turned into the "Temple of the Lord." It was considered too holy a site to alter very much. They extended the small cave to use as a chapel, covered the cave floor, and cut a hole in the center of the rock for smoke to dissipate from the lanterns. (They may have also slightly extended the next lower cave before they covered its

---

167 Hamilton, R. W., *The Structural History of the Aqsa Mosque* (Oxford, 1949)

entrance.) The Templars merely put a marble floor over the central rock, possibly also leveled the rock in various places for the marble floor and added a metal guardrail around the rock inside the building.

This was added because many Christian pilgrims would cut away pieces of the rock for souvenirs, or to sell in their homeland for exorbitant prices. In this way, these earlier pilgrims actually destroyed part of the original Temple site, cutting away at least four to six feet of the original stone in several places.

The destruction of the rock face also dispels any doubt to the legendary hoofprints of Barak, the horse of Muhammed who the Muslims say jumped from this rock to heaven. The hoofprints they like to show you inside would have been cut away by the Crusader pilgrims. The rock face is now four to six feet lower in various places than when the Crusaders arrived. However, the Arabs do have a small shrine inside that supposedly houses three hairs from the beard of Muhammed! And the presence of Muhammed in Israel is only a later legend because he never came to Jerusalem. The Muslims repeat this story to give legitimacy to their presence in Jerusalem by trying to create an earlier presence of Muhammed there, although this story is only legend.

Had the Crusaders been able to read Arabic, they would have doubtlessly changed some of the decoration inside the dome that includes writing that is blasphemous to the Christian faith. Apparently, the interior must have been covered with Christian decoration, and later changed to the Muslim decoration after they recaptured the Temple Mount.

The Dome of the Ascension was erected by the Crusaders to the north of the Dome of the Rock for use as an elaborate baptistery. (It was recently remodeled in 2022–2023, which caused many Jews to surmise that the Arabs were also destroying evidence of the earlier Herod Temple Altar which stood only a few feet under the current ground level.) The Dome of the Chain was celebrated as a shrine to Saint James, the first Christian pastor to die as a martyr. The entire Temple Mount complex was adorned with great splendor and venerated with utmost reverence.

Shrines Returned to the Muslims

The Muslim invasion in A.D. 1187 under Saladin brought the Temple Mount into Muslim control, where it remained until A.D. 1967. The former Muslim shrines were returned to Islamic worship and have gone through various stages of remodeling or reconstruction to the present.

As of the Six-Day War in A.D. 1967, Israel regained control of Jerusalem and the Temple Mount, but, continuing a tradition of religious leniency and freedom, have allowed the Muslims to continue their worship in both the El Aqsa Mosque and the Dome of the Rock.

Will this soon be the site of a new Temple? To determine the possibility of rebuilding, we have looked at the Temple's amazing past. Many people wonder if the Dome of the Rock must be removed to rebuild the Temple. Some people have asked, "Will the Temple be rebuilt as a result of a religious war?" To examine the future of the Temple, we need only to look at the prophecy of the next Temple, the Tribulation Temple of Antichrist.

CHAPTER TWELVE
The Tribulation Temple

The most explosive, tumultuous, destructive period of the world is coming, the dreaded Tribulation Period. This period is described in the Bible as a time of the unleashing of the wrath of God upon the world. This will be the most devastating time of trial and destruction of all of earth's history. Never before has the world experienced the intensity of the wars, famine, pestilence, and death of the coming Tribulation and we may be standing on the threshold of this very hour!

The Tribulation Period

This period begins with a war and then sudden peace is brought about by a renowned world leader who combines the world into a great unified government and universal religion. The Antichrist will be a monumental, astonishing, brilliant, all-powerful figure. He will suddenly rise to power, he will later have a miraculous healing, and he will pull all the world under his sway.

The man of sin will promise peace to the world and a new and greater era for mankind. He may even first appear to be kind and compassionate. But soon his true character will be manifested as he tries to kill all the Christians and Jews of the world.

This Antichrist will establish a numbering system, based upon 666, that will be designed to force all people to be under his control. It will be a means to control the world economically and, ultimately, to cause people to worship him.

Christians saved during this time will turn to Jesus and refuse to take the number of the Antichrist. Untold numbers of people will be martyred by Antichrist's forces.

Mass famine, pestilences, and wars will ensue, and death will be commonplace. In the middle of this seven-year period, the Antichrist will desecrate the Jewish Temple and declare himself God, demanding that all people worship him (2 Thess. 2:3-4; Rev. 6-18).

The Time of Rebuilding

For these things to happen the Temple must be rebuilt. Yet, when will this happen?

The rebuilding of the Temple is usually placed sometime before the Rapture of Believers and the beginning of the Tribulation Period. One reason for this is the assumption that rebuilding the Temple will take many years. The Temple of Herod was begun in 20 B.C. and it took many years to build, going through added embellishments right up until its destruction in A.D. 70.

In our modern time, reconstruction of the Temple could be accomplished in a relatively short period of time. It is not unusual for modern skyscrapers to be erected in the span of six months. If all hindrances were removed, the Temple could be built in a relatively short amount of time. The Temple could also be built during the Tribulation Period. We know that the Temple is in full operation in Jerusalem for some time before the Antichrist will desecrate it in the middle of the Tribulation. But before the Temple can be rebuilt, whether quickly or in the future, several obstacles must be overcome.

How can the obstacles to rebuilding be overcome?

Obstacles to Rebuilding the Temple

There are several obstacles to rebuilding the Temple today. Some liberal Jews do not believe it is necessary to worship God in a Temple with sacrifices. They view the rebuilding as a vain effort by more "radical" Jews and a needless part of their religion, which they see today operating as only through internal faith. Some Jewish groups emphasize other metaphysical ideas.

CHAPTER TWELVE

The Christian Objection

Certain Christians are opposed to the idea because they view the rebuilding of the Temple as a denial of Jesus' atonement for sin made on the cross. Jesus was the one-time sacrifice for the sins of the world. His death paid for our sins and His resurrection proved His deity. By Jesus' substitutionary death on the cross, He paid for all the sins of the world. He is now able to become our personal Savior if we will just call on Him to save us from Hell and forgive us of our sins, accepting His payment for our sin. We do not need a sacrificial system for salvation.

Hebrews 9:12 tells us, *"Neither by the blood of goats and calves, but by his own blood he entered in once into the holy place, having obtained eternal redemption for us."*

All people are born into sin. We live a life continually plagued with temptations, carnality, and sin. This sin separates us from a holy God. We will all be judged for this sin and must be saved from God's wrath in judgment. If not saved, we face an eternal damnation in a lake of fire, tormented for our sin. But in love, Jesus came to earth to die for the sins of the world (Rom. 3:10, 23; 5:8, 12; 6:23; 10:9–10, 13).

God left the celestial throne of glory and came to earth. He lived a sinless life and was worthy to die for our sins on the cross.

The sacrifice Jesus made was the only true sacrifice for sin. Only by realizing your sinfulness and need of cleansing from your sin, believing in Him and accepting His personal salvation can you escape the Judgment of God.

The rebuilding of the Temple in no way denies Jesus' salvation for us. This unfolding drama is seen prophetically as a sign of our Lord's Return. While the Jews that rebuild the Temple do reject Jesus as their Messiah, they are being used of God to fulfill His plan to re-establish Temple worship in the Temple for the Tribulation Period. This event is viewed by Christians as only a part of the end-time prophetic plan of God.

The Arab Objection

Arabs are opposed to the rebuilding of the Temple, viewing the idea as unthinkable that their third holiest site could fall into the hands of "infidels." They would quickly move to fight in a *jihad* (holy war) to protect their holy site. But one Egyptian Muslim leader mentioned that Jerusalem is unimportant, and today there is a movement to make other places in Saudi Arabia more relevant.

How could the existence of the Temple be resolved? How could the Arab holy houses be removed?

How Will the Obstacles Be Overcome?

The possibility for changing the Muslim holy sites usually mentioned is by some natural disaster which could be interpreted as the will of God. The intervention of an earthquake has been often mentioned to me by Jews at the Temple Mount, which is prophesied to come at the beginning of the Millennium (Zech. 14:2-4). Also, the destruction of the Temple Mount site in a war is sometimes expressed by Jews and Christians.

Rabbi Getz believes that the Dome of the Rock will be removed by such an event as an earthquake. He tells us:

> *In the time of the Redemption, there will be a huge earthquake. Everything will blow up! the mosques—everything! It is written in Zechariah chapter 14. It is the same as the Christian [interpretation]. But all of the churches around will [also] be destroyed by the earthquake. And the Temple Mount will be raised up, and there will be no mosques then—so of course we'll have enough opportunity to build the Temple.*

The Muslims have always repaired or rebuilt any of these buildings when damaged in the past, and it seems logical that they would just rebuild them again. The Israelis have ownership of the land but have allowed the Arabs to maintain the Temple Mount. Would an earthquake specifically change that policy?

Sometimes the possibility of negotiations with the Arabs for dual control or total Jewish control is suggested. Similar suggestions include attempting to purchase the "rights" to use the land, to auction the buildings, or to pay to move the Muslim shrines to Mecca.

Notwithstanding, the land is also sacred to the Muslim Arabs, and I am not convinced that any amount of money could accomplish these negotiations.

The land issue could be settled as a result of a religious war. However, the Temple Mount was recaptured in the Six-Day War of 1967, and other land in 1972. In spite of this, the land boundaries of Israel are being questioned to this very day. It would be difficult to imagine the Arab nations ever allowing the mosque and shrine to be removed and the Temple built.

The Antichrist's Covenant of Peace

How could the control of the Temple Mount be resolved? It is my opinion that the Antichrist will accomplish this feat as part of his rise to prominence. The Bible says that he will make a covenant of peace with Israel, implying peace from all enemies including the Muslims.

Daniel 9:27 tells us, "And he shall confirm the covenant with many for one week. ..."

We do not know how he will accomplish this covenant of peace. One possibility is the weakening of all of Israel's enemies as a result of the Russian Invasion of Israel, mentioned in Ezekiel 38–39, sometimes called the war of Gog and Magog.

Because there are two different conflicts mentioned in the Bible with a connection to the titles Gog and Magog, they can be distinguished because they each include different parties of conflict and happen at different times. But they can be referred to as Gog and Magog I and Gog and Magog II, in the same concept as World War I and World War II. These earlier world wars involved different nations fighting on a global scale at different times about distinct issues, but they were both global in scale. The first Gog and Magog War, Gog and Magog I, involves the Russian invasion of Israel at the beginning of the Tribulation Period, when Russia is joined by many other nations. The second Gog and Magog War, Gog and Magog II, is the final rebellion of the world against Christ when Satan deceives many people to follow him rather than God. This war happens at the end of the Millennium, a thousand and seven years later, yet each are global in involvement.

Gog and Magog I

In this war, Russia is joined by Iran and a host of other nations that are made up of all of Northern Africa except Egypt, some parts of the nations of black Africa, parts of Europe, and parts of Middle Eastern nations. Russia is apparently pulled into the conflict against her will, or against the logical situation at the time, because the Bible says hooks are in her mouth drawing her to battle with Israel.

These nations move to attack Israel but are stopped by falling fire and brimstone on the invading armies coming to Israel, and also destruction in each of their individual home countries. The destruction is so severe that five-sixths of each of these nation's attacking armies are destroyed and they are never again able to raise an invasion to attack Israel.

The Bible mentions that the destruction is so severe that it takes an entire valley to bury the dead in Israel, and seven years to burn the weapons. Because of the continual burial of the dead for about a year, and the burning of the weapons for seven years, it is often thought that this short war happens at the beginning of the Tribulation Period, so that the land is cleansed and ready for the reign of Christ after the Tribulation seven years later. And because of the weakening of all of Israel's opponents and their armies, this is why the Antichrist can rise to power in this time and guarantee peace, because there are no opponents to Israel left to fight. They have become so weak that they can never again raise an army to oppose Israel.

Because the Antichrist enters the Temple to desecrate it with the abomination of desolation in the middle of the Tribulation, it must be built and in operation by that time. Thus, the building of the Temple is possible before the Rapture, but more likely after the Rapture, when the Russian invasion of Israel will occur as the next event.

As a result of this Russian invasion, the invading forces' armies will be so decimated by the judgment of God that these nations could never invade Israel again. The soon rise of the Antichrist with his peace covenant will pave the way for a peaceful atmosphere in which the Temple could be quickly built, and Jewish worship completely restored.

It is my opinion that this peace pact will include the ability of Jews to rebuild their Temple on the Temple Mount and the removal of the Dome of the Rock. It is not clear if the El Aqsa Mosque must be removed, but many scholars believe that the Mosque will be removed; the Orthodox Jews see it as essential.

Will the El Aqsa Be Removed?

The book of Revelation gives us a picture of the Temple as it will stand in the Tribulation Period. Revelation 11:1-2 says,

> *And there was given me a reed like a rod: and the angel stood, saying, Rise, and measure the temple of God, and the altar, and them that worship therein.*
>
> *But the court which is without the temple leave out, and measure it not; for it is given unto the Gentiles: and the holy city shall they tread under foot forty and two months.*

The El Aqsa Mosque, or possibly one of the Muslim schools, may remain on the Temple Mount because the exterior court was not to be measured. This area was given to the Gentiles and was considered profane. Some Christian religious leaders believe the area does not appear to be part of the Tribulation Temple Complex, being "given to the Gentiles."

Many Jewish Rabbinical leaders insist that the El Aqsa Mosque must be removed. The area would be needed for the outer courtyard, called the Court of Women. The Southern Gate of the Temple would also stand exactly over the El Aqsa Mosque's southern section.

It is my opinion that the mosque will be removed to please the Jewish leaders and to make the necessary area available for each part of the Jewish Temple and its respective outer buildings, gates, and bridges. The Gentile section could be another place on the Temple Mount. Consequently, the location of this Gentile court and the removal of the El Aqsa Mosque is open to debate.

Where Will the Rebuilt Temple Stand?

The traditional location of the Temple of Solomon, Zerubbabel, and Herod has always been at the foundation stone in the Dome of the Rock. And the Jews are adamant that the Temple must be rebuilt on its earlier foundations. To accomplish this, the Dome of the Rock would have to be removed.

In an attempt to reconcile the placement of the Temple with the existing Muslim buildings, several alternative locations have been presented.

The Northern Location

Dr. Asher Kaufman has investigated a theory that the Temple was originally built to the north of the Dome of the Rock.[168] While excavating a cistern for water storage on the northwest edge of the platform supporting the Dome of the Rock, the Supreme Muslim Council discovered an ancient wall. Following standard policy for any discovered remains, they

---

[168] Kaufman, Ashers, "Where the Ancient Temple of Jerusalem Stood" *Biblical Archaeological Review*, IX: 2(March/April 1983): 40

called for government archaeologists. These archaeologists identified a wall made of massive stones that could have been Herodian. The wall was five meters long, two meters thick, and several courses high.

This could have been the eastern wall of the Herodian Temple Mount complex. In this view, the Temple would have been placed on the north side of the raised Temple Mount platform in line with the Eastern Gate. It is believed that the Temple was aligned with a gate on the east side. This location would place the Temple in alignment with the Eastern Gate.

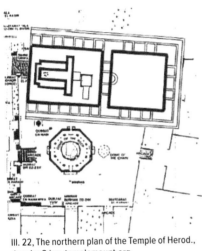

Ill. 22, The northern plan of the Temple of Herod., drawing3.jpg templemount.org

The Dome of the Spirits is a small cupola in this area covering exposed bedrock like that inside the Dome of the Rock. Some people believe that this rock served as the Holy of Holies area in the Temple. Dr. Kaufman believes this location would be correct because the Herodian wall fits his theory for the placement of the Temple, the exposed rock would fit the location for the Holy of Holies, and the Temple would align with the Eastern Gate.

There are several difficulties with this theory. The archaeologists who examined the stones disagree as to whether they could be from the Herodian Second Temple period. The wall could have been the remains of another Herodian structure or of a different historical period, such as a later Roman structure. We have already shown evidence that many scholars believe that the Romans built a profane Temple on the north side of the earlier Jewish Temple in the time of Hadrian, in the location of the "Kaufman plan."

Also, the Jewish historian Josephus describes a moat between the Roman Antonia fortress and the Temple of Herod. This moat has been discovered underground and the moat would encompass part of the land area of the Temple of the "Kaufman plan."

The Eastern Gate is not the only gate on the eastern side of the Temple Mount. At least four gates have existed in the past and possibly others also. The existing Eastern Gate was not built until the Sixteenth Century. Thus, the Temple could have been aligned with another gate, such as the nearby gate referred to (mistakenly) as the Shushan Gate.

Archaeologists are very hesitant about supporting this theory until more evidence can be found to prove it. And that would be very difficult because excavations are not allowed on the Temple Mount.

The Southern Location

Another little-known theory was presented by Franciscan scholar Father Bellarmino Bagatti, sometimes known as the southern location, near to the front of al-Aqsa Mosque.[169]

Father Bagatti believes the Temple once stood to the south of the Dome of the Rock, with the Al Kas (Muslim washing fountain) serving as the Holy of Holies. Others have proposed this theory by trying to line up the gates of the Temple Mount with a shorter bridge to the Mount of Olives.

He based his theory on observations of the Temple Mount walls, belief that the Temple was situated at a lower elevation than the Dome of the Rock platform—closer instead to the City of David on the Hill of Orphel, belief that the Dome of the Rock has no real historical significance, and the reading of an ancient account of a pilgrimage to the Temple site in A.D. 438.

An early group of pilgrims to the Temple Mount, led by Barsauma, describes the Jews gathering on the Temple Mount

---
169 Bellarmino Bagatti, *Recherches sur le Site du Temple de Jerusalem*, 1979.

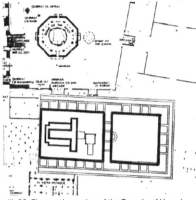

Ill. 23, The southern plan of the Temple of Herod., drawing3.jpg templemount.org

to venerate their ruined Temple "at the gates which lead to Siloam." This would place the Temple near the El Aqsa Mosque which stands on the remains of the Huldah Gate in the southern wall, an ancient underground double gateway that leads to the Pool of Siloam.

This view has very little significant support and is based largely on supposition. The account of the pilgrimage in A.D. 438 was very interesting but does not necessarily discount the Dome of the Rock Site. Jews have always been restricted from treading the exact Temple site for fear of accidentally crossing the Holy of Holies and causing a further desecration to the site. These Jews may have known the location of the Temple was in the center of the platform and have gathered a little to the south in respect for the other location.

The Traditional Location

The Dome of the Rock is the traditional location of the past temples of Solomon, Zerubbabel, and Herod, and also the site of various other Biblical references. Many centuries before the Temple of Solomon was ever built there, Abraham led his son Isaac to the top of this mountain to offer him as a sacrifice to God. The Lord stopped Abraham from sacrificing his son, providing a ram caught in a thicket to die in his stead. Some people believe that this is the traditional location of Jacob's dream. Jacob, the father of the original twelve tribes, had a dream upon this mountain where he dreamed of a ladder with angels ascending and descending from heaven. (There is also another possible location of Jacob's dream, but it is this location that is held by tradition.) King David purchased this mount as a place dedicated to build a house for the Lord. His son Solomon built the first Temple to the Lord there about 950 B.C. and that is where the Temple location has always remained.

The Dome of the Rock was first built as a Byzantine church over the Foundation Stone at the Temple Mount. Why would the Byzantines build a church over this exposed rock? It is my opinion that the early Christians believed that this was the location of the Jewish House of God, where the Shekinah glory cloud resided over the Ark of the Covenant, and that it was the holiest place on earth. So, they built the church at this site to preserve and venerate the location. Many traditions name this exact position as being the correct area of the past Temples, and it has been the setting of the Temple traditionally upheld by the Jewish rabbis.

The Foundation Stone as the Site of the Holy of Holies

There has long been a belief that the Ark of the Covenant stood on the bedrock of the Temple Mount, presumably the highest point of the Mount. The large, exposed rock, called the Even Shetiyyah or "Foundation Stone" is the highest point of the Temple Mount platform, and is possibly the rock where the Ark of the Covenant rested.

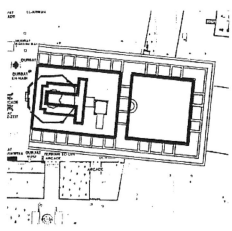

Ill. 24, The Temple with the Rock as the Holy of Holies., drawing1.jpg templemount.org

The book *Ready to Rebuild* recounts a July 1991 interview of the Jewish scholar Dan Bahat. In it, he states his opinion of where the Temple stood:

> I will say right now that the Temple is standing exactly where the Dome of the Rock is today on the Temple Mount. I want to say explicitly and clearly that we believe that the Rock under the Dome is the precise site of the Holy of Holies. [To be more accurate], the Temple extended exactly to the place where the Dome is today. The "Foundation Stone" (the Rock within the Dome) is actually that stone which comprised that Holy of Holies.[170]

Further proof of the Temple location at the Dome of the Rock is provided by Leen Ritmeyer. Explained in detail in the pages of the *Biblical Archaeological Review*, Dr. Ritmeyer describes the significance of the large stones at the northwestern entrance to the Dome of the Rock platform.[171] The stones at the base of the steps are massive, ancient stones and are of a different size, color, and cut from the other stones in the steps, carrying typical characteristics of Solomonic stones. It is Dr. Ritmeyer's contention that these stones are the remains of the earlier Temple platform of Solomon, and measuring from this location and other wall remains, the location of the Temple would be placed at the Dome of the Rock.

Thus, tradition, rabbinical scholars, and archaeological opinion agree that the Dome of the Rock is the correct location of the past Temples and the only possible location for the future Temple.

There are two slight variations of this location. One opinion identifies the Foundation Stone as the place of the Holy of Holies inside the back of the Temple building proper. The other possibility locates the Foundation Stone at the Altar of the Temple complex in the front of the Temple building.

The Foundation Stone as the Site of the Altar

When the Western side of Jerusalem was captured in the

---

170 Thomas Ice, Randall Price, *Ready to Rebuild*, Ibid., 166-167.
171 Ritmeyer, Leen, "Locating the Original Temple Mount" *Biblical Archaeological Review* (XVIII: 2, March/April 1992), 24-45

war of 1967, Chief Rabbi Goren led a group of soldiers to the top of the Temple Mount and meticulously measured the Temple Mount walls to establish the location of the walls of the inner Temple.

Chief Rabbi Goren tells us:

> The Holy of Holies is not ... beneath, nor is it located within the Dome of the Rock. The Moslems are mistaken. I made the measurements right after the Six-Day War, and I came to the conclusion, and it is 100 percent [certain], that the Holy of Holies is outside the Dome of the Rock, to the west side.[172]

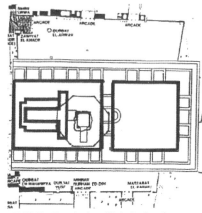

Ill. 25, The Temple plan with the Rock as the Altar., drawing1.jpg templemount.org

One interesting consideration is that the altar of the Temple rested on natural bedrock and was approached by ascending a ramp on the south side. This would be the highest bedrock on the Temple Mount. Ancient rabbinical sources tell of drainage channels and a sewer at the altar.

In the Foundation Stone is evidence of drainage channels cut into the stone and underneath are several underground chambers which once held fluid and lead off in a great distance, presumably all the way to the Kidron Valley. These channels would fit the description of the drainage channels used for the altar and the chambers (or caves) would have possibly been the sewage system.[173]

According to rabbinical descriptions, the distances were given for the area of the Temple from the southern, northern, and western walls.[174] Assuming the cubit equals 1.6 feet, or about 19 inches, the Altar must have stood over the Foundation Stone

---

172 Ice, Thomas and Price, Randall, *Ready to Rebuild*, Ibid., 164-165.
173 Tiferes Yisroel, Rashi, Pesachim 22a
174 Shiltai HaGiborim

and the Holy of Holies would have stood 176 feet to the west, near the western steps of the platform. Thus, there is strong evidence that the Foundation Stone probably would have been the place of the Temple Altar because of the height of the rock required for the Altar, the rock included drainage channels and a sewer, and it matches the measurements from rabbinical sources, such as Rabbi Goren.

Consequently, according to this view the Temple will be built to the west of the Dome of the Rock with the Rock servings as its Altar. The Holy of Holies would be placed at the western steps to the Dome of the Rock platform. Either of these views must be proven archaeologically—and probably will sometime in the future—which will tell us the full evidence in stone of which view is correct.

What Will the Temple Look Like?

The Temple will be built in the same fashion as the earlier Temples. The book *The Holy Temple Revisited* is one of many recent attempts to establish the exact dimensions of the earlier Temples in order to enable a rebuilding of another sanctuary. This book outlines in great detail the specifics of the Temple and its furniture.[175] The Temple was a building of simplicity and yet adorned in great splendor with fine gold, cedar wood, and beautifully spun curtains in a myriad of colors.

The exterior of the building will be majestic, and the courtyard will be expansive, such as befitting the glory of the Lord. The courtyard and exterior walls are different to the Temple of the Old Testament.

The Temple of Solomon was built with a courtyard that surrounded the Temple in a rectangular fashion. But the Temple of the Tribulation will be surrounded by a larger square courtyard and the interior courtyard arrangement will be different.

---

[175] Leibel Reznick, *The Holy Temple Revisited* (Jason Aronson, Inc., 1985), 120-139.

The book of Ezekiel describes the future Temple as being over a mile long and wide. The Bible gives its dimensions in lengths called reeds. But this would make the Temple larger than the entire Temple Mount! Because of the impossibility of building the Temple on the existing Mount on such a grand scale, it is generally assumed that the Temple must be measured in cubits (about 18-24 inches) instead of reeds (about 126-144 inches).

Using the measurement of cubits, and assuming that a cubit is about 19 inches, the Temple would exactly fit the Dome of the Rock platform! Adjusting the Ezekiel Temple size to 550 feet by 540 feet, the Temple could be replaced on the existing platform.

The Bar Kokhba Temple

The Dome of the Rock's platform was first built to house the Temple of Bar Kokhba in A.D. 130. This Temple could have been built in the plan outlined by Ezekiel in Ezekiel 40–48. But in the Second Temple period, the plans for another Temple already existed.

In the Dead Sea scroll caves, a famous scroll was discovered in Cave Eleven called the Temple Scroll. This scroll outlined the building of a future Temple. Yigael Yadin researched this scroll and explained that the Temple of the Scroll was not the final Temple of the Lord. It was not exactly like the Temple of the Old Testament or the Temple of Ezekiel's prophecy. Yadin explains:

> *The one [the Temple] in the scroll purports to be the Temple which the Children of Israel are commanded to build. The one in the vision of Ezekiel is the Temple of the future which the Lord himself will create. The two, therefore, need not be identical. And the author could find backing in the fact that in certain significant details Ezekiel himself departs from the plan of Solomon's Temple as depicted in Kings and Chronicles.*[176]

[176] Yadel Yadin, *The Temple Scroll: The Hidden Law of the Dead Sea Sect* (Random House, 1985).

CHAPTER TWELVE

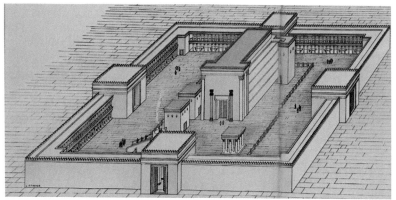

Ill. 26, The Temple Scroll Temple., Temple-Scroll-bog.jpg ritmeyer.com

This Temple plan was known to the leaders of the Jews during the Second Temple period and was found very close to the letters of Bar Kokhba in a nearby cave. It is Yadin's opinion that the Temple plan of the Temple scroll was known to Josephus and was a part of the description we find in his writing, Antiquities, which reflects this Temple plan. Although very similar in some ways, again the courtyards and gates and some buildings are quite different. This plan might well have been the plan used by Bar Kokhba to rebuild or plan to build the Temple on the Temple Mount.

The Temple of Ezekiel

The Jews today believe that they are preparing to rebuild the last great Temple of the Lord and begin the Kingdom Age. In their view, the Messiah will soon return to rule in His Kingdom and the Millennial Age of peace will commence. So, the Temple that the Jews want to rebuild is the Temple of Ezekiel's prophecy. They will actually build the Temple of the Tribulation Period, but they believe that it will establish the Millennial Kingdom. Thus, to identify the coming Tribulation Temple, we must look at the Temple of Ezekiel's prophecy that they propose to raise.

It has already been mentioned that the Ezekiel Temple would be too large for the Temple Mount, and so the size of the reed is assumed to be adjusted to the cubit.

The Temple Building itself will be built in the same manner as the Temple of Solomon and Herod but the outer buildings and courtyard will be different. The courtyard plan is based upon a square instead of a rectangle and will include much more room, enabling the inclusion of many more buildings and a more expansive open area.

A Description of Herod's Temple

To get a picture of what the building would be fashioned like, let us examine a description of the Sanctuary built by Herod as seen by Josiphon, a historian from the Roman period.

Josiphon describes the Temple:

> *The stones with which the king [Herod] built the Sanctuary were white as snow. A single stone was twenty-five cubits in length, twelve cubits in width, and eight cubits high, marble stones. Each stone was identical, from the foundations until the top of the building. The sanctuary rose very high. It could be seen anywhere in the city and from afar.*
>
> *The doors were fashioned most ornately. The doorposts, lintels, the knobs, and the hinges were all made of silver. Over each door hung a curtain the same size as the door. Woven curtains, made of gold, blue wool, purple wool, and scarlet threads, set with precious gems and points of gold and blue wool, most beautiful. Each curtain had a border of a golden floral design.*
>
> *There were pillars of gold with silver bases and golden hooks. He fashioned a sculpture of grape clusters and leaves and vines out of the purest gold and hung the sculpture atop the pillars. One thousand talents [approximately 2.4 million ounces] of the purest gold was its weight. These clusters were fashioned with the greatest wisdom. The tendrils, leaves, and blossoms were of sparkling gold, the clusters of greenish gold, and the berries of precious gems. All the work was intricate and detailed. It was a*

wonder to behold, and brought joy to all that saw it. Many in Rome testified to this, for they saw it in the house that was destroyed.[177]

Thus, the Temple of Herod was a magnificently beautiful structure. It was considered the most beautiful ancient building ever made. The coming Tribulation Temple will look something like this description, being patterned closely after Herod's Temple.

A Walk Through the Tribulation Temple

The Main Sanctuary itself will be 100 cubits high and 100 cubits wide (240 feet by 240 feet) fashioned something like the letter "T."

The Portico (porch) will be similar to the top of the "T" with the rest of the building extending out perpendicularly. The Portico will be a shallow but very wide and tall porch with two large windows in the front.

The Holy Place will extend out from the Portico and will include paneled walls overlaid with gold, engraved with palm trees, vines, flowers, and angels. Inside this room will be placed the Temple furniture, such as the Table of Showbread, the Altar of Incense, and the Menorah (the seven-branched candlestick). In ancient times, the curtain to the Holy Place and the Holy of Holies were only opened at the festival feasts so that the people could see the beauty of the engravings on the walls and the golden furniture.

The Holy of Holies will be entered by passing through two curtains which veil the Ark of the Covenant from view. Only on the Day of Atonement can the high priest pass inside to sprinkle the blood of anointing on the Mercy Seat of the Ark.

The entire Temple building will be surrounded by Treasury rooms that will be built on three different levels. In front of the Temple is the Altar. The Altar will be built on natural bedrock

---
[177] Josiphon, *History of the Jews During the Period of the Second Temple, and the War Between the Jews and the Romans* (Hominer Publication, 1967) Chapter 55, 193.

and will be elevated. There will be a ramp on the south side of the Altar to ascend to the place of sacrifice. The Altar will stand centered in front of the doors of the Temple, and it will be surrounded by the Court of the Priests. The Altar will be the center and focal point of the entire Temple Complex, once again offering sacrifices as a sweet savor to the Lord.

In the Priest's Courtyard that surrounds the Altar in front of the Temple, there will be another courtyard. On the east side there will be a platform that is called the Courtyard of the Israelites (or Courtyard of Men). In ancient times, you would enter this courtyard by passing through the Gate on the east side called the Nicanor Gate. There will now be three gates similar to this gate on the north, south and east of the Courtyard of the Priests.

Differences Between the Tribulation Temple and Solomon Temple

Solomon's Temple complex contained a courtyard in the very front of the east side called the Courtyard of Women. This courtyard was shaped in the shape of a Greek cross and the Temple Sanctuary was formed in the manner of an Egyptian cross. In these courtyards were various rooms such as rooms for the priests, the Supreme Court, the Nazarites, pregnant women, lepers, temple vessels, music instruments, and wood for the sacrifices.

The Tribulation Temple will have the same inner Sanctuary, the inner courtyard for the priests containing the Altar, and the three gates similar to the Nicanor Gate. It will also have a Court of Women, but then it will be

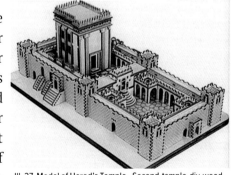

Ill. 27, Model of Herod's Temple., Second-temple-diy-wood-kit-made-Israel.jpg zaksjerusalemgifts.com

CHAPTER TWELVE

much larger, surrounding the entire Temple Complex. In each corner of the expansive Court of Women will be a cooking chamber.

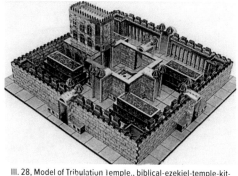

Ill. 28, Model of Tribulation Temple., biblical-ezekiel-temple-kit-detail.jpg zaksjerusalemgifts.com

Another significant difference to this Temple will be that there will only be three gates into the surrounding walls instead of thirteen. In Solomon's Temple there were three gates to the Women's Courtyard and separate gates to the Priest's Courtyard, but then the Women's Courtyard will encompass the entire complex, giving only three gates of access. The inner Priest's Courtyard will also only be accessible by three gates in the Women's Courtyard, picturing the Trinity of God: the Father, the Son, and the Holy Spirit.

This will be a glorious Temple, possibly exceeding the glory of all Temples before it. It will be a very sacred site. Jewish law, worship, and sacrifice will be rigorously maintained to follow the Lord's Old Testament commands.

The Tribulation Temple Destroyed

Sadly, this Tribulation Temple will only stand for about seven years. Antichrist will come to desecrate it, and the "people of the prince that shall come shall destroy the city and the sanctuary ..." (Dan. 9:26).

All the glory, all the beauty, all the magnificence will be gone as the madman of the universe unleashes his vile work of desecration on the Temple and on Jerusalem. But never fear. The Lord is coming to fight this "man of sin" and He will overcome him valiantly in the great Battle of Armageddon.

Then Jesus will usher in His final Kingdom and establish a greater Millennial Temple where all the world will come to worship the Savior and King.

CHAPTER THIRTEEN

The Millennial Kingdom

The coming Millennium marks the beginning of the reign of Jesus on this earth. Peace has finally come to the world. All the wars of the earth are ended. The Antichrist has been subdued and soundly defeated and is cast into the Lake of Fire, together with the False Prophet, the evil man who helped bring him to power. Jesus will begin His reign on earth from Jerusalem, His holy city, and His Temple will be erected on His holy mount.

The World in Chaos

At the beginning of this Kingdom, the world will be in chaos. The earth has just experienced the most disastrous time of destruction, disease, famine, and divine judgment ever known. At the beginning of the Millennium, it is estimated that only one-third of the Jews and one-third of the Gentiles will be left alive, about one-quarter dying in the first half, and another one-third or more dying in the second half of the Tribulation. One estimate is two-thirds of 9 billion, being 6 billion people, dying at this time.[178]

Society has fallen to mass anarchy, businesses have failed, and even the cities are laid waste. The financial market has collapsed, money is scarce, food is difficult to find, and there is not a family in which there is not someone dead.

Zechariah 8:10 describes the scene on earth in those days, "For before these days there was no hire for man, nor any hire for beast; neither was there any peace to him that went out or came in because of the affliction." Now, Jesus will bring order to chaos, peace to a world of war. He will bring political, financial, and spiritual stabilization, and God will rule on earth as the King of all mankind.

---

[178] Tiff Shuttlesworth, *How Many People Will Die During the Tribulation?* Accessed on Feb. 1, 2023, https://lostlamb.org

The Judgment of All Nations

At the beginning of the Millennium, Jesus will judge all the nations. Jesus will be seated on His throne on the holy mountain and He will judge both Jews and Gentiles who have served the Antichrist and not followed the Lord. All those who were followers of the Antichrist, not believers in Jesus, will be judged. This will include those people living on earth at that time but not include resurrected saints (who were already judged and rewarded at the Judgment Seat of Christ). In other words, the people of this world will be judged while still in their natural bodies. Those nations who have treated the Christians with compassion and fairness will be rewarded. But those who have oppressed God's servants shall be sent to eternal damnation.[179]

The Bible tells us that this judgment will happen at the Valley of Jehoshaphat in Jerusalem. Jesus will be seated on Mount Moriah and will look over the Valley of Jehoshaphat, sometimes called the Kidron Valley. This valley is between the Temple Mount and the Mount of Olives. As Jesus descends to earth, the Olivet Mount will be split and fall, and the Valley of Jehoshaphat will be much enlarged.

In Joel 3:1-2, 12 the Bible describes the scene:

> *For, behold, in those days, and in that time,*
> *When I shall bring again the captivity of Judah and Jerusalem,*
> *I will also gather all nations,*
> *And will bring them down into the valley of Jehoshaphat,*
> *And will plead with them there for my people and for my heritage Israel,*
> *Whom they have scattered among the nations,*
> *and parted my land. ...*
>
> *Let the heathen be wakened, and come up to the valley of Jehoshaphat: for there will I sit to judge all the heathen round about.*

---
[179] Arno Fruchtenbaum, *The Footsteps of Messiah* (San Antonio, Tx: Ariel Ministries, 1983)

This judgment is usually seen as the Judgment of the Sheep and the Goats in Matthew 25. In this judgment, all the sheep nations that have treated well the believers of Christ by feeding the hungry, giving drink to the thirsty, housing the homeless, clothing the naked, visiting the sick, and aiding the oppressed will be rewarded. Matthew 25 tells us that the righteous saints will "… inherit the kingdom prepared for you from the foundation of the world." (Matt. 25:33-34)

These will be the people who inherit the Kingdom of God on this earth, and who enter this inheritance. The evil nations will be judged and found sinful and sent to everlasting punishment. Thus, all those who enter this future Kingdom of God will be Christian followers of Jesus Christ, and it is probably only these believers who would have helped the Jewish people who were also being persecuted by the Antichrist. Thus, those people would now be revealed as true followers of God and enter into His Kingdom.

Although previous saints, followers of Jesus, have been resurrected or raptured and received glorified, eternal bodies, these people living on earth who enter the Millennium will enter in their natural bodies and continue to live out the next thousand years on earth. They will still be able to procreate, and they will have children born to them during the entire Millennium. Because there will be a world of peace with no sickness, death will be so rare that if someone dies at a hundred years of age, it is considered that a small child has died. These are the people that glorified saints will help to rule and reign over. They will teach, and they will witness of God's working in earlier times. It is believed that the world population can grow to as many as fifty billion people during this Millennial Kingdom of Peace!

God Establishes His Kingdom on Earth

God has always planned to rule the earth in a Theocratic Kingdom.

George N. H. Peters reminds us,

> Stanley ... correctly says, "The Theocracy of Moses was not a government of priests as opposed to kings; it was a government by God Himself, as opposed to government by priests or kings. It was indeed, in its highest sense, as appeared afterward in the time of David, compatible both with regal and sacerdotal (priestly) rule." Originally and primally, all civil and religious law proceeded from God; and others in the government were subordinates to carry into execution the supreme will of the King, i.e., God. The Theocracy then is something very different from Divine Sovereignty and must not be confounded with the same.[180]

God has always ruled over the universe in the Universal Kingdom of God. Yet, at times, God exercised more direct contact and control over the earth, and at other times ruled through the workings of men. Sometimes this is oversimplified and explained as the theocracy, the rule of God, and kingdom, the rule of men, but God has always had an influence and leading over mankind.

In the Garden of Eden, when God first created mankind as Adam and Eve, He commanded that they should subdue the earth, be fruitful, and multiply. God placed Adam as the ruler over his animal creation, and also as ruler over his own race of mankind; God gave him dominion over all of creation. But because of Adam's fall into sin, and the subsequent fall of mankind into being born as sinners, God moved to the order of people living while guided by Conscience. Mankind grew more and more sinful, so much so that God was sorry that He even made man and He sent the universal Flood in judgment, yet by grace saved a remnant of Noah and his family. Through the rule of Human Government, when mankind rebelled with building the tower of Babel, God then sent the judgment of confusion of tongues (languages), and even divided the land into continents.

---
180 George N. H. Peters, *The Theocratic Kingdom* (New York: Funk & Wagnalls, 1884; Grand Rapids: Kregel, reprint edition), Vol. I, 217.

CHAPTER THIRTEEN

God chose to reveal Himself and His plan of redemption and Promise, and He next spoke to Abraham and his family, who after several generations moved to Egypt. Later, after Israel was freed from Egyptian slavery in the Exodus, under the time of Moses, God sent the Law, and the entire Tabernacle/Temple worship system to show mankind his need for a savior and to bring people to God. When Gideon was offered the kingship, he refused and said, "... I will not rule over you, neither shall my son rule over you: The LORD shall rule over you" (Judges 8:23). Although Israel soon wanted an earthly king and monarchy, with many successive kings such as Saul, David, Solomon, and then the divided kingdoms, Israel continually rebelled against God, went into idolatry, repented, and returned to God, and then returned to idolatry.

After the Exile and Return of the Jewish people, God did send the Savior, Jesus Christ, as prophesied in Isaiah 9:6; 7:14, Daniel 9:26, and many other places, and Jesus came to offer the Kingdom to the Jewish people. His offer and Kingdom were rejected, and they crucified their Savior, but He rose from the grave, proving that He is God in the flesh. However, this also was foreseen by God as His ultimate plan to provide the way of salvation by His grace through our believing faith, that we accept His gift of salvation, and receive Jesus Christ as Savior because "... as many as received him, to them gave he power to become the sons of God, even to them that believe on his name." (John 1:12) During the Church Age, Christ continually works spiritually in the hearts of men and through His Church, and these believing saints will be raptured at the end of the Church Age.

During a short Tribulation Period, many cataclysmic things will occur as the Antichrist comes to power to rule over the world. During his short reign, he will try to kill all believing Christians who are saved at this time, and he will later attempt to kill all of the Jews. In the Battle of Armageddon, he gathers the armies of this world to fight against the Jews and bring final total destruction of the entire Jewish race, but Christ appears in the clouds to fight the Antichrist and his forces. At this time, the Jews will see Him whom they have pierced, will cry in anguish, and will be saved as a nation physically and spiritually in one day. Then, Jesus will establish the prophesied coming Kingdom of God on earth, during the Millennium, where Jesus rules as Priest and King.

To slightly review the working of God in a theocracy, let us look at The Greatness of the Kingdom:

> *This theocratic kingdom began with Moses, continued under Joshua and the judges, developed and reached its highest degree of extension and prosperity under the first three kings, declined after Solomon and the division of the tribes, and came to a melancholy end with the departure of the Visible Presence at the Captivity. If, in the beginning, it seems strange to have a kingdom without a king, we must not forget that in this kingdom it is God, not man, who rules. And this theocratic rule could be, and was historically, mediated directly through chosen leaders of various types, whether prophets or judges or kings. The important idea is not to be found in the title these various leaders bore, but rather to their common function of mediatorial rule. Considered as individuals, there were vast differences between them both in ability and faithfulness. But all alike were held responsible to God for the manner in which they exercised their divinely appointed mediatorial function in the only kingdom ever established by God Himself on earth over a single nation in human history.*[181]

At the beginning of the Millennium, God now finally establishes the Kingdom of Theocratic rule on earth, where Jesus reigns personally, literally, and bodily as King of Kings and Lord of Lords. It will be a Spiritual Kingdom.[182] Salvation will come from God, and He will save all who believe on Him

---
181   Alva McClain, *The Greatness of the Kingdom*, Ibid., 92-93.
182   Alva McClain, *The Greatness of the Kingdom*. Ibid., 218.

by His grace. Isaiah tells us men will draw from the "wells of salvation" (Isa. 12:1-6), they will be clothed in the "garments of salvation" (Isa. 61:10), and even the walls of Jerusalem will be called "Salvation" (Isa. 60:18). When the men of the city shout, "Thy God reigneth," then they will also proclaim, "The Lord hath made bare his holy arm in the eyes of all the nations; And all the ends of the earth shall see the salvation of our God" (Isa. 52:7, 10).

Salvation will be accomplished only by the grace of God. During all the existence of mankind on earth, there is only one way of salvation: being saved by believing in the grace of God. Just as the Old Testament saints looked forward to the prophecies of a coming Deliverer, a kinsman-redeemer and Savior, Immanuel (God with us)—namely, Jesus Christ of Nazareth and His provision of salvation by His death on the cross, burial, and resurrection—so too, future people will be saved by looking back to the cross of Jesus. They will know the fulfillment of these prophecies to the last detail; they will know the understanding of salvation and its effects to a vastly in-depth degree; and they will believe in God by grace through faith.

God's grace is also a key feature of His reign on earth in mercy and justice. At the beginning of the Kingdom, when describing the wondrous King of Glory, the first thing about the majestic King mentioned in Psalm 45 is "Grace is poured into thy lips" (Ps. 45:2). And with the outpouring of the "spirit of grace" in Zechariah 12:10 is the portrayal of a coming kingdom when God gives both "grace and glory" (Ps. 84:11).

During this Kingdom, there will be repentance for sin (Jer. 31:19), forgiveness by God ("... let him return unto the Lord ... for he will abundantly pardon"—Isa. 55:7), justification for sinners when we are covered with God's righteousness (Jer. 23:6), the Holy Spirit will be poured out on Israel and all flesh (Joel 2:27–28), and there will be sanctification of human life (Zeph. 3:11-13).

Jesus, as King, will be the central figure of the Kingdom. "Behold, a king shall reign in righteousness ... And a man shall be as an hiding place from the wind, And a covert from the tempest; ... As the shadow of a great rock in a weary land" (Isa. 32:1-2). His salvation is available to all who believe ("Ho, every one that thirsteth, come"), is free to all ("without money and without price"), and the saved are given lasting, eternal salvation they can never lose, because it is "sure" (Isa. 55:1-3).

The Kingdom will bring joy to all of the world, and it will be a world full of singing and music. Jeremiah 31:12 tells us, "... they shall come and sing...their soul shall be as a watered garden, And they shall not sorrow any more at all." Isaiah 51:11 beautifully describes this exuberant, joyful time: "Therefore the redeemed of the Lord shall return, And come with singing unto Zion; And everlasting joy shall be upon their head: They shall obtain gladness and joy; And sorrow and mourning shall flee away."

Moral values will be changed, and the world will have proper ethics and social conditions. In Isaiah's day, he told us there were men who called "evil good and good evil; That put darkness for light, and light for darkness" (Isa. 5:20). But when Jesus rules on earth as King, moral values will be measured by God's law and have to stand up to God's righteousness. Thus, "the crooked shall be made straight" (Isa. 40:4). When men are taught by the Master Teacher, the King of Righteousness, the Word of God will go forth and be spread across the world (Isa. 2:3). God will bring forth justice in truth and God's truth will rule the earth.

The Blessings of the Millennium

Ezekiel 36 gives us a unique view into many aspects of the Millennium in one magnificent tapestry of majestic glory. All of these aspects are part of the blessings of God on the Earth during the Millennium. The gracious blessings are social, physical, and even spiritual in nature.

Here, God demonstrates that the future spiritual blessings are tangible in their result and we will see and experience these astounding events. In Ezekiel 36, Israel is regathered into their own land (verse 24), there is divine cleansing from sin (verse 25), a new spiritual heart (verse 26), the gift of God's Spirit (verse 27), an increase in agricultural production with no more famines (verse 29-30), genuine repentance for sin (verse 31), a work of repentance and divine grace (verse 32), wasteland will be reclaimed and waste cities rebuilt (verses 33-35), the nations shall see that God is doing all of this (verse 36), and a great increase in population shall fill the devastated cities (verses 37-38). Thus, the Kingdom is a spiritual kingdom with physical, moral, political, and worldwide effects.

Topographical Changes in the Middle East

Topographical changes are also abundant in the land of God during this time. A great earthquake has rent the Mount of Olives into a huge valley. This calamity has also brought forth a mighty river that runs along the valley's side all the way from the Mediterranean Sea to the Dead Sea. A spring shoots forth a fountain from the area of the Temple which becomes a great river and it flows to the Mediterranean and to the Dead Sea. This will become a waterway for future shipping traffic and commerce and people can even be moved by sea, as well as by land.

The Bible tells us the multitude of geologic changes in a graphic picture given in Zechariah 14:2-4 and 8-9.

> *For I will gather all the nations against Jerusalem to battle; and the city shall be taken, and the houses rifled, and the women ravished; and half of the city shall go forth into captivity, and the residue of the people shall not be cut off from the city.*
>
> *Then shall the LORD go forth, and fight against those nations, as when he fought in the day of battle.*

> And his feet shall stand in that day upon the mount of Olives, which is before Jerusalem on the east, and the mount of Olives shall cleave in the midst thereof toward the east and toward the west, and there shall be a very great valley; and half of the mountain shall remove to the north, and half of it toward the south.
>
> And it shall be in that day, that living waters shall go out of Jerusalem; half of them toward the former sea, and half of them toward the hinder sea: and in summer and winter it shall be.
>
> And the LORD shall be king over all the earth: in that day shall there be one LORD, and his name shall be one.

Changes in Jerusalem

Topographical changes will occur to modern Jerusalem in the Millennium. The Bible tells us that as a result of this earthquake that the Mount of Olives is fallen and a great valley is left in its place. A mighty river appears in the Kidron Valley, running from the Mediterranean Sea to the Dead Sea.

Not only is Jerusalem to be elevated to be the center of God's kingdom politically, but it will also physically be recognized from a great distance as the "city of the great King." One result of this earthquake is that the surrounding land is leveled down to a plain while the city proper is lifted up to a conspicuous elevation, and becomes at least the largest mountain in that part of the world. The Temple Mount (also called Mount Moriah) will merge with the Zion Mount and become one huge combined mountain. The Tyropoeon (cheesemaker's) valley will be raised and all the city of Jerusalem will be lifted up to become the center of the land of the Millennial Kingdom.

Noted scholar, F. Gardiner, says that the prophecy of Ezekiel describing the size of the city and the changes in the surrounding area could not possibly be taken literally "without changes in the surface of the earth."[183] This, of course, is exactly what God predicted and what happens at the beginning of the Millennium.

---
183 F. Gardiner, *Elliot's Commentary on Ezekiel* (Grand Rapids: Zondervan Publishing House, reprint 1954), 315.

CHAPTER THIRTEEN

Ill. 29, A topographical map of the changes for the Millennial Temple, Topological Map, Temple of Ezekiel's Prophecy, H. Sulley Public Domain

Hebrew Christian author, David Barron, notes, "As the 'city of the great King' (Ps. 48:2), whose dominion extends to earth's utmost bounds, and as the center whence God's light and truth shall go forth among all the nations, Jerusalem is also to be physically exalted above the hills by which she has hitherto been surrounded and overshadowed."[184]

Notice the line on the upper right side of the map that shows the line of cleavage for the Mount of Olives. Also notice that the Millennial Temple will encompass the Temple Mount, the Zion Mount, and the Russian compound, as seen in Illustration 29. It covers almost two entire mountains!

These changes in the city are so vital that God Himself calls upon men to pray "and to give him no rest, till he establish, and till he make Jerusalem a praise in all of the earth." (Isa. 62:6-7)

According to Zechariah 14:10:

> All the land shall be turned as a plain from Geba to Rimmon

---

[184] David Baron, *Visions and Prophecies of Zechariah* (4th Impression; London: Hebrew Testimony to Israel, 1951), 510-513.

> *south of Jerusalem: and it shall be lifted up, and inhabited in her place, and from Benjamin's gate unto the place of the first gate, unto the corner gate, and from the tower of Hananeel unto the king's winepresses.*

As the city is lifted up and exalted above the other land, the Muslim shrines and the foundation of the former Temple and the various churches will be abolished. This will be a hill wholly dedicated to the Lord Jesus.

The Dead Sea Comes to Life

The new river will reach the Dead Sea (the Salt Sea) and this sea will come to life again. No living thing can survive in the Dead Sea today. Today, the waters will poison you. But the Bible tells us that these waters will be healed and a great multitude of fish will be found in the sea.

Ezekiel 47:8-11 relates:

> *Then said he unto me, These waters issue out toward the east country, and go down into the desert, and go into the sea: which being brought forth into the sea, the waters shall be healed.*
>
> *And it shall come to pass, that every thing that liveth, which moveth, whithersoever the rivers come, shall live: and there shall be a very great multitude of fish, because these waters shall come thither: for they shall be healed; and every thing shall live whither the river cometh.*
>
> *And it shall come to pass, that the fishers shall stand upon it from En-gedi even unto En-egla-im; they shall be a place to spread forth nets; their fish shall be according to their kinds, as the fish of the great sea, exceeding many.*
>
> *But the miry places thereof and the marishes thereof shall not be healed; they shall be given to salt.*

Because the fishing is done "from En-gedi even unto En-egla-im" and the "miry places...shall not be healed" but "given to

CHAPTER THIRTEEN

salt," not all the Dead Sea will be changed. The upper portion will be merged with fresh water and come to life but the southern portion will remain the Dead Sea.

Interestingly, the Dead Sea has been receding for many years, although there is no water outlet. The waters have receded so drastically that it has already divided itself and is basically two sections of the same sea. I have been to the Dead Sea on numerous occasions and have seen the water continually recede. But I was very surprised to find the sea had completely divided by the time of my trip in 1993. The southern portion will remain lifeless and salty but the northern portion will be healed and have living fish again.

The Nile River is Stopped

According to Isaiah 11:15,16 and 19:23-25, the Nile River will be stopped and possibly diverted to another channel. This will make a dry passage (or highway) from Egypt to Assyria.

New rivers stretching across the land are also mentioned in Isaiah 35:1, 6 and 7. These rivers possibly will also form pools or lakes in other areas of Israel. The entire land of Israel is elevated and comes to life. Meanwhile, Egypt has an additional 40-year judgment before she is blessed.[185]

Isaiah 35:1 and 7 says:

> *The wilderness and the solitary place shall be glad for them; and the desert shall rejoice, and blossom as the rose.*
>
> *And the parched ground shall become a pool, and the thirsty land springs of water: in the habitation of dragons, where each lay, shall be grass with reeds and rushes.*

New Boundaries for Israel

Israel will be blessed as a nation and given new and enlarged borders. These boundaries are outlined in many places in the

---

[185] Daniel Woodhead, *Ezekiel 30:1-19 – the Impact of the Day of the Lord on Egypt and Her Allies*, Accessed on Feb. 1, 2023, https://bibleoutlines.com

Bible. Genesis 15:18 says the boundaries run "from the river of Egypt unto the great river, the river Euphrates." The northern boundary runs from the northern Euphrates River to the Mediterranean Sea. The southern boundary would include all of the Sinai Peninsula, or at least a large part of the peninsula, with the southern border extending east from Israel's lower current boundary including all the land in a straight line east unto the Persian Gulf. Thus, the borders would include all of current Israel and the West Bank, Lebanon, Jordan, and part of Saudi Arabia, Iraq, Syria, and Egypt, and probably be shaped something like a large triangle.

The boundaries could even include the Arab Emirates, Yemen, Kuwait, and a part of Turkey, depending on possible interpretations taken to their most extreme possibilities, but this is unlikely, while others limit the borders to the time of David and Solomon. The land of Israel will be divided by tribal sections and the area of Jerusalem will be called the Holy Oblation. (Ez. 45:1-8)

Jerusalem is Given a New Name

The city of Jerusalem will be given a new name. Jerusalem will become the capital of the world and the seat of God's government on Earth. This will be the political and religious center of the world, where God's Temple will stand and all the world will come to worship. "For out of Zion shall go forth the law, and the word of the LORD from Jerusalem" (Isa. 2:2). This city of peace will become Jehovah Shammah, (meaning "the Lord is There"). Isaiah 62:2-4 also calls the city Hephzibah (meaning "My Delight Is in Her") and the land of Israel will be named Beulah (meaning "Married to the LORD").

There will be new divisions of land for the individual tribes, running from north to south and becoming something like individual states. In Jerusalem itself, the Temple area is given to God, and a section of this area is called the Holy Oblation and it is an area for the priests of God. Usually, that means it would be for the Levites, but one verse relates that it may be possible that priests are also taken from the Gentiles during the Millennium. This may be a special occurrence in the same way that there were Jewish proselytes in the Old Testament. These proselytes were Gentile followers of the Jewish faith. In the Millennium, there will be believers from all over the world. What is unusual would be the possibility of Gentile believers serving as priests with the Levites in the worship of the Millennial Temple.

God's Political System

God will establish the seat of his throne and government in Jerusalem and the political world will be vastly changed.[186] All the world will operate in a theocracy, but it is a unique form of government. Here, God bodily rules over the world as an international authority. Thus, it can also be seen as a monarchy, but not by a human king, but by God Himself! Thus, it is a unique form of combined theocracy and monarchy.

The kingdom foretold through Old Testament prophecy is a monarchy whose ruler is a King, who will sit upon a "throne," and the "government shall be upon his shoulder." (Isa. 9:6-7) He is God's king, established upon his throne by the supernatural power of "the God of Heaven," and whose regal authority is from Heaven. (Ps. 2:6, Dan. 2:44; 7:14) Yet, this monarchy is not ruled by a mere man, but by the God-man, Immanuel – God with us; namely the Lord Jesus Christ. Therefore, the government is a unique blending of a Theocracy and monarchy into a new form.

All the functions of government are centered in the Messiah-king, and the eyes of man "shall see the king in his beauty" ruling upon the Earth as "judge," "lawgiver" and "king." (Isa. 33:17, 22)

God will rule in truth, holiness, righteousness, and peace.

---
186 Walvoord, John F., *The Return of the Lord*, (Grand Rapids, MI: Zondervan Publishing House, 1978)

"Righteousness and justice are the foundation of his throne." (Ps. 97:12) He will keep to the forms of the law "judging," he will use his own knowledge to get to the truth of every case "seeking judgment," he will quickly exercise the verdict "hastening righteousness" (Isa. 16:5) and he will also rule in strictness. Revelation 19:15 says "He shall rule with a rod of iron." Psalm 2:7-9 remind us, "Thou art my son…Ask of me, and I shall give thee the heathen [nations] for an inheritance…Thou shalt break them with a rod of iron; thou shalt dash them in pieces like a potter's vessel." As a result of this just and righteous rule, with clear consequences for disobedience, Isaiah 26:9 tells us, "The inhabitants of the world will learn righteousness."

And Isaiah reminds us about God's judgment being balanced by his tender mercies when he recounts in Isaiah 16:5, that "in mercy shall the throne be established." The mighty king that rules "with a strong hand" is the same king who will "feed his flock like a shepherd: he shall gather the lambs with his arm, and carry them in his bosom, and gently lead those that are with young." (Isa. 40:9-11) As a result, the people who see this justice and righteousness and those who live in this kingdom will say, "Blessed are they that put their trust in him." (Ps. 2:9, 12) They will experience and know in a personal and vital way, *"Mercy and truth are met together, righteousness and peace have kissed each other."* (Ps. 85:10)

His world will be a world of peace and a world of righteousness. No nation will dare to rise up in war and violence will be unknown. Jesus will be a priest after the order of Melchizedek, and a King from the line of David of Judah. So, He will rule with both the concepts of a religious kingdom which spreads the Word of God, and a political kingdom where He reigns in peace over all of the world. God Himself will "judge among the nations" and peace becomes eternal and an actual reality among the nations. Therefore, "neither shall they (the nations) learn war anymore."

CHAPTER THIRTEEN

Isaiah 2:2-4 describes the scene:

> And it shall come to pass in the last days, that the mountain of the LORD's house shall be established in the top of the mountains, and shall be exalted above the hills; and all nations shall flow into it.
>
> And many people shall go and come and say, Come ye, and let us go up to the mountain of the LORD, to the house of the God of Jacob; and he will teach us of his ways, and we will walk in his paths: for out of Zion shall go forth the law, and the word of the LORD from Jerusalem.
>
> And he shall judge among the nations, and shall rebuke many people: and they shall beat their swords into plowshares, and their spears into pruning-hooks: nation shall not lift up sword against nation, neither shall they learn war anymore.

Ruling and Reigning with Christ

The saints of God will rule and reign with Jesus in this coming Kingdom. (Rev. 5:9-10) In Matthew 19:28 the Bible tells us of the apostles sitting on twelve thrones, ruling over the twelve tribes of Israel. The Lord has promised us that great promise, that we can rule and reign with Him![187]

In Revelation 3:21 Jesus says, "To him that overcometh will I grant to sit with me in my throne, even as I also overcame, and am set down with my Father in his throne." There are two entire chapters of blessing in Revelation 2 and 3 on those who overcome and part of that blessing includes position of power and influence in the kingdom, probably given in relation to those who were more faithful in their continual life with a heart of dedication to God and a life that demonstrates that total consecration. Those who serve God faithfully will probably have a greater position of service in the future Millennium.

The entire world will be transformed at this blessed time. Happiness will fill the air. Singing will be heard in the streets as people rejoice in the goodness of God.

[187] Walvoord, John F., *The Millennial Kingdom*, (Grand Rapids, MI: Zondervan Publishing House, 1976)

Will David Be King Again?

One interesting thing to consider is the opportunity to not only meet many of the people of the past such as people of the Bible, after we are taken to heaven and later return to Earth in our glorified bodies, but this would also include the opportunity to serve God together and to work in His kingdom together with these past saints.

Earlier, it was mentioned that the twelve apostles will rule with Christ and judge Israel, but apparently, King David also returns to serve the Lord. (While these may be some of the key positions of service in the Kingdom, perhaps many of the people of the Bible will have key positions of service, and we can interact and possibly serve with them.)

The Lord Jesus Christ will reign over all the Earth as King of Kings and Lord of Lords, serving as the supreme ruler of all the Earth for "He is a great King over all of the earth," (Ps. 47:2, "He is the governor among the nations," (Ps. 22:28), and "the Lord shall be king over all the earth." (Zech. 14:9) Jesus will rule the world sitting on the throne of his father David as an emperor, a King of all Kings. Revelation 11:15 tells us, "The kingdoms of this world are become the kingdoms of our Lord, and of his Christ, and he shall reign for ever and ever." Thus, Jesus will have many kingdoms, and He will have many saints serving and ruling with Him as lower-level kings, princes, and governors.

Jeremiah 30:9 makes references to King David serving as King to Israel, "But they shall serve the LORD their God, and David their king, whom I shall raise up unto them."

Ezekiel 37:24 tells us, "And David my servant shall be king over them, and they all shall have one shepherd...and my servant David shall be their prince for ever."

There are several verses that refer to Jehovah and a separate prince or prince David in the same verse. It seems that there are two distinct people in these verses.

Notice again, Jeremiah 30:9 tells us they shall serve God and David their King, "But they shall serve the LORD their God, and David their king, whom I shall raise up unto them."

Ezekiel 34:24 says, "And I will be their Lord, and my servant David a prince among them."

In Ezekiel 44:1-3, the Prince sits to eat bread in front of the LORD, and only the prince is allowed to enter by the Eastern Gate, by command of the Lord. In Ezekiel 45:9-25, we find the Prince offering sacrifices for himself and for the people before the Lord. Although Jesus is without sin and would not require a sacrifice, the Prince is not without sin and his offerings are appropriate.

In Ezekiel 46:18, the Prince will take the people's inheritance by oppression and give it to his sons, and he will have a land allotment along with the Ten Tribes of Israel. David had earthly sons, and Jesus does not. The Prince also performs priestly functions in Ezekiel 45:16, 17, 22 and in Ezekiel 46: 4, and 12.

Apparently, King David is resurrected and returns to serve as a prince, a lower king, or a vice-regent over the people of Israel and he has authority only over Israel, while Christ Jesus reigns a King of all the Earth, and also as the King of Glory, even ruling over the domain of the celestial skies of the heavens and outer space. (Eph. 1:9-10, Col. 1:16-20)

Beneficial Climate Change

During the Millennium, the climate of the world will experience change worldwide. Today, man is limited in how he might affect the weather. While man's ability has made astonishing advances in predicting and following the weather patterns of the Earth, his ability is still limited in his control of the weather. The climate of the Earth is an effect of cosmic and geological causes. These factors are affected and changed during the Millennium. Isaiah 30:26 mentions that in the coming day that "the light of the moon shall be as the light of the sun, and the light of the sun shall be sevenfold, as the light of seven days." Whatever these changes may be, they are associated with climatic changes on the earth which will result in more plenteous agricultural results and an increase of cattle. (Isa. 30:23-25)

Franz Delitzsch gives us insight into this time:

> *This also is not meant figuratively...it is not of the new heaven that the prophet is speaking, but of the glorification of nature, which is promised by both Old Testament prophecy and by that of the New at the closing period of earth's history. No other miracles will be needed for this than the wonder-working power of God, which even now produces these changes of weather, the laws of which no researcher of natural science have enabled us to calculate, and which will then give the greater brilliancy and most unchangeable duration to what is now comparably rare: namely, a perfectly unclouded day, with sun or moon shining in all its brilliancy, yet without scorching from the one, or injurious effects from the other. Heaven and earth will then put on their sabbath dress, for it will be the Sabbath of the world's history.*[188]

Consequently, each day will be a perfect day of peaceful tranquility, and the weather will seem invigorating, mild, beautiful, and always in perfect balance. It will look like a brilliant, sunny day, yet without excessive heat, and the most illuminating, clear moon to light each night. And the effects will be constant worldwide.

Increased Fertility and Productivity

As a direct result of improved climate conditions and controlled rainfall, there will be an increase of fruitfulness and agricultural productivity. Instead of "thorns and briars," the wilderness will become a fruitful field. (Isa. 32:13-15) Isaiah 35:1-2 describes this wondrous farming productiveness:

---

188 Franz Delitzsch, *Commentary on Isaiah* trans. J. Martin (Grand Rapids: Eerdmans Publishing Co. reprint, 1950), Vol. II, 39.

CHAPTER THIRTEEN

> *The wilderness and the solitary place shall be glad for them, and the desert shall rejoice, and blossom as the rose.*
>
> *It shall blossom abundantly, and rejoice even with joy and singing: the glory of Lebanon shall be given unto it, the excellency of Carmel and Sharon, they shall see the glory of the LORD, and the excellency of our God.*

There will be no more famines as the hills, the mountains, the valleys, and even deserts and far-off isolated places will become a land of plenty. (Ez. 36:4-11) Psalm 72:16 tells us that even the most remote and barren places will bring forth in abundance. "Then shall be an handful of corn in the earth on top of the mountains, the fruit thereof shall shake like Lebanon." Amos 9:13 recounts, "the plowman shall overtake the reaper, and the treader of grapes him that soweth seed."

Because this fertility of the ground is associated with a special outpouring of God's Spirit, He shall be "poured upon us from on high, and the wilderness be a fruitful field." This is a supernatural restoration of ground fertility (Isa. 32:15; Ps. 104:29-30).

The Disappearance of Physical Disease and Deformity

In spite of all of man's amazing progress and astounding discovery in medical advancement and surgery, we still live in a world of suffering and death. Almost every family has already experienced death or serious medical problems, and if not yet, it is only a matter of time until it comes to everyone. Yet, this will not be the case in the future Kingdom of God on earth.

People will still live out their lives in the normal manner of procreation, birth, and growth. The rejoicing of the bride and bridegroom is heard (Jer. 33:11), the children play in the streets of the cities (Zech. 8:5) and the little ones shall become "a thousand" (Isa. 60:22).

All physical infirmities and deformities will be rectified. People will not be born with deformities, and any physical problems with be quickly remedied.

Isaiah 35:5-6 gives us the scene of the future: "Then the eyes of the blind shall be opened, and the ears of the deaf shall be unstopped. Then shall the lame man leap as an hart, and the tongue of the dumb sing." The inhabitant shall not say, I am sick." (Isa. 33:24) People will have the energy and ability to leap like "an hart," to run, jump and leap like a deer! They will know how to be healed with natural means, such as through knowledge of what to eat, or how to use herbs and vegetation for healing. Ezekiel 47:12 explains, "the fruit thereof shall be for meat, and the leaf thereof for medicine." In some cases, tangible means may be used for healing and also at time these various illnesses may also be dealt with by divine power, when God steps forth to heal quickly.

Longevity of Life

Aging will be a thing of the past and longevity will be commonplace. In the early book of Genesis before the flood, people could live for many hundreds of years and long life was a common occurrence for mankind. So, it shall be in the coming Kingdom. People will live for many hundreds of years and may live throughout the entire 1,000-year period. During the early time of Genesis, men waited longer to have children, and probably had more children over their lifetime. These same characteristics will occur in the time of the Millennium.

Notice Isaiah 65:20, "There shall be no more thence an infant of days, nor an old man that hath not filled his days: for the child shall die an hundred years old; but the sinner being an hundred years old shall be accursed." This means that the old people will have vitality of life, energy, full mental comprehension, and physical agility even into old age, after living several hundred years. Not only will there be a lack of people with mental problems in the future Millennium, mankind will be able to use more of their brain for many more centuries of life. Can you imagine how brilliant people will become, and how advanced civilization can grow in that kind of world?

People will be shocked if someone dies living less than one hundred years and they will think and refer to this as the death of a child. Also, God graciously gives mankind a hundred years to believe in the Lord Jesus as their Savior, but they may not live beyond this first one hundred years because they are considered a "cursed sinner." Thus, all mankind who are past one hundred years are those who have believed in God as their Savior, and they will live out their days, living a life of vitality, energy, and activity even into extreme old age.

Because of the lack of medical illness and deformity, long life will become the rule. Isaiah 65:22 informs us, "for as the days of a tree are the days of my people, and mine elect shall long enjoy the work of their hands." Today, trees commonly live to be hundreds of years old, and people will age slowly and live hundreds of years. Yet they will retain their vitality and enjoy working long hours with their hands even into their advanced age. Infancy will be measured by years instead of by days and there will be no more "an old man that hath not filled his days." Even those living into very advanced age such as 900 years will still have the energy and stamina to enjoy extreme old age and "live out" their days. Today, people sometimes retire without the strength to enjoy their retirement age with travel or other exciting pursuits, but in the Millennium, even the extreme elderly near 1,000 years old will have the energy to enjoy a life of vitality.

The Barrier of Language

During the time of the Millennium, every obstacle to human understanding will be removed. Differences of racial groups, distinct tribal, social, and financial classes and nations have also been empowered by various languages. One of the problems of bringing people together is understanding and the foundation of understanding is language. Attempts to bring about a common language (*lingua franca*) have been made, but usually frustrated by the desire of various groups to keep their distinct culture and identity.

However, Zephaniah 3:9 tells us, "For then will I turn to the people a pure language, that they may call upon the name of the LORD, to serve him with one consent." Zephaniah seems to understand the difficulty with language and that God will one day remedy the problem of understanding the truth about God, and the problem of united worship by bringing all people to pray and worship together with a single language. When commenting on this passage, A. C. Jennings has said, "The discord of Babel shall, as it were, give place to the unity of language."[189] The curse of various languages is taken away to enable all people to speak, know, and understand the same words, nuances, and inflections even in concepts and implications. E.B. Pusey adds, "Before the dispersion of Babel the world was of *one lip*, and that, impure, for it was in rebellion against God. Now it shall be again of *one lip*, and that, purified."[190] We will be unified in language and understanding!

Peace in the Animal Kingdom

Even the animal kingdom shall be transformed. Dangerous animals will no longer hurt us or each other. The curse of the land will be removed. Peace will abound in the land even to the animal kingdom. Originally created to cohabit peacefully with mankind, the animals also experienced a change at the time of Adam's fall, and there became a wildness and danger to interact with many of the animals. Yet, the fascination of mankind with animals, and the love, taming, and interworking with men

---

189   A. C. Jennings, *Elliot's Commentary on Zephaniah* (op. cit.) in loc. See also Hoffman; and Jamieson, Fausset and Brown.
190   E.B. Pusey, *Commentary on Minor Prophets* (New York: Funk and Wagnalls, 1886), in loc.

CHAPTER THIRTEEN

has been an interesting part of man's history and a current captivation today. Hosea 2:18 foresaw a future change in the animal kingdom. "And in that day will I make a covenant for them with the beasts of the field, and with the fowls of heaven, and with the creeping things of the ground: and I will break the bow and the sword and the battle out of the earth, and I will make them to lie down safely." Ezekiel 34:25 adds, "They shall dwell safely in the wilderness, and sleep in the woods." No longer is there fear of other animals as predators, or of mankind hunting the animals, because they can now sleep in perfect safety in the woods. Animals will no longer want to attack or hurt mankind, and apparently, even the ability of reptiles to kill with poison no longer exists. At that time, even an innocent small child can play with a viper or cobra and not be hurt. The lamb no longer fears being eaten by the wolf, and the lion is seen as eating straw, rather than the flesh of other animals. Truly, there must be a change across all of the mammals of the animal kingdom, and this would include reptiles such as snakes and alligators, birds such as eagles and hawks, and fish, such as sharks and other dangerous sea life.

Isaiah 11:6-9 tells us:

> *The wolf also shall dwell with the lamb, and the leopard shall lie down with the kid; and the calf and the young lion and the fatling together; and a little child shall lead them.*
>
> *And the cow and the bear shall feed; their young ones shall lie down together: and the lion shall eat straw like an ox.*
>
> *And the suckling child shall play on the hole of an asp, and the weaned child shall put his hand on the cockatrice' den.*
>
> *They shall not hurt nor destroy in all my holy mountain: for the earth shall be full of the knowledge of the LORD, as the waters cover the sea.*

God's Special Love for the Jewish People

Although the Church is referred to as the Bride of Christ in the New Testament, Israel is the wife of Jehovah in the Old Testament, and there is a special love of God for the Jewish people. They are loved as God's chosen people. They are used to bring about the Word of God and even to provide the Messiah and Savior through the line of David, and they are preserved as a chosen people throughout history. God knew they would be dispersed around the world, but in the last days, they would return to the land in unbelief, and eventually be saved in one day as the people of God. Hosea describes this special relationship of God with Israel in Hosea 2:19-20:

> And I will betroth thee unto me for ever;
> yea, I will betroth thee unto me in righteousness,
> and in judgment, and in lovingkindness, and in mercies.
> I will even betroth thee unto me in faithfulness:
> and thou shalt know the LORD.

Today, many Jews do not know the Savior and are living in unbelief. But God loves the Jewish people, and He will reclaim them and they will return to their God and Savior, even believing in Jesus as their personal Savior. God still has His hand on the Jewish people and He will save them.

God Building His Temple

The Millennial Temple will be rebuilt by God himself and all the world will assist Him. Zechariah 6:11-12 tells us that the coming Messiah will build the Temple of the Lord. The Bible also promises that many people will be allowed to help in the building. Can you imagine the joy of people as they assist in the building of this future final Temple of Glory?

Zechariah 6:15 says,

> And they that are far off shall come and build in the temple of the LORD, and ye shall know that the LORD of hosts hath sent me

unto you. And this shall come to pass, if ye will diligently obey the voice of the LORD your God.

Consequently, God will build his Temple and we will have the privilege to help Him in the work. Artisans will come from around the world to use their handicrafts. Just as Bezalel and his assistants were given special ability in craftmanship, learning, talent, and refined beauty in creating many articles for the Tabernacle and for the building itself, so God will again use and specially gift his people for the task. They will have special imagination for the ability to create with great splendor.

Stone is Provided for Building

Stone for the rebuilding will be exposed, resulting from the earthquake. The First and Second Temples were built from stone quarried from the Temple Mount itself, from within its deep recesses. The Jews believed that the mountain was holy and it was to encompass a holy house. Thus, when building these earlier temples, they quarried stone from the mountain, to only use holy stone for God's sanctuary.

The earthquake would expose new stone for the building. Jerusalem could not only provide limestone as in the earlier temples, but may also exhibit marbles of red, white, pink, and yellow colors, which could be worked to a fine polish.

According to Zechariah 14:10, a new valley is created around the outer boundaries of Israel similar to the great valley in the Dead Sea area. This valley would extend from "Geba to Rimmon."

Sacrifices Renewed in the Temple

This will be a Temple for sacrifices unto the Lord. Isaiah 40:40-42 states that the priests will offer burnt offerings and sacrifices. According to Isaiah 66:21-23, the annual feasts are observed by the entire world. This same passage describes a wonderful event: Priests will be chosen to join in service in the Temple from Gentile nations around the world.

These sacrifices and feasts are observed by all Christians on the Earth. This, in no way, diminishes or replaces the sacrifice of Jesus for our sins on the cross. The sacrifices and feasts are commemorative and venerate his death at Calvary as a memorial, much as our church ordinance of the Lord's Supper shows forth our Lord's death "till he comes."[191] But by the Millennium, Jesus has come! These feasts and sacrifices now look back to his sacrificial death as a memorial to all generations of the salvation of the Lord.

This is also a way for people to comprehend this sacrifice of Jesus dying on the cross for the sins of the world. If Jesus was sitting on his throne displayed in all his glory, ruling on earth in his glorified body as the King of Glory, it would be very difficult to imagine Jesus coming to Earth as the babe of Bethlehem, and then later providing salvation through the cross and resurrection. The sacrificial system is an illustration to the people of the Millennium of the one-time sacrifice of Jesus, atoning for the sins of the world.

The Later Gog and Magog War

The children born to these Millennial people will still need to believe in Jesus as their personal Savior, to be given eternal life. That is why the sacrificial system is restarted, as a memorial to the Cross of Jesus and His payment for the sins of the world. And at the end of the Millennium, some of these children do not yet believe in Jesus as Savior and are deceived by Satan, after he is released from the bottomless pit, in the later episode of the second Gog and Magog war of rebellion, sometimes called Gog and Magog II (Rev. 20:7-9).

This final rebellion is viewed as a rebellion of youth, because

---
191 J. Dwight Pentecost, *Things to Come: A Study in Biblical Eschatology*, (Grand Rapids, MI: Zondervan, 1958), 525 - 527.

CHAPTER FOURTEEN

it is believed that all people involved are less than a hundred years old. They rise in such vast numbers they are described as the sand of the sea, coming against the Lord Jesus Himself.

By the end of the Millennium, with no wars, sickness, disease, and death is almost unknown, it is conservatively estimated that the population of the Earth could grow to as many as fifty billion people. That is why there are so many people, that it looks like the sand of the sea. If an estimated number, such as only five billion people tried to invade the land area of Israel, it would look so vast, that seeing the "sea of people" would look innumerable, something like the sand of the sea.

Even though Satan has been imprisoned for a thousand years, he is "loosed for a season." Mankind has had Jesus ruling on Earth as their priest-King in a glorified body. Other glorified saints have also ruled with Him in the kingdom in various stages of service and salvation is freely taught worldwide. Mankind has had every opportunity to be saved. But men are born sinners in need of a savior, and no matter what situation they may be in, God has shown their need of salvation. In the Garden of Eden, mankind fell into sin, and in the different administrations of his working throughout history (sometimes called the various dispensations of grace), mankind always needs to know God, repent, and believe on Him as Savior. Whether living under the time of Innocence, Conscience, Human Government, Promise, the Mosaic Law, the Church Age, the Tribulation Period, or the Millennium, mankind always falls into sin because they are inherently sinners. No matter what their living environment, mankind can be deceived and turn against God. This shows how extreme is the patience of God and how amazing is the grace of God in saving mankind.

Satan is then loosed from the bottomless pit. He comes and deceives many of the yet unsaved on Earth into following him and trying to take over the Kingdom from God, as a final rebellion of the people and his last desperate attempt at taking God's place on Earth. Jesus, the holy and just King, who rules with a "rod of iron" and cannot allow rebellion, injustice, and the extreme sin of following Satan instead of Christ, responds and calls fire down from heaven on the rebellious in judgment.

While it is certainly important to understand the concept and many aspects of the coming Kingdom of God, for this study, one of the most interesting things is to understand certain details such as the coming Temple of the Millennium. As previously stated, there will be two future temples: the Tribulation Temple, which the Antichrist will desecrate and destroy, and the Millennial Temple, where Jesus Himself will rule and reign during the last thousand years. We will now examine the Millennial Temple.

CHAPTER FOURTEEN

The Millennial Temple

What Will the Millennial Temple Look Like?

The description of the Millennial Temple given by Ezekiel in Ezekiel 40-48 is fascinating. In the vision of Ezekiel, he is set upon a high mountain and views the Temple of the Lord from a distance. In Ezekiel 40:2 he describes the Temple building as looking "like the frame of a city." In his mind, the one building looks as large as any ancient city he has ever seen.

Ezekiel wrote this book while in the ancient city of Babylon, one of the largest cities of the ancient world. From Babylon, he was taken in a vision to the city of Jerusalem and watched as a man took a reed and measured the Temple. This man, "whose appearance was like the appearance of brass," was probably an angel.[192] (Ezek. 40:3)

This man used an ancient measuring flax called a reed to measure the city. The length of a reed was twelve feet. As he watched the man take measurements, Ezekiel was amazed by what he saw. This Temple was not just a large building situated in the middle of a city. To the mind of Ezekiel, the Temple itself looked like an entire city!

The man measured the Outer Wall around the Temple building and found each wall was 500 reeds long. The Temple building was placed inside this outer square wall. Each side of the wall was 500 reeds long which is equal to 6,000 feet or 1.136 miles on each side, making the entire circumference over four and a half miles! The total circumference would be 4.544 miles. It would be that long to walk around one building. That is why Ezekiel thought that the building looked like an entire city, because the Temple was probably larger than any city he had ever seen in antiquity.

---

192 Charles Fienberg, *Ezekiel*, (Grand Rapids, MI: Zondervan, 1958)

The Outer Wall would contain a courtyard encompassing all the rest of the Temple complex. This courtyard would be so expansive that it would be over a mile square and could contain eight hundred and twenty-six acres. The current Temple Mount only contains 37 acres.

Ezekiel's Description of the Temple

Ezekiel now proceeds to tour the Temple while the angel takes measurements. As he walks close to the wall he tells us,

> And behold a wall on the outside of the house round about, and in the man's hand a measuring reed of six cubits long by the cubit and a hand breadth: so he measured the breadth of the building, one reed; and the height, one reed. (Ezek.40:5)[193]

Ill. 30, The Gates of the Millennial Temple. Temple Gates, Temple of Ezekiel's Prophecy, H. Sulley Public Domain

The wall described here is one reed high and one reed broad (or thick). This would mean that the wall is twelve feet high and twelve feet thick on the first floor. Ezekiel 40:3-5 and 42:15-20 informs us that the inside of each of the four sides (north, south, east, and west) were measured first and then the outside.

---

193   For this study, the reed measurement used is 144 inches (12 feet), although the actual measurement is 147 inches (12 feet 3 inches) by this verse. So, the final measurements are approximate.

CHAPTER FOURTEEN

Verse six tells us that the gate was measured and two thresholds (doorways) were measured, each twelve feet wide and tall. One was probably used for entrance and the other as an exit. He then went through the gateway and took measurements from the other side.

This gate would have been massive in size and would have been fashioned much like a building, including the entrance, chambers, pedestals, porches, boundaries, "Palm trees," arches, and arabesques or "narrow windows." The entire gate-building would have been one hundred feet long by fifty feet broad. This gate was one of many magnificent structures built into each of the walls. The Bible describes several gates in the Temple in Ezekiel 40:8, 32, but it seems most likely that there are three gates, one for each side: east, north, and south. And each gate is multistoried with many narrow windows, sections, arches, and palm tree-like columns, and the first story is 12 feet.

Ill. 31, A half-mile vista down the outer court of the Millennial Temple. Half-mile view, Temple of Ezekiel's Prophecy, H. Sulley Public Domain

On the inside of these gates is the Outer Court. Flanking the Outer Court were Chambers. Inside these Chambers were the gates of the Outer Court. In between these Chambers and the gates of the outer wall was the width of the Outer Court, given as one hundred cubits, or 200 feet wide if a cubit measurement is the royal cubit of 24 inches (Ezek. 40:17-19, 24-28).

Thus, the outer wall of the Temple complex contained several gate-buildings. Inside this outer wall were Chamber buildings with gates of the Outer Court in them. This outer wall and the Outer Chambers were separated by the Outer Courtyard between them.

The Corner Courts are mentioned in Ezekiel 46:19-24. Here, the prophet talks about four buildings at the corner of each of the outer walls, which connect each of the outer walls and the Outer Court Chambers together. Measuring thirty reeds broad and forty reeds high, the square structure would be 360 feet broad by 480 tall, or wide! It would look something like a combined city built as one building with a skyscraper in each corner that would connect the four sides of the house together.

This entire outer Temple structure is referred to as the Sanctuary by Ezekiel. The term "Sanctuary" can be used in a broad sense and can mean not only the Temple building proper, but also the entire Temple Complex, which would include the Outer Courtyard, the interior Temple, and the Altar at the center of the complex. Chapter 41:21 tell us that the Sanctuary is squared, and the Corner Courts were squared.

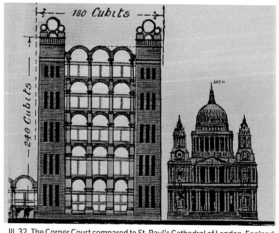

Ill. 32, The Corner Court compared to St. Paul's Cathedral of London, England. Corner Court, Temple of Ezekiel's Prophecy, H. Sulley Public Domain

In between this Outer Courtyard and its chamber buildings

CHAPTER FOURTEEN

and the Temple building proper was the Inner Courtyard. After receiving the measure of the porch and before he was given the measurement of the Temple, Ezekiel was brought to the Temple inside of the Inner Courtyard. Ezekiel 41:1 tells us, "Afterward he brought me to the Temple." This must mean that the porch is not joined to the Temple building but that there is space between them. The amount of space is given as five cubits (10 feet) to the beginning of the next temple area. (Ezek. 41:11)

The Inner Temple

The Inner Temple building is described in small segments. It is much like viewing the Empire State Building with a small magnifying glass one brick at a time. Because of the method of description in the Bible, there are several different views about Millennial Temple design and various details. I have seen five different proposals. Some of these views are a mix of the earlier Temple of Herod's time with Ezekiel's, a mix of the Temple Scroll Temple with Ezekiel's, a straight-forward view of the Temple Scroll Temple, and or a straightforward view of Ezekiel's Temple with differences in sizing Ezekiel's Temple. There are also different views of interpretation with Ezekiel's Temple in some details. This presentation is only one possibility, based on research by weighing differing views.

The Temple measurements and description is given in Ezekiel 40:44-49 and 41:1-26. The Temple is the

Ill. 33, The Inner Temple. Inner Temple, Temple of Ezekiel's Prophecy, H. Sulley Public Domain

central building to the Temple complex and is explained as having porches, posts at the entrances, rooms for singers, beautiful windows, the Great Hall, the "place left" and adorned with cherubs possessing the faces of a man and a lion.

One unusual feature of the Temple building is that it is possibly round. Ezekiel 40:44 tells us of chambers in the Temple that were beside the east gate and had its prospects toward the north. This has long puzzled scholars. How can a chamber flank an east gate and face north and not face east? One possible answer is that the inner Temple building is circular. This would also match the description given in Ezekiel 43:12: *"This is the law of the house; Upon the top of the mountain the whole limit thereof round about shall be most holy. Behold, this is the law of the house."* The phrase "round about" could mean that the law of building the Inner Temple is to be circular.

The Sanctuary is 500 reeds square, equal to 3,000 cubits or 6000 feet square. The circumference of the circle which is 2,220 cubits in diameter is 6,974 cubits. The radius would be 1,120 cubits. Thus, the Inner Temple is also vast and expansive.

The Altar of the Temple

Inside this Temple is the round section on the top of the mountain called the Most Holy. This section is reserved for the Lord himself and certain priests to commit the sacrifices. In the center of this area of the Most Holy is the Altar, at the peak of the mountain. (Ezek. 43:13-17)

The Altar is twelve reeds by twelve reeds (144 feet square) and it sits on a platform that is fourteen reeds square (168 feet square). The altar is 84 cubits wide. The size would translate to 168 feet at 24 inches to a cubit or 126 feet at 18 inches a cubit! This would be an enormous Altar to fulfill the sacrifices of the world.

In summary, the Temple will have a giant square outer wall with three gates. Inside this square wall is the Outer Courtyard

CHAPTER FOURTEEN

Ill. 34, The Millennial Temple Covered with the Shekinah-glory Cloud. Shekinah over the Temple, Temple of Ezekiel's Prophecy, H. Sulley Public Domain

which is enclosed by the Chambers, a set of buildings built in a square that houses the Outer Courtyard Gates. Immediately inside the Chambers is the Inner Courtyard. This Courtyard contains the possibly circular Inner Temple. The Most Holy place is enclosed by the Inner Temple and the Altar is at the very center of the circle at the mountain's peak.

This entire beautiful edifice is the future Throne and coming Temple of God. Inside the Temple will be many different buildings. The Temple Complex will house all the buildings of the earlier Temples. The Bible specifically mentions many chambers, such as the Chamber of Singers, Storehouses for presents to the Lord, a portion of the Temple reserved for the tribe of Levi, and Thrones of Judgment.

The Temple Thrones of Judgment

As mentioned earlier, in the Millennial Kingdom we will rule and reign with Christ. We will be made joint-heirs of his covenant of promise.

The Temple buildings are wonderfully fashioned for judicial as well as religious use. By the way the buildings are fashioned, it seems that God had this in mind. Each double gateway would give access to a space about twenty-two feet wide which could give approach to judgment seats that could be placed all the way around the house. It is estimated that there would be room for at least three hundred and eighty-nine stations for judges to sit with Him on the "thrones of the House of David." (Ps. 122:1-5)

The Temple of Ezekiel's prophecy is truly a wonder of the world. Today, there is not enough room on the Temple Mount for a building of that size. But when the Mount of Olives is divided and the other mountains merge to become the holy Mount of the Lord, there will be room to place the entire Temple complex on the top with the Altar of God in the center. The Altar was in the center of the earlier Temple complexes and so it will be in the coming Millennial Temple.

Christ will be the high priest of the next Temple, the supreme ruler in the courts of the Temple, and the overseer of the world. He will establish peace, justice, and righteousness and the world will be a place of wonderment. We have never seen a world entirely made up of righteousness, a world of peace without any violence or wars, and blessed with such manifold blessings. This world is literally beyond our full comprehension.

The beauty and wonder of the city of Jerusalem will be beyond our current understanding. It is impossible to fully comprehend the exquisite beauty of the city and kingdom of God. But God reminds us of this scene in Psalm 48:1-2.

> *"Great is the LORD, and greatly to be praised in the city of our God, in the mountain of his holiness. Beautiful for situation, the joy of the whole earth, is mount Zion, on the sides of the north, the city of the great King."*

CHAPTER FOURTEEN

Other Possible Temple Designs

Because of the size of the Temple described in Ezekiel, the Bible is not always interpreted literally in these passages. As we mentioned earlier, the Temple is measured in reeds, and one reed is twelve feet. A royal cubit would be 24 inches (or two feet) while a reed is twelve feet. This quickly makes a vast difference in size, so we must know what the Scripture means. To take the measurement literally seems impossible because no mountain in Jerusalem is large enough to contain a Temple complex of that enormous size. Thus, the passages are often interpreted to mean measurements in cubits instead of reeds. Yet, we know that an earthquake will occur, taking away the Mount of Olives and leaving a great valley in its place. The Mount Moriah and Mount Zion will rise and become one new combined mountain where the Millennial Temple will stand. A fountain will burst from this mountain and will become a new river running to the Dead Sea and to the Mediterranean Sea, and there will be a general settling of the surrounding area of Israel. You will then be able to see Jerusalem from a great distance, sitting on the mountain, covered with the Shekinah glory of God.

The earlier drawings of the Millennial Temple presented are the concepts of an architect of the 1800s, Henry Sulley, who took the concepts literally and then drew them as he interpreted them. These drawings are being used by several Christian organizations, such as the Church of God, the Church of Christ, and some Bible institutes in the Far East. While we do not agree with any of the heretical teachings of the group with which Sulley was involved, we find it captivating to continue to study various possibilities of the Temple's design and we only include these pictures as a point of interest and comparison.

Differences of interpretation exist about the Temple design, such as the dimension of the Inner Temple. Ezekiel 41:12 tells us that it was seventy cubits wide and ninety cubits long, which sounds like a rectangular building that is 140 feet wide and 180 feet long with walls ten feet thick.

The following are more traditional interpretations of the Millennial Temple. The first design is very close to the design and dimensions from the Temple Scroll Temple plan.

Ill. 35, A Jewish Model of the Millennial Temple, Plantemple.png thirdtemple.org

This model of the Temple of Ezekiel is much more similar to the Temples of Solomon and Herod. However, the outer courtyard is square and much enlarged. It includes several additional buildings, a cooking chamber in each corner, and three inner and outer gates. The walls are much higher and the Temple building proper is multistoried, often depicted as much as five times higher than the Temple in Jesus' day. It is my belief that the model is constructed this way because the Jewish interpreters are trying to compensate for the enormous size of the Temple. Because it is impossible to fit the Biblical size of Ezekiel's Temple on the current mountain, due to its width, the Jews design a Temple that is very tall. (Apparently, if you cannot build it out, you must build it up.)

There are several models of the Temple of Ezekiel, both

in Israel and in the US, and they usually follow this same basic design. One of the best examples of this design is next presented. This complex is very beautiful and impressive.

Ill. 36, Another Jewish Model of the Millennial Temple, phototemple.jpg thirdtemple.org

In this model, the dimensions of the outer courtyard are larger and more correct and there are buildings for the priests, such as living quarters and other additional buildings. But the gates do not seem to be as elaborate as the Biblical description. An improved interpretation of the Temple was created as an illustration for the magazine *Israel My Glory* by The Friends of Israel Ministry.

Ill. 37, The Millennial Temple concept from Israel my Glory, Consummation.jpg israelmyglory.org Public Domain

This last depiction displays more extravagant gates and also includes the fountain of water that flows from the Temple to become a great river. In each of these designs, you will find many of the Biblical particulars followed with great detail, with exacting specifics to even small essentials. Yet, in each design, some area is often overlooked.

This is the design you usually find in Bible research notes such as Logos software and various Bible study reference works. But the dimensions are often reduced from a reed to a cubit.

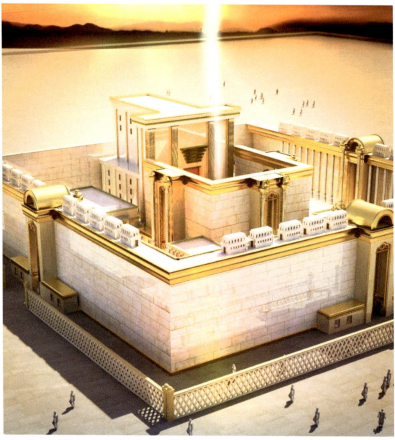

Color Image 24, The Temple of Ezekiel, temple-3-jerusalem-maquette.jpg thirdtemple.org

The Bible is very clear that the Temple complex is a huge square, with specific gates. The size is so large that it is difficult to imagine and comprehend. The fountain that flows from the Temple and becomes a river is unheeded in many designs. It may be that the researchers know these variations but do not know where to place certain details. There are also very large corner courts and some of the details are assumed, usually based on earlier Temples.

The more traditional concepts appear to be more correct because of the size and dimensions of the Inner Temple of Ezekiel 41:12 which sounds rectangular, while the heavenly Temple, which Moses saw and upon which the Biblical Tabernacle and Temples are based, must still have a bearing on the Millennial Temple structure, resulting in some similarity. Yet, it would seem that there are still parts of the Millennial Temple concept to discover!

It is mesmerizing to learn about and contemplate the design of the future Temple of God during the Millennium, when God rules on Earth as King of Kings and Lord of Lords! It seems that we know many elements of the Temple, and yet there are still parts to determine or reconcile. Yet, the most exciting thing is not to see and experience this coming Temple of God. The most thrilling event of all will be residing in the very presence of God Himself, to see Jesus personally, and abide with Him every day!

How thrilling and glorious that time will be when we will live with Christ personally on Earth and serve Him in the future Temple of God, covered with the Glory of God.

The Purpose of the Ark and the Temple

To the religious Jew today, the purpose of the Ark is not just a display of a piece of furniture with amazing abilities, an object of mystery or of overwhelming Divine power. The Jews respect the Ark because it was the receptacle for the written Word of God. They cherish and study the whole of the Old Testament, and their relationship to God is not measured today by how physically close they are to the Ark, but by how they adhere to the Covenant. In the Millennium, the Ark will not be placed in the Temple of God. Jeremiah 3:16-17 says,

> *"And it shall come to pass, when ye be multiplied and increased in the land, in those days, saith the LORD, they shall say no more, The Ark of the Covenant of the LORD, neither shall it come to*

> mind: neither shall they remember it, neither shall they visit it, neither shall that be done any more.
>
> At that time, they shall call Jerusalem the throne of the Lord; and all the nations shall be gathered unto it, to the name of the LORD, to Jerusalem: neither shall they walk any more after the imagination of their evil heart."

To regard the Ark as the only place of God's presence was incorrect. God is always everywhere present in all the world and the universe. *"Can any man hide himself in secret places that I shall not see him? saith the LORD. Do I not fill heaven and earth? saith the LORD."* (Jer. 23:24)

The Ark, the Temple, or even the holy city is not the actual home of God. For Isaiah 66:1 tells us, *"The heaven is my throne and the earth is my footstool. Where could you build a house for me? What place could serve as my abode?"*

Deuteronomy 16:6 tells us the answer as to the real purpose of the Ark, Temple, and Jerusalem:

> *"But at the place which the LORD thy God shall choose to place his name in, there thou shalt sacrifice the passover at even, at the going down of the sun, at the season that thou camest forth out of Egypt."*

The central temple is not God's home, or the only place where He resides. It is simply the place where He chooses to rest His name. The place of His name is for people to remember God.

In the past Old Testament, the Jews gathered there for sacrifice, to hear the reading of the law (Deut. 31:12), and as a physical reminder to the Jews of God's presence and law. In the Millennium, it will also be a place of sacrifice, where we hear the Word of God, and can see the physical presence of God seated on His throne and see His Presence in the Shekinah Glory of God.

CHAPTER FIFTEEN

The Glory of God on the House

Previously, Ezekiel was given a vision to see the earlier Temple of Solomon and to see the Glory of God depart, when Ichabod (the glory has departed) was written above the door. In the vision for the future temple, Ezekiel saw the return of the Shekinah glory, to this temple, and identifies it specifically with the "Glory" he had seen departing from the historic temple (compare Ezek. 43:2-5 with Ezek. 11:23). Furthermore, as the Glory enters the future temple in his vision, the prophet hears the voice of Jehovah saying, *"Son of man, this is the place of my throne...where I will dwell in the midst of the children of Israel for ever."* (Ezek. 43:7) After this first departure of the Glory, there was no Shekinah Glory in the second Temple of Zerubbabel or in the later remodeled Temple of Herod.

This return of the Glory shows that God is returning to bless, honor, and dwell in the Millennial Temple, and there has never been a time like this since the Temple of Solomon. God first dwelt in the Shekinah cloud of glory with Israel in the Tabernacle of the wilderness. God will tabernacle (or dwell) with his people again!

Jesus had earlier come to dwell with the people and to show God's glory. John 1:14 says, *"And the Word [Jesus] was made flesh and dwelt [tabernacled] among us, (and we beheld his glory, the glory as of the only begotten of the Father), full of grace and truth."* Jesus showed his glory on the Mount of Transfiguration. Jesus was the human incarnation of God, God clothed in human flesh, and his glory was enclothed in this flesh. When Jesus returns in His glorious appearing at the Battle of Armageddon, he will appear arrayed in the Shekinah Glory, the glory of the Father. He will look like the sun shining in its strength, from the east unto the west, the brilliance of God filling the entire sky! And when this final Temple is built, the glory of God returns and covers the house of God. This glory is a symbol of the presence of Jehovah God.

One of the most beautiful and amazing prophecies of all is that God will become a pillar of fire and surround the beautiful city of Jerusalem. (Zech. 2:4, 5) He will cover the Temple with His glory. The Shekinah-Glory cloud of God will blanket the Temple and provide a Tabernacle of fellowship with God and protection from our enemies.

Isaiah 4:2-6 says,

> *In that day shall the branch of the LORD be beautiful and glorious, and the fruit of the earth shall be excellent and comely for them that are escaped of Israel.*
>
> *And it shall came to pass, that he that is left in Zion, and he that remaineth in Jerusalem, shall be called holy, even every one that is written among the living in Jerusalem.*
>
> *When the LORD shall have washed away all the filth of the daughters of Zion, and shall have purged the blood of Jerusalem from the midst thereof by the spirit of judgment, and by the spirit of burning.*
>
> *And the LORD will create upon every dwelling place of mount Zion, and upon her assemblies, a cloud and smoke by day, and the shining of a flaming fire by night: for upon all the glory shall be a defense.*
>
> *And there shall be a tabernacle for a shadow in the daytime from the heat, and for a place of refuge, and for a covert from storm and rain.*

The glory of God will once again be on Israel, but also His Presence will be on the entire world. His glory will be a defense, a shadow from the heat, a refuge and covert from the storm, and a symbol of His eternal love and presence. God will be with us and we can live in the presence of the Lord every day. We will see Jesus, our Savior and Lord, and abide with Him who loved us and gave Himself for us.

CHAPTER FIFTEEN

We can worship Him in His holy Temple and see Jesus on His omnipotent throne. We will serve Him daily in the Kingdom of Peace. Jesus will also be that loving shepherd who watches over us and carries us in His arms, who gently leads us every day. And He will be that "friend that sticketh closer than a brother." We can experience the glory of God personally and live and serve in His presence forever!

EPILOGUE

To know God personally is an amazing experience. Many people do not know that this is possible and have never experienced the joy of having God in their life. Then, for others, the search for God is often an unfulfilled mystery. Some people look for God in nature, while others look for God in good works and in various forms of religion, but the mystery of knowing God can be discovered and experienced because God has revealed Himself to mankind. 1 Timothy 3:16 tells us, *"And without controversy, great is the mystery of godliness: God was manifest in the flesh, justified in the Spirit, seen of angels, preached unto the Gentiles, believed on in the world, received up into glory."*

The path to God and understanding of God are revealed through Jesus Christ. By meeting Jesus, you can know God and find the way to heaven.

The Hidden Meaning of the Jewish Sacrifice Revealed

In the days of the Old Testament, while many Jews kept the Jewish law and offered the sacrifice of a lamb to God, the full meaning of this sacrifice was not always known to them. Each sacrifice was a picture or example of a future sacrifice that would bear the sins of the person who was offering it to God. That is why each sacrifice had to be perfect, and free from blemishes, to show that the prophesied redeemer would also be a pure, sinless sacrifice. A person could never pay for his own sins, or even die for someone else, because each person is a sinner and God will only accept a pure, sinless offering for sin. Because all men are sinners, men cannot pay for their own sin, but they need a pure sacrifice.

Romans 3:10 says, *"As it is written, There is none righteous, no, not one,"* and Romans 3:23 says, *"For all have sinned, and come short of the glory of God."*

God requires a judgment and payment for sin. God is holy and cannot allow sin into his presence in heaven. So, all sin must be paid for and that payment applied to each sinner, and they must also be cleansed of their sin to enter heaven. God knew that mankind could never pay for their own sin and no sinner could ever earn salvation by doing good works. So, God sent His Son Jesus to be the Lamb of God that could be offered as a sacrifice to pay for the sins of the world.

John 3:16 tells us, *"For God so loved the world, that he gave his only begotten Son, that whosoever believeth in him should not perish, but have everlasting life."*

When Jesus first began his ministry, John the Baptist immediately recognized who Jesus was and his real purpose in coming to this world when he exclaimed, *"Behold the Lamb of God, which taketh away the sin of the world"* (John 1:29).

He knew that Jesus was the prophesied Savior who could pay for the sins of the world and provide salvation from hell and a home in heaven to all who would believe in Him.

Jesus, the virgin-born, sinless Son of God, came to die on the cross, paying for the sins of the world. He also proved that he was God in the flesh by rising again the third day.

We must all pay for our sin and the only payment we can offer is death and hell. But Jesus loves you and he came to pay for your sin on the cross and to offer you heaven as a free gift.

Romans 6:23 says, *"The wages of sin is death; but the gift of God is eternal life through Jesus Christ our Lord."*

Jesus is the only way of being saved and receiving eternal life. Many people are sincere and live lives of good works, yet these works will never buy your way to heaven or even pay for your personal sin. There is only one way to heaven. In John 14:6, *"Jesus saith unto him, I am the way, the truth, and the life: no man cometh unto the Father, but by me."*

How Do You Accept Eternal Life?

How do you receive the gift of eternal life? You must believe the gospel: that Jesus Christ is the sinless, Son of God who died on the cross for your sin, was buried, and came out of the grave in the resurrection. And if you believe in your heart, then you ask Jesus to be your personal Savior.

Romans 10:9 *"That if thou shalt confess with thy mouth the Lord Jesus, and shalt believe with thy heart that God hath raised him from the dead, thou shalt be saved."*

Romans 10:10 *"For with the heart, man believeth unto righteousness; and with the mouth confession is made unto salvation."*

Romans 10:13 *"For whosoever shall call upon the name of the Lord shall be saved."*

Then Jesus will save you eternally, promising you a home in heaven. He will be with you personally in your heart and take you through each day of your life. Have you ever called upon Jesus to save you?

For those reading this book who do not know Jesus as their Savior, how imperative it is that you accept Him today! You must realize that you are a sinner and cannot save yourself. Jesus died on the cross, paying the debt for your sin, and was resurrected, proving that He is the Son of God. Call upon Jesus to be your personal Savior, to come into your heart, to forgive you of your sins and to take you to heaven.

What a wonderful blessing it is to know Jesus as your Savior, have heaven as your home and experience the presence of God now in your life! If you are not saved, why not be saved today?

If you realize your need to be saved and you will call upon God, believing in Him to save you, pray right now:

> "Dear Lord, I confess that I am a sinner, I believe that Jesus Christ is the Son of God who provided salvation by dying on the cross for the sins of the world and I need you as my living Savior. Please come into my heart and forgive me of all my sin. Save me from Hell and take me to Heaven to live with you eternally. In the name of Jesus I pray, Amen."

How wonderful it is to know God as your personal Savior and to know that heaven is your eternal home. God tells us in 1 John 5:13, *"These things have I written unto you that believe on the name of the son of God; that you may know that ye have eternal life, and that ye may believe on the name of the son of God."*

And we can know that this life is eternal because it is not resting on our ability to keep ourselves saved and to keep ourselves in God's family. We can know that we have eternal life because we are kept in the hand of God, and he guarantees us to keep our future promise of eternal life in heaven. John 10:28 tells us, *"And I give unto them eternal life; and they shall never perish, neither shall any man pluck them out of my hand."*

In the light of the Lord's soon return, Christians of this world should be alerted to watch for His coming and work diligently for His kingdom. Because the Jews are preparing for a future temple by renewing the sacrifice of the Red Heifer and are looking for the earlier Ashes to cleanse the Temple, that means we are living close to the time of the rebuilding of the Temple. These Jews are also searching for the Ark of the Covenant to place in the Temple and then will rebuild the Temple that will exist in the Tribulation Period. Yet, we know the Antichrist will desecrate this temple in the middle of the Tribulation Period, and that the Rapture occurs three-

and-a-half years before this time. That means we are living in the last days and that Jesus could come at any moment!

These last days should awaken us to a renewed vision of service for God. We must all be busy about the Father's business, winning souls to Jesus. Truly, the "fields are white unto harvest" and we should "work for the night is coming." We must maintain a pure testimony of a holy life so that we would not be ashamed at His coming, but be gloriously received into the heavenly kingdom. Be faithful because Jesus is coming soon!

For any questions or comments, please contact

Dr. Lonnie Shipman

103 Bleriot Place

Grand Prairie, Texas 75051

lonnie@lonnieshipman.com

BIBLIOGRAPHY

A. BOOKS

Allegro, John Marco *The Dead Sea Scrolls*
2nd Edition, Harmondsworth: Oxford, 1975

Allegro, John Marco *The Treasure of the Copper Scroll*
New York: Oxford University Press, 1959

Archer, Gleason L. *Encyclopedia of Biblical Difficulties*
Grand Rapids, MI: Zondervan Publ. House, 1982

Arnold, William R. *Ephod and Ark*
Cambridge Harvard University Press, 1969

Ariel, Rabbi Yisrael and Richman, Rabbi Chaim
The Odysscy of the Third Temple
Jerusalem: 1993

Bahat, Dan *Carta's Historical Atlas of Jerusalem*
Jerusalem: Carta, 1986

Bartlett, W.H. *Jerusalem Revisited*
London: Thomas Nelson & Sons

Beckwith, Isbon T. *The Apocalypse of John*
New York: Macmillan Publishing Co., 1919

Ben-Dov, Meir *In the Shadow of the Temple*
Jerusalem: Keter Publishing House, 1985

Ben-Dov, Meir *Jerusalem Man and Stone:*
An Archaeologist's Personal View of His City
Tel Aviv, Israel: Modan Publishing House, 1990

Bloomfield, Arthur *Where is the Lost Ark of the Covenant and What is Its Role in Bible Prophecy?*
Minneapolis: Dimension Books, 1976

Burrows, Millar *The Dead Sea Scrolls*
New York: Viking Press, 1955

Carter, Howard *The Tomb of Tutankhamen*
U.S.A.: Excalibur Books, 1954

Casson, Lionel *Great Ages of Man: Ancient Egypt*
New York: Time-Life, 1965

Church, J.R.	*The Ark of the Covenant – We Have Found It* Oklahoma City: Prophecy Publications, 1993
Combs, James O and Lewis, David A., editors	*Mysteries of the Bible Now Revealed* Green Forest AK: New Leaf Press, 1999
Combs, James O.	*Rainbows Through Revelation* Springfield, MO: Tribune Publishers, 1996
Combs, James O.	*Mysteries in the Book of Daniel* Springfield, MO: Tribune Publishers, 1996
Couch, Mal, editor	*The Dictionary of Premillennial Theology* Grand Rapids: Kregel Publishing Co., 1995
Davies, A. Powell	*The Meaning of the Dead Sea Scrolls* New York: New American Library, 1956
De Mol, J.J.	Bruges and its Beauties Bruxelles: Thill, n.d.
DeVaux, Roland	*Archaeology and the Dead Sea Scrolls* New York: Oxford University Press, 1959
Dobson, Cyril C.	*The Mystery of the Fate of the Ark of the Covenant* Haverhill, MA: Anglo-Saxon Federation of America, 1939
Eisenman, Robert and Wise, Michael	*The Dead Sea Scrolls Uncovered* Rockport, MA: Element Inc., 1992
Edersheim, Alfred	*The Temple: Its Ministries and Services as They Were at the Time of Christ* Grand Rapids: William B, Eerdmans Publishing Co., reprint 1972
Fereday, W. W.	*Solomon and His Temple* Kilmarnock: John Ritchie Limited, 1941
Flaherty, Thomas H., managing editor	*Lost Civilizations: The Holy Land* Alexandria, VA: Time-Life, 1992
Furnivall, Fradrick J. editor	*The History of the Holy Grail* London: Roxburghe Club, 1863-64

Futterer, Antonia F.   *Palestine Speaks*
　　　　　　　　　　　Los Angeles: A.F. Futterer, 1931

Futterer, Antonia F.   *Search is on for Lost Ark of the Covenant*
　　　　　　　　　　　Los Angeles: A.F. Futterer, 1927

Gaverluk, Emil and Hutchings, Noah
　　　　　　　　　　　The Search for the Ashes of the Red Heifer
　　　　　　　　　　　Oklahoma City, OK: Southwest Radio Church, 1981

Ginsburg, Christian D.   *The Essenes and the Kabbalah*
　　　　　　　　　　　New York: MacMillan Co., 1992

Goodrich, Norman Loore
　　　　　　　　　　　The Holy Grail
　　　　　　　　　　　New York: Harper Collins Publishers, 1992

Grogan, Geoffrey F.   *The Expositors Bible Commentary*, Vol. 6
　　　　　　　　　　　Frank C. Gaebelein, general editor
　　　　　　　　　　　Grand Rapids: Zondervan, 1986

Habechirah, Hilchos Bias
　　　　　　　　　　　Mishneh Torah
　　　　　　　　　　　New York/Jerusalem: Moznaim Publ. Co., 1992

Hancock, Graham   *The Sign and the Seal:*
　　　　　　　　　　　The Quest for the Ark of the Covenant
　　　　　　　　　　　New York: Touchstone Books, 1992

Hamilton, R.W.   *The Structural History of the Aqsa Mosque*
　　　　　　　　　　　Oxford, 1949

Haran, Menachem   *Temples and Temple-Service in Ancient Israel*
　　　　　　　　　　　New York: Oxford University Press, 1988

Ice, Thomas and Price, Randall
　　　　　　　　　　　Ready to Rebuild: The Imminent Plan
　　　　　　　　　　　to Rebuild the Last Days Temple
　　　　　　　　　　　Eugene, OR: Harvest House Publishers, 1992

Jeffrey, Grant R.   *Armageddon: Appointment With Destiny*
　　　　　　　　　　　New York: Bantam Books, 1990

Jeffrey, Grant R.   *Messiah: War in the Middle East*
　　　　　　　　　　　and the Road to Armageddon
　　　　　　　　　　　New York: Bantam Books, 1991

Jeffrey, Grant R.	*Heaven: The Final Frontier* New York: Bantam Books, 1990
Kenyan, Kathleen M.	*Digging up Jerusalem* London: Praeger Publishing Co., 1974
Kiene, Paul F.	*The Tabernacle of God in the Wilderness of Sinai* Grand Rapids, MI: Lamplighter Books, 1977
Lasor, William Sanford	*The Dead Sea Scrolls and the New Testament* Grand Rapids, MI: William B. Eerdmans Publishing Co., 1972
Lewis, David Allen	*Prophecy 2000* Green Forest, AR: New Leaf Press, 1992
McClain Alva J.	*The Greatness of the Kingdom* Winona Lake, IN: BHM Books, 1959
Mears, Kenneth	*The Crown Jewels* London, Historic Royal Palaces Agency, 1994
Murphy-O'Connor, Jerome	*The Holy Land*, 3rd Edition Oxford/New York: Oxford University Press, 1992
Payne, J. Barton	*Encyclopedia of Biblical Prophecy* New York: Harper and Row Publishers, 1973
Pearlman, Moshe	*Digging up the Bible* New York: William Morrow and Company, 1980
Pearlman, Moshe	*The Dead Sea Scrolls in the Shrine of the Book* Tel Aviv: Sabinsky Press Ltd., 1988
Pfeiffer, Charles F.	*The Dead Sea Scrolls and the Bible* Grand Rapids, MI: Baker Book House, 1969
Price, Randall	*In Search of Lost Temple Treasures: The Lost Ark and the Last Days* Eugene, OR: Harvest House Publishers, 1994
Reznick, Rabbi Leibel	*The Holy Temple Revisited* Northvale, NJ/London: Jason Aronson Inc., 1990
Richman, Rabbi Chaim	*The Mystery of the Red Heifer: Divine Promise of Purity* Jerusalem, Israel, 1997.

Richmond, A., and Tatham, Earnest	*The Sites of the Crucifixion and the Resurrection* London, 1943.
Santini, Loretta	*Rome and Vatican* Narni-Terni: Plurigraf, 1975
Schaffer, Rabbi Shaul	*The Divine Dwelling: Israel's Temple Mount* Jerusalem: Schaffer, 1975
Scherman, Rabbi Nosson and Zlotowitz, Rabbi Meir	*History of the Jewish People:* *The Second Temple Era* Jerusalem: Mesorah Publications Ltd., 1990
Seiss, J.A.	*The Apocalypse* 3 vols., New York: Charles C. Cook, 1909
Shafer, S.	*Construction of the Holy Tabernacle* Jerusalem: Tzvi Shaffer, 1990
Shorrosh, Anis A.	*The Exciting Discovery of the Ark* Winona, MN: Justin Books, 1984
Silberman, Niel Asher	*Digging for God and Country:* *Exploration, Archaeology and the Secret* *Struggle for the Holy Land, 1799-1917* New York: Knoft Publishing Co., 1982
Smith, Arthur E.	*The Temple and It's Teaching* Chicago: Moody Press, 1956
Smith, G.A.	*The Historical Geography of the Holy Land* London, 1894
Smith, G.A.	*Jerusalem from the Earliest Times to A.D. 70* London, 1907
Soltau, Henry	*The Holy Vessels and Furniture of the Tabernacle* Grand Rapids: Kregel Publishing Co., 1971
Steinberg, Rabbi Shalom Dov	*The Mishkan and the Holy Garments* Jerusalem: Toras Chaim Institute, 1992
Stewart, Don	*In Search of the Lost Ark:* *The Quest for the Ark of the Covenant* Orange, CA: Dart Press, 1992

Waeholder, Ben Zion	*The Dawn of Qumran* Cincinnati: Hebrew Union College Press, 1983
Walvoord, John F.	*The Rapture Question* Grand Rapids, MI: Academic Books of Zondervan Publishers, 1979
Walvoord, John F.	*The Revelation of Jesus Christ* Chicago: Moody Press, 1966
Walvoord, John F.	*The Return of the Lord* Grand Rapids, MI: Zondervan Publishing House, 1978
Warren, Charles	*Recovery of Jerusalem* London, 1871
Warren, Charles	Underground Jerusalem London, 1876
Warren, C. and Conder, C.R.	*The Survey of Western Palestine: Jerusalem* London, 1884
Wead, Doug and Lewis, David and Donaldson, Hal	*Where is the Lost Ark?* Minneapolis, MN: Bethany House Publishers, 1982
Wilson, Charles	*Ordinance Survey of Jerusalem* London, 1865
Yadin, Yigael, editor	*Jerusalem Revealed* *Archaeology in the Holy City 1968-1974* New Haven and London: Yale University Press and the Israel Exploration Society, 1976

B. PERIODICALS

Adkins, Harry R.   "Ark of the Covenant: Not in Ethiopia"
Biblical Archaeological Review,
Nov./Dec. 1993: 78

Bray, Hiawatha   "*Raiders of the Lost Ark* Puts God in a Box"
Christianity Today, Vol. XXV, No. 14,
August 7, 1981: 48

Hoberman, Barry   "The Ethiopian Legend of the Ark"
Biblical Archaeologist, Vol. 46, No 2,
Spring 1983: 113

Isaac, Ephraim   "Is the Ark of the Covenant in Ethiopia?"
Biblical Archaeological Review,
July/Aug. 1993: 60-63

Kaufman, Ashers   "Where the Ancient Temple of Jerusalem Stood"
Biblical Archaeological Review, IX: 2,
March/April 1983: 40

Millard, Alan   "Does the Bible Exaggerate King Solomon's Golden Wealth?"
Biblical Archaeological Review, XV: 3,
May/June 1989: 20

Myers, Eric M. and Carol L.
    "American Archaeologists Find Remains of Ancient Synagogue Ark in Galilee"
Biblical Archaeological Review, VII: 6,
Nov./Dec. 1981: 24

Porten, Bezalel   "Did the Ark Stop at Elephantine?"
Biblical Archaeological Review,
May/June 1996: 54-77

Ritmeyer, Kathleen and Leen
    "Reconstructing Herod's Temple Mount in Jerusalem"
Biblical Archaeological Review, XV: 6,
Nov./Dec. 1989: 23

Ritmeyer, Leen   "Locating the Original Temple Mount"
Biblical Archaeological Review, XVIII: 2,
March/April 1992: 24-45

Ritmeyer, Leen	"The Ark of the Covenant: Where It Stood in Solomon's Temple" *Biblical Archaeological Review*, Jan./Feb. 1996: 46-53
Shanks, Hershel	"Ancient Remains on the Temple Mount Must Not Be Destroyed" *Biblical Archaeological Review*, IX: 2, March/April 1983: 60
Shanks, Hershel	"Tom Crotser Has Found the Ark of the Covenant - Or Has He?" *Biblical Archaeological Review*, IX: 3, May/June 1983: 66
Silberman, Neil A.	"In Search of Solomon's Lost Treasures" *Biblical Archaeological Review*, VI: 4, July/August 1980: 30
Tushingham, A. Douglas	"The Men Who Hid the Dead Sea Scrolls" *National Geographic*, Dec. 1958: 784-808
Yeivin, Ze'ev	"Has Another Lost Ark Been Found?" *Biblical Archaeological Review*, IX: 1, Jan./Feb. 1983: 75
Zimmerman, Michael A.	"Tunnel Exposes New Areas of the Temple Mount" *Biblical Archaeological Review*, VII: 3, May/June 1981: 34

ABOUT THE AUTHOR

Traveling in a worldwide ministry as an evangelist and concert pianist, Lonnie Shipman was born into a preacher's family and saved at age 6. Trained as a concert pianist, he won six national piano competitions and toured 48 states and Canada as a teenager. After being called to preach at age 15, Lonnie graduated from high school as valedictorian and entered Bible college.

A product of a musical family that has toured nationally, Lonnie Shipman is dedicated to reaching souls with the gospel of Christ. He travels throughout America and the world preaching the gospel, performing concerts, teaching in colleges, giving prophetic, Biblical, archaeological and Biblical heritage conferences and music seminars.

As his testimony acclaims, *"My consuming desire is to see a heaven-sent revival that will reach the lost and awake the church to a total commitment to Jesus. There is nothing more important than winning souls to Christ."*

An author, Dr. Shipman's writings give insight on Biblical, prophetic, musical, archaeological, and historical subjects and include on-location photographs of Biblical places, original prophecy charts and Biblical maps.

When first led to enter evangelism, Dr. Shipman felt burdened to travel the world preaching the gospel to reach souls in the regions beyond. He has now preached in 27 countries on 31 international tours.

He has preached and presented concerts in North America, including Canada, Mexico, and the continental 48 states, as well as South America, the Caribbean, the Middle East and Eastern and Western Europe appearing personally to over

10,000,000 people and to millions on television in America and Europe.

Dr. Shipman has preached with two prime ministers of Europe, and has performed piano in many European concert halls, two royal palaces of Europe, Oxford University, and Madison Square Gardens of New York.

In May 2003, he presented a theological prophecy paper at Louisiana Baptist Theological Seminary, Shreveport, Lousiana.

In May 2009, Dr. Shipman was a presenter at Piano Texas 2009, at Texas Christian University, Fort Worth, Texas, along with professors from the Julliard School.

In March 2013, he was part of the Bible exposition at the Washington Capital Mall and participated in "The Significance of the 400th Anniversary of the King James Version of the Bible," at George Washington University, Georgetown, Virginia.

Lonnie Shipman has attended eleven colleges and graduated from Arlington Baptist University (B.S. in Bible), Dallas Baptist University (B.M. in Piano Performance and Violin), Baptist Christian College (B.A.), Louisiana Baptist University (M.A.), Baptist College of Florida (M.M. in Worship Leadership, with emphasis in Piano Performance and Sacred Music), Louisiana Baptist Theological Seminary (M.Div., Th. D. in Bible Prophecy) and Pacific International University (D.S.M. in Music Composition).

He has done graduate work at Pensacola Christian College, Southwestern Baptist Theological Seminary and has done a special research study at Christ Church, Oxford University, Oxford, England.